W9-CEV-449

Low and
Outside

William B. Mead

A
REDEFINITION
BOOK

Low and Outside

It was a rough and tumble decade, as the power of the Yankees and the aggressiveness of the Cardinals' Gashouse Gang typified—and dominated—their respective leagues. Jimmy Brown (right), a Cardinal rookie in 1937, tried to show he belonged by crashing into Dodger catcher Babe Phelps.

Hack and the Rabbit Ball

No tougher player ever lived than Hack Wilson.
—Joe McCarthy, manager,
Chicago Cubs, 1930

The Yankees had Babe Ruth. The Chicago Cubs had Hack Wilson, and for one dramatic season he lit up baseball with a display of slugging that some consider the greatest in baseball history. In that 1930 season he drove in more runs than anyone before or since and appeared ready to break Ruth's record of 60 home runs. But Wilson's fireworks faded like a dying flare, and he is remembered mostly as a symbol of that one great season—the Year of the Hitter.

Baseball changes only in response to earthshaking events. In 1920 the earth shook twice—from revelations that eight members of the Chicago White Sox conspired with gamblers to throw the 1919 World Series, and from the power with which players, especially the young Babe Ruth, were slugging the "lively" ball. The Black Sox scandal, as it was called, caused the owners to appoint baseball's first commissioner—Judge Kenesaw Mountain Landis—to preside over the game, keeping it straight by whatever means he saw fit. The sudden upsurge of long hits in 1920 had its effect on the sport, too: as hitting increased, so did attendance, and so the owners naturally tried to encourage even more slugging. The spitball was outlawed, and umpires were ordered to throw in a new ball when the one in play got dirty or scuffed—moves that only increased the liveliness of the cork-center ball, in use since 1910.

Traditionalists like Ty Cobb and John McGraw yearned for the old dead-ball days, but the fans preferred to see runs cross the plate and balls soar over the outfield wall. The era of hit-and-run baseball—a style that

In 1930 Hack Wilson (opposite) performed a remarkable feat: he drove in his weight.
The 5' 6", 190-pound center fielder for the Cubs drove in a record 190 runs. Cubs
Kiki Cuyler and Woody English—who hit ahead of him—combined to score 307 runs.

Hack Wilson (above, left) chafed under the stiff management style of new Cubs manager Rogers Hornsby (center) in 1931. A year after Wilson set the all-time record for RBI in a season, his slugging percentage plunged almost 300 points, and at the end of the season the 31-year-old Wilson was traded for 38-year-old spitballer Burleigh Grimes.

had typified the game for more than half a century—was as dead as the dead ball itself.

The stock market crashed on October 29, 1929, jolting baseball with a shock of another kind. Connie Mack's Philadelphia Athletics had beaten the Chicago Cubs in the World Series just 15 days before, and baseball was at the crest of what came to be called the Golden Age of Sports—the era of Babe Ruth, Red Grange, Jack Dempsey, Bobby Jones and Bill Tilden. But club owners had feared an economic downturn, and National League owners were tired of playing second fiddle to the slugging mastery of Ruth and Lou Gehrig. So in 1930 the National League juiced up its baseball a little more, and both leagues lowered the height of the stitches on the ball, making it hard for pitchers to get a good grip for throwing a breaking pitch.

Hack Wilson and the other sluggers of 1930 were fed a rabbit, and they feasted on it. The whole American League, pitchers included, hit .288, and the National League batting average came in at .303. Bill Terry of the New York Giants led the NL in batting at .401, followed by Babe Herman of the Brooklyn Dodgers at .393 and Chuck Klein of the Philadelphia Phillies at .386. No National Leaguer since Terry has hit .400. For that matter, no National Leaguer since Herman has hit .390, and none since Klein has topped .385.

In the American League, Babe Ruth got off to a fast start, belying his bulging waistline and his 35 years. He predicted he would hit about 75 homers. But by midseason his pace slowed, and he ended up slugging a mere 49 homers to lead the league, while driving in 153 runs and batting .359—your average Babe Ruth season. His teammate Lou Gehrig hit 41 homers, drove in 174 runs

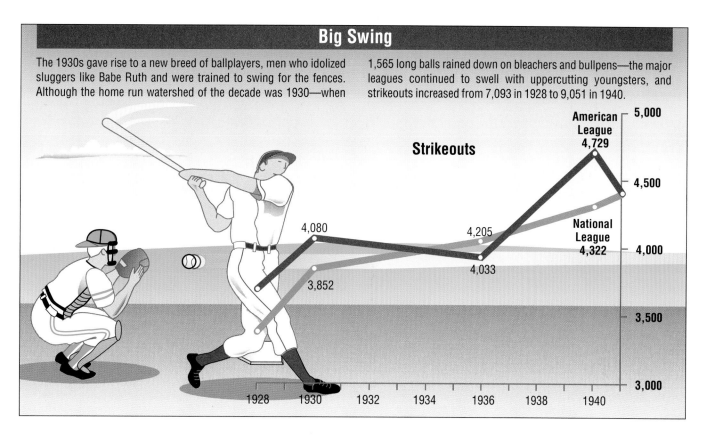

Big Swing

The 1930s gave rise to a new breed of ballplayers, men who idolized sluggers like Babe Ruth and were trained to swing for the fences. Although the home run watershed of the decade was 1930—when 1,565 long balls rained down on bleachers and bullpens—the major leagues continued to swell with uppercutting youngsters, and strikeouts increased from 7,093 in 1928 to 9,051 in 1940.

Strikeouts

American League 4,729

National League 4,322

4,080

4,205

3,852

4,033

5,000

4,500

4,000

3,500

3,000

1928 1930 1932 1934 1936 1938 1940

to lead the league, and batted .379. Not bad, but the Athletics' Al Simmons posted a .381 batting average to lead the league, and had 36 homers and 165 RBI. No one, however, could match Hack Wilson. He batted .356—high enough to lead the league most any season nowadays, but 11th among the NL's over-achievers of 1930. He hit 56 homers, a National League record that still stands. He drove in 190 runs, a record that remains to this day as untouchable as any in baseball. Lou Gehrig came close in 1931 with 184 RBI for the American League record, but since 1938, no hitter in either league has driven in as many as 170 runs; since 1962, no one has reached 150.

Lewis Robert Wilson did not look the part of a heroic athlete. He stood only 5′ 6″ tall, and most of his 190 pounds were packed in a hugely muscular upper body. He wore size 5½ shoes. Wilson was signed by the New York Giants in 1923, and after spending time in their major league lineup, was sent down to the minors during the 1925 season. He was drafted by the Cubs at the end of the season, and in 1926 he promptly garnered the NL home run title with a modest 21. He kept the title for three years, hitting 30 in 1927—half as many as Ruth hit to take AL laurels—and 31 in 1928. In 1929 he belted 39 homers but relinquished the crown to Chuck Klein, who hit 43. Wilson also led the league in strikeouts from 1927 to 1930, but his 1928 high of 94 remains admirable compared with the numbers compiled by today's liberal swingers. Wilson was a respectable, if far from spectacular, center fielder, but in 1927 he led the league in putouts with an even 400.

Stories differ as to why he was called "Hack"; one suggested that he resembled a famous wrestler named Hackenschmidt. But sportswriters and opposing players teased him with other nicknames: they called him "Caliban," after

6' 1" 195 lbs.   b 10/15/1909
BR TR

MEL HARDER
Pitcher

"I guess I'll be remembered as the pitcher who held [Joe] DiMaggio to a .180 average," Cleveland's Mel Harder once said. Holding a .325 career hitter to .180 is no small feat, but it obscures Harder's other achievements—he pitched for 20 years, and compiled 223 career wins, more than any other Indian except Bob Feller.

Cleveland picked up Harder in 1927, when he was an 18-year-old fastballer with an awkward-looking delivery. By 1930 he had developed a mean curveball and went on to average 14 wins a season for the Indians through 1933. His best year came in 1934, when he won 20 games, posted a 2.61 ERA and led the league in shutouts with six. He faced the NL's best hitters in four All-Star games from 1934 through 1937, and didn't allow a run in 13 innings.

Although 1947 marked the end of Harder's pitching career, it was not the end of his baseball career. In 1948 Cleveland hired Harder as one of the first pitching coaches in the major leagues. He had a remarkable eye—one that could spot the slightest flaw in a pitch. Hurlers under his tutelage included Bob Feller, Mike Garcia, Bob Lemon and Early Wynn. Behind such great pitching—and coaching—Cleveland won the 1948 World Series.

On his ability to continually baffle DiMaggio, Harder said, "I had good luck against him. It kept me around for a long time." But he was around the game for more than 40 years; it had to be more than luck.

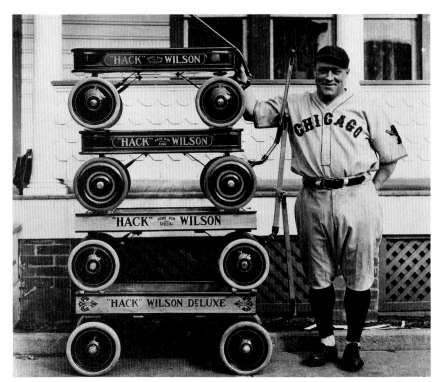

After his incredible 1930 season, the affable Wilson was a merchandiser's dream. He toured with a vaudeville show and endorsed a line of kids' wagons (above).

the deformed slave in Shakespeare's *The Tempest,* "the Hardest-Hitting Hydrant of All Time," "the Boy With the Mountainous Chin" or "a sawed-off Babe Ruth." Since the Cubs had picked him up after the 1925 season for a measly $5,000, some pop-song parodists called him "A Million Dollar Slugger from the Five and Ten Cent Store." After the 1929 World Series, they called him "Sunny Boy Hack" because of two fly balls Wilson lost in the sun in the seventh inning of Game 4, helping the Philadelphia Athletics score ten runs to wipe out an 8–0 Cub lead, and setting up the Athletics for a 4–1 Series victory.

Wilson had a hot temper, but he took most of the razzing about his size and his performance lapses with good humor. "Let them yowl," he said. "I used to work in a boiler factory and noise doesn't bother me. I don't mind hearing the fans yell. If they think my legs look funny, maybe they've got a point."

In 1930 Wilson was a man with missions. Teammate Rogers Hornsby, the National League's Most Valuable Player in 1929 and for years its premier hitter, broke an ankle on May 30, 1930. With Hornsby out most of the season, Wilson had to take up the slack as the Cubs fought hard to try to win a second straight pennant.

Wilson also wanted fame and fortune. He was popular in Chicago; he used to walk along the box seats before games, signing autographs and chatting with fans. He reveled in the speakeasies of Al Capone's Chicago and was arrested twice for violating Prohibition laws; on one occasion he was caught climbing out the window of a speakeasy. All this was considered rakish good fun in the Chicago of 1930, and Wilson felt right at home.

Hack Wilson may not have been as physically imposing as Yankee sluggers Babe Ruth (center) or Lou Gehrig (right), but pound-for-pound he was probably the strongest player in the game. He built up his upper body as a teenager pounding hot rivets with a sledge hammer at a locomotive works.

Wilson loved nightlife, and drinking and carousing cut short his career. By 1938 he was out of baseball but back in Brooklyn—where he had once played—getting tap dancing lessons from Edith Delaney (above).

But Wilson wasn't well known outside Chicago. His fly-ball swing was perfect for the close-in, high walls of Wrigley Field, but until 1930 he never had a Ruthian season. Like many other players, Wilson aspired to match Ruth in fame and achievement. It was uphill work, then as now; no player has ever done it. By 1930 Ruth was America's most luminous celebrity. He was paid $80,000—$5,000 more than President Herbert Hoover. "I had a better year than he did," the Babe was quoted as saying. Ruth's salary—which would be roughly $630,000 today—was not dramatically higher in value than the current major league *average* salary, which is close to one million dollars. Still, no other ballplayer at the time earned nearly as much, and Wilson was considered fortunate to get a raise to $40,000 for 1931 on the strength of his spectacular 1930 season.

At World Series time, newspaper syndicates used to hire baseball stars, pairing them with ghostwriters to compose feature stories about the games. Four Cubs players rated ghostwriters for the 1929 Series, but Wilson wasn't among them. "I'll have a ghost writer in the next World Series, even if it's played at the Polo Grounds," he said. "I notice that Babe Ruth sits in the press box in civvies with his ghost writer as a body guard. Just watch my home run smoke next year!"

On June 1, 1930, Wilson smoked his 15th and 16th homers and was mentioned as a threat to Ruth's record of 60. On July 21 he hit two more, and on July 26 Wilson hit three home runs in a single game against the Phillies. On August 10 the Cubs swept a doubleheader from the Boston Braves thanks to three more homers by Wilson, and on August 19 he hit his 43rd to tie Chuck Klein's year-old National League Record. A week later, Wilson let a line drive get past him in center field for an inside-the-park homer. By way of apologizing to the Cub pitcher,

Continued on page 14

Ruth's Called Shot

nly Babe Ruth could be credited with such a flamboyant gesture. It came during Game 3 of the 1932 World Series between Ruth's Yankees and the Chicago Cubs at Wrigley Field. The score was tied, 4–4, when Ruth came to bat in the fifth inning. He took a called strike, two balls, and another called strike. Before the next pitch, he stood holding the bat loosely in his left hand, raised his right arm, and seemed to point at center field. Then he knocked the next pitch over the center field wall.

There is no question that he raised his right arm; photographs show it. Some witnesses said he pointed at the center field wall, just as the legend has it. Others insisted Ruth didn't point toward the field at all, but merely waved his hand at the Cub bench while exchanging pungent insults with his opponents. Lou Gehrig, who was in the on-deck circle, said Ruth was pointing not at the wall but at the Cub pitcher, Charlie Root. Gehrig explained, "Babe was jawing with Root and what he said was, 'I'm going to knock the next pitch right down your goddamned throat.' "

Root claimed Ruth had not predicted his homer. "Ruth did not point at the fence before he swung," Root said. "If he had made a gesture like that, well, anybody who knows me knows that Ruth would have ended up on his ass." Gabby Hartnett, the Cub catcher, said Ruth had held up two fingers to indicate the number of strikes on him and said, "It only takes one to hit it."

Ruth had never played at Wrigley Field before, but that didn't intimidate him. In batting practice before Game 3 he hit nine balls into the stands. "I'd play for half my salary if I could hit in this dump all my life," Ruth yelled at the Cubs. In his first at-bat, Ruth slugged a three-run homer into the right field bleachers.

When Ruth returned to the plate in the fifth, he knocked Root's curveball hard and deep to center; it was the longest home run ever hit at Wrigley Field. Ruth enjoyed every step around the bases. He spoke to Charlie Grimm, the Cub first baseman, and to Billy Herman, the second baseman. He clasped his hands over his head like a victorious boxer.

Joe Williams, sports editor of the Scripps-Howard newspaper chain, wrote a spot story for afternoon newspapers that day focusing on the called shot. The *New York World-Telegram* headlined it, "RUTH CALLS SHOT AS HE PUTS HOMER NO. 2 IN SIDE POCKET."

Ruth said he meant to call his shot. "I didn't exactly point to any spot, like the flagpole," he told sportswriter John P. Carmichael. "Anyway, I didn't mean to. I just sorta waved at the whole fence."

Radio listeners believed that he did, too. Tom Manning of NBC Radio called it this way: "And Babe Ruth steps out of the batter's box again! He's holding up his two and two. Oh, oh, and now Babe Ruth is pointing out to center field. And he's yelling at the Cubs that the next pitch over is going into center field! Someone just tossed a lemon down there. Babe Ruth has picked up the lemon and now he tosses it over to the Cubs' bench. He didn't throw anything, he sort of kicked it over there. After he turns, he points again to center field! And here's the pitch. It's going! Babe Ruth connects and here it goes! And it's a home run! It's gone! Whoopee! Listen to that crowd! "

No one remembers, but Gehrig followed Ruth's homer with a homer of his own. The Cubs were finished. The Yanks won the game, 7–5, and completed the sweep the next day, winning 13–6. Gehrig was the Series star, batting .529 with three homers and eight RBI. But Ruth, as always, stole the show.

Babe Ruth's "called shot" in Game 3 of the 1932 World Series was one of the most dramatic—and artistic—homers in history. But even the Babe realized he was more slugger than seer—as he rounded the bases he admitted saying to himself, "You lucky, lucky bum."

6' 2" 207 lbs.
BL TR
BB 1946

b 11/11/1912
d 6/18/1979

HAL TROSKY
First Base

World War I ended on Hal Trosky's sixth birthday. Sixteen years later, Trosky declared war on American League pitchers and turned in one of the most powerful rookie seasons ever. In 1934 Trosky hit .330 and set major league rookie records, which still stand, with 374 total bases and 89 extra-base hits. He set another major league rookie record with 142 RBI, and an AL rookie record—both since broken—with 35 homers.

Trosky began his baseball training by hitting corncobs with a broomstick on his parents' farm in Norway, Iowa. A pitcher in high school, he moved to first base in the minors and was tutored in the field every step of the way. What Trosky never needed was hitting lessons. After a slight sophomore slump in 1935, he exploded in 1936, hitting .343 with 42 homers. He led the league with 162 RBI, 405 total bases and 96 extra-base hits.

Trosky hit over .330 in 1938 and 1939 and drove in at least 104 runs every year from 1934 through 1939. Unlike many power hitters, he struck out rarely, and in 1939 had just three more strikeouts than home runs, 28–25. But severe migraine headaches cut short what may have been a Hall of Fame career. Trosky didn't play in 1942, 1943 and 1945 due to illness, and he retired after the 1946 season. He was one of the most productive hitters of the 1930s, yet because he played in the shadow of fellow AL first basemen Lou Gehrig, Hank Greenberg and Jimmie Foxx, Hal Trosky never was named to an All-Star team.

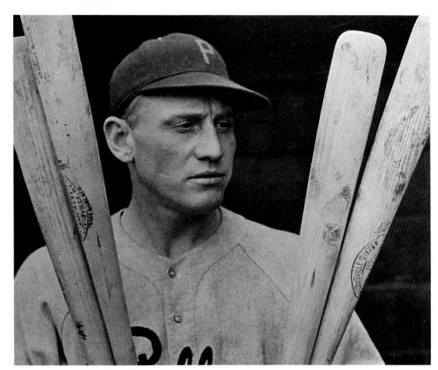

In most seasons Chuck Klein's .386 average, 40 home runs and 170 RBI would have won the Triple Crown. But in 1930 the Phillie outfielder was second to Hack Wilson's in homers and RBI, and third to Bill Terry and Babe Herman in batting.

Sheriff Blake, Wilson promised to hit a homer himself. He did, and the Cubs won, 7–5.

The National League that year was embroiled in one of history's closest pennant races. The Cubs, Dodgers and New York Giants vied for the lead, and in August the St. Louis Cardinals also looked like a possible contender, with a lineup that boasted a .300 hitter at every position except pitcher, and four more on the bench. Not that the Cubs were exactly slackers at the plate; right fielder Kiki Cuyler finished the season with a .355 batting average, and third baseman Woody English, with .335; they finished second and third behind Chuck Klein in runs scored with over 150 each. Even though it was a hitter's season, Chicago's Pat Malone was a 20-game winner tied for the league lead with Pittsburgh's Ray Kremer. But through it all, Wilson paced the Cubs. In August he hit 13 homers and drove in 53 runs. In September he hit ten more. In the season's final five weeks he drove in 41 runs.

On September 6 Wilson's 47th homer helped the Cubs score ten runs in the last two innings to overcome a 12–8 Pittsburgh lead. On September 27 Wilson hit his 55th and 56th homers to beat the Reds. The next day, the final day of the season, Wilson batted in two runs to set the new major league RBI record, having already surpassed his own 20th-century NL record 159 of the previous season and Gehrig's 175 of 1927. But the pennant race was going right down to the wire, and wins, not records, were what counted. The Cubs put on a final burst to win their last six games, but it wasn't enough. The dark-horse Cardinals rushed past everybody and took the NL pennant with just two games to go.

Winning the home run and RBI titles in 1930 gave Wilson two jewels of the triple crown; Bill Terry snatched the third with a .401 batting average. Yet

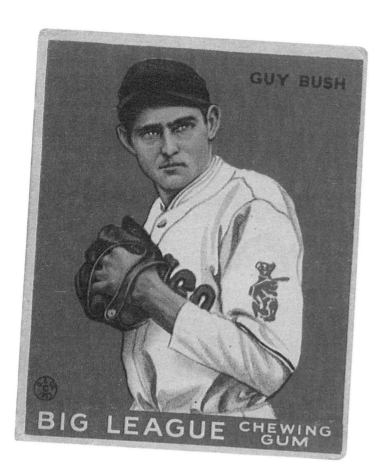

A 6.20 ERA generally will get you a trip to the minors, but in 1930 it earned the Cubs' Guy Bush a winning record. Despite allowing opposing hitters a .358 on-base percentage, Bush went 15–10, largely because his Cubs averaged 6.48 runs per game that season.

Wilson's achievement was barely mentioned in the press. His records were not paired with a pennant, as Ruth's had been when he hit 60 homers in 1927, and as Roger Maris' were when he hit 61 for the Yankees in 1961. Wilson's only real accolades came later, from Cubs manager Joe McCarthy: "I never saw a guy win games the way he did that year. We never lost a game all year if he came up in the late innings with a chance to get a hit that would win it for us."

The Cubs' second-place finish in the pennant race proved a tough blow for both Wilson and McCarthy, and not only because they were denied a second World Series opportunity. William Wrigley Jr., owner of the Cubs, was so disappointed at his team's failure to win that he fired McCarthy and replaced him with Rogers Hornsby, who had managed the Cardinals to a world championship in 1926. Though McCarthy recovered—the Yankees snatched him up, and he won eight pennants for them—the change in managers didn't help Hack Wilson.

Besides being an outstanding manager, McCarthy was also a master psychologist who knew how to get the most out of rambunctious characters like Wilson. Hornsby, on the other hand, preferred a drill-sergeant approach. In the clubhouse, where players relax, Hornsby forbade chewing, smoking, eating, reading and drinking—and not just drinking beer, which was illegal, but soft drinks, too. He told his players they should never read, not even on long train trips; reading, he said, wore out the eyes. Most humiliating to Wilson, Hornsby often gave him the "take" sign on counts of 2 and 0 or 3 and 1—counts that real sluggers feast upon.

The rabbit ball of 1930 lost some of its hop in 1931. Major league attendance set a record in 1930, proving again that fans like lots of hitting. But baseball elders feared that the delicate balance between offense and defense was out of whack. John McGraw, the aging manager of the Giants, campaigned for a

Hitting .324 with 18 doubles in 92 games just wasn't good enough in 1930, the first and last major league season for Phillies first baseman Monk Sherlock (right). His brother Vince (left) had an even shorter major league career, consisting of nine games with the 1935 Dodgers. He hit .462.

Big numbers didn't necessarily translate into big salaries in the hitting frenzy of the late 1920s and early 1930s. The Phillies' Lefty O'Doul hit .398 with 254 hits, 122 RBI and 152 runs scored in 1929, and earned a $500 raise. In 1932 he won the NL batting title with a .368 average and wound up taking a $1,000 cut.

FRANK (LEFTY) O'DOUL

BIG LEAGUE CHEWING GUM

While everyone else was swinging for the fences in 1930, Athletics second baseman Max "Camera Eye" Bishop helped his club by keeping his bat on his shoulder. Although he hit just .252—36 points below the league average—he walked 128 times, setting the table for A's sluggers Jimmie Foxx, Al Simmons and Mickey Cochrane.

restoration of the old days. He thought dirty baseballs should be kept in play and suggested that the pitching rubber be moved a couple of feet forward. Nothing that radical was done, but both leagues raised the stitches on the baseball again, giving pitchers a break, and the National League put a heavier horsehide cover on the ball, subtracting some of its zip. As a result, NL teams scored 21 percent fewer runs in 1931 than in 1930. Wilson was a right-handed hitter with most of his power to right-center, and many of his long drives—drives hit with no less power than they were in 1930—settled into outfielders' gloves. He hit so poorly that Hornsby benched him from time to time. Wilson finished the 1931 season at .261, with 13 homers and 61 RBI.

Wilson's frustration and his temper continued to strike sparks with Hornsby, and heavy drinking contributed to his downfall. The Cubs traded him to the Dodgers at the close of the 1931 season, and the Dodgers sent him to the Phillies, who released him as the 1934 season wound down. He played a few years in the minors and for a time owned a Chicago saloon, a venture that didn't exactly improve his health.

In August 1948, Babe Ruth, the man Wilson had tried to emulate, died. More than 80,000 people came to see Ruth's body as it lay in state at Yankee Stadium. Three months later, at the age of 48, Hack Wilson died in Baltimore. He was a pauper. The National League wired $350 to pay for a small funeral.

Wilson's slugging and Bill Terry's 254 hits and .401 batting average tended to obscure other hitting exploits of 1930. The Cardinals boasted balanced hitting of a kind unseen before or since. Cardinal catchers Jimmie Wilson and Gus Mancuso hit .318 and .366, respectively. Outfielder George Watkins hit .373, platooning with veteran Ray Blades, who hit

Hack Wilson was signed by the Giants in 1923, but manager John McGraw was unimpressed at first glance. "He ain't got no neck," McGraw said.

Wilson was buried in Martinsburg, West Virginia (above), where he had begun his professional career in the Blue Ridge League in 1921. Ten months after his death, Wilson's teammates and friends dedicated a ten-foot high memorial at his grave site.

.396. The Cardinals averaged 6.52 runs a game, scoring 1,004 runs on the season, a modern-day NL record that still stands. As a team, the New York Giants batted .319, another post-1900 record. They finished third. The Phillies hit .315, but their 1,783 hits amounted to yet another major league record from that rabbit-ball year. Chuck Klein hit 40 homers and drove in 170 runs to go with his .386 batting average; Lefty O'Doul hit 22 homers, 97 RBI and batted .383. But the Phils were never in contention—even for seventh place. They finished last, as their pitchers posted a 6.71 ERA, yielding 1,993 hits and 1,199 runs. Those, too, are records. But the Phils had an excuse: they played their home games in ancient Baker Bowl, a pitchers' hell even when the ball was dead. It was only 300 feet to the right-center power alley. "Standing on the mound it looked like you could reach back there and thump that wall," recalled Ray Benge, a hapless Phillie pitcher of 1930.

Lots of pitchers and lots of walls got thumped in 1930. Baseball was loaded with superior sluggers—Ruth and Gehrig of the Yankees, Al Simmons and Jimmie Foxx of the Athletics, Heinie Manush and Joe Cronin of the Washington Senators, Bill Terry and Fred Lindstrom of the Giants, Klein and O'Doul of the Phillies, Herman and Del Bissonette of the Dodgers, Pie Traynor and the Waner brothers of the Pirates, Frankie Frisch and company of the Cardinals. The Cubs, too, had a strong supporting cast with Gabby Hartnett, Riggs Stephenson, Kiki Cuyler and Woody English. But no one hit that rabbit ball like Hack Wilson. It took until 1979, but that one great season finally won him a niche in the Baseball Hall of Fame. ◐

The Waner Brothers

The Waner brothers combined for 5,611 hits and a .326 average in 38 major league seasons, but Lloyd claimed neither he nor his brother Paul was the best hitter in their family. "Our sister Alma was the best," Lloyd said. "We used to soak corncobs in water so they wouldn't fly so far when we hit them. Alma was the first to hit one far enough to break a window in the barn."

Even without Alma, Paul and Lloyd were the most productive siblings in baseball history. They had 517 more hits than the three Alou brothers, 758 more than the three DiMaggio brothers and 1,400 more than the five Delahanty brothers. From 1927 to 1940 they played alongside each other in the Pirates' outfield, and sprayed hits at a record pace all over Forbes Field.

Paul, the elder by three years, came to Pittsburgh via San Francisco. He hit .401 in 1925 for the San Francisco Seals of the Pacific Coast League, then followed that up with a .336 rookie season and a league-leading 22 triples, all the while telling Pirates owner Barney Dreyfuss that little brother Lloyd was even better. Lloyd also broke in with the Seals, but was declared a free agent during the 1926 season. The Pirates signed the 20-year-old outfielder and sent him to Columbia of the South Atlantic League, where he hit .345 in 1926.

The following season, the Waner brothers took the National League by storm. Paul won two-thirds of the Triple Crown, leading the league with a .380 average, 131 RBI, 237 hits and 17 triples. Lloyd hit .355 and led the league with 133 runs scored. While his 223 hits were second to Paul's, they remain an all-time NL rookie record. The Waners helped the Pirates win the pennant and set a club record for attendance at Forbes Field that lasted for the next 20 years. And that fall, the Waners made their only World Series appearance against the Yankees of Murderers' Row fame. The Yankees beat the Pirates in four games, but did it with great pitching, limiting Pittsburgh's hitters to just .223 in the Series—82 points below their regular season average—yet the Waner boys hit a combined .367, and Lloyd scored five of the Pirates' ten runs.

Despite the Yankee sweep, the Waners gained star status, and received a hero's welcome in their hometown of Harrah, Oklahoma. Then they took to the stage and went on a nationwide vaudeville tour for an astounding $2,100 a week. Paul played the saxophone, Lloyd the violin; the show's highlight came when Lloyd rushed onto the stage, out of breath, and Paul asked where he'd been. "I've just finished chasing the last ball hit by Babe Ruth," Lloyd replied.

In the spring they returned to the less lucrative practice of destroying NL pitching. Both were unusually small players—each standing about 5' 9" and weighing around 150 pounds—extremely fast and nearly impossible to strike out. Lloyd was the faster of the two, and got a lot of hits on ground balls that would have been routine outs for most hitters. "He had unbelievable speed for those days," said catcher Al Lopez. "Infielders would have to play him differently. I don't know if he was the reason why, but soon after he came up, you started hearing about teams looking for fast ballplayers." Lloyd used his speed to blanket the huge power alleys in right and

Hits were the Waner brothers' stock-in-trade. Each had six in a single game, and Paul (right) used six different bats to get his. Paul topped 200 hits in a season eight times, while Lloyd did it four times.

left center at Forbes Field, led NL outfielders in putouts four times and set a major league record with 18 in a 1935 doubleheader. He also had amazing bat control, and ranks as the third all-time toughest hitter to strike out. He fanned just 173 times in his career, an average of once every 45 at-bats. Lloyd's batting eye was so keen, wrote William Curran, "most umps would delay the call until they saw what [Lloyd] thought."

Lloyd was the Pirates' leadoff hitter, Paul batted third and they were on base incessantly. Their nicknames—"Big Poison" for Paul and "Little Poison" for the younger Lloyd—came from a frustrated Dodger fan and the effect his heavy Brooklyn accent had on the word "person." During a Pirates-Dodgers

game at Ebbets Field, a sportswriter overheard a fan say, "Every time you look up those Waner boys are on base. It's always the little poison on third and the big poison on first."

Like Lloyd, Paul struck out rarely, an average of just once every 25 at-bats. But Paul had more punch in his stroke, and while Lloyd blooped, bunted and bounced his hits, Paul was the master of the frozen rope. He ripped shots down both lines and into both outfield gaps, and in his first 14 years in the majors he averaged 39 doubles and 13 triples per season. In June 1927 he set a major league record that still stands—getting at least one extra-base hit in 14 consecutive games—and eight times had at least 200 hits in a season. Dick Bartell, an 18-year veteran

PAUL WANER

Outfield
Pittsburgh Pirates 1926–1940
Brooklyn Dodgers 1941, 1943–1944
Boston Braves 1941–1942
New York Yankees 1944–1945
Hall of Fame 1952

GAMES	2,549
AT-BATS	9,459
BATTING AVERAGE	
Career	.333
Season High	.380
SLUGGING AVERAGE	
Career	.473
Season High	.547
BATTING TITLES	1927, 1934, 1936
HITS	
Career	3,152
Season High	237
DOUBLES	
Career *(9th all time)*	603
Season High *(5th all time)*	62
TRIPLES	
Career *(10th all time)*	190
Season High	22
HOME RUNS	
Career	112
Season High	15
TOTAL BASES	4,471
EXTRA-BASE HITS	905
RUNS BATTED IN	
Career	1,309
Season High	131
RUNS	
Career	1,626
Season High	142
WORLD SERIES	1927
MOST VALUABLE PLAYER	1927

and teammate of such greats as Mel Ott, Hank Greenberg and Bill Terry, said, "Paul was the greatest hitter I ever saw. He had broad shoulders and steel springs in his wrists and he hit line drives. He made solid contact whether they threw him spitballs or knuckleballs or whatever." He didn't care what kind of bat he used either, and in 1926 went 6 for 6 in a game, using a different bat for each hit. Buddy Hassett, who played with Paul on the Boston Braves in 1941, quoted Paul's hitting philosophy: "He said he just laid his bat on his shoulder and when he saw a pitch he liked he threw it off."

Both Waners were intelligent, educated men. Paul was said to be fond of reading Seneca, a Roman philosopher, in his free time. But he was more famous as one of the era's biggest carousers. He admitted to playing while drunk or hung over, but maintained that it gave him a certain advantage. "Paul thought you played best when you relaxed," Lloyd said, "and drinking was a good way to relax." He also claimed the ball looked a bit blurry to him after a long night on the town, and that there was therefore "more of it to hit." In 1938 the Pirates looked to be pennant contenders, and Paul's manager and former teammate Pie Traynor asked him to give

Paul Waner was one of the most popular players of his time, and it probably didn't hurt that, at 5' 8½" and 153 pounds, he was an undersized star. "People like to pull for a little fellow," said teammate Pie Traynor.

Leading off a great Pirate lineup, Lloyd Waner paced the NL in at-bats three times, including a then-major-league-record 681 trips in 1931.

up drinking for the season. He agreed, but when his average was hovering around .240, Traynor took him out for a drink. He ended the season at .280, the first time in 13 years he failed to hit .300. Casey Stengel admired Paul's ability to handle his liquor. "He had to be a graceful player," Stengel said, "because he could slide without breaking the bottle on his hip."

The Waners left Pittsburgh in 1941, when Lloyd was traded to the Braves and Paul went to Brooklyn. Paul was struggling with the Braves in 1942 when he bounced a grounder off an infielder's glove. It was ruled a hit—the 3,000th of his career. But Paul didn't agree, and motioned to the official scorer in the press box that he wanted the call changed to an error. The scorer obliged, and two days later Paul got his 3,000th hit on a clean single to center.

The Waners hung on in the majors through most of World War II, since baseball needed all the players it could get. As a 41-year-old outfielder with the Yankees in 1944, Paul was a shadow of his former self, with the exception of his good humor. "Some fan in the bleachers yelled at me, 'Hey, Paul, how come you're in the outfield for the Yankees?' 'Because,' I said, 'Joe DiMaggio's in the army.' "

LLOYD WANER

Outfield
Pittsburgh Pirates 1927–1941,
  1944–1945
Boston Braves 1941
Cincinnati Reds 1941
Philadelphia Phillies 1942
Brooklyn Dodgers 1944
Hall of Fame 1967

GAMES	1,992
AT-BATS	7,772
BATTING AVERAGE	
Career	.316
Season High	.355
SLUGGING AVERAGE	
Career	.394
Season High	.479
HITS	
Career	2,459
Season High	234
DOUBLES	
Career	281
Season High	28
TRIPLES	
Career	118
Season High	20
HOME RUNS	
Career	28
Season High	5
TOTAL BASES	3,060
EXTRA-BASE HITS	427
RUNS BATTED IN	
Career	598
Season High	74
RUNS	
Career	1,201
Season High	134
WORLD SERIES	1927

The Last of the Breed

Connie Mack broke into professional baseball as a catcher in 1884; Clark Griffith, as a pitcher in 1888. But they are best remembered as owner-managers. When the American League was formed in 1901, its first pennant-winning manager was Griffith, at the helm of the Chicago White Sox; Mack followed with the Philadelphia Athletics in 1902. Mack had retired as a player by then. Griffith, a pitcher, won 24 games for his 1901 champions; he won 20 or more seven times in his 21-year playing career.

Thirty years later, Mack's Philadelphia Athletics and Griffith's Washington Senators were again among the best teams in baseball. Mack was approaching his 70th birthday yet was still managing, in addition to running the front office. He was kindly, soft-spoken and revered. He sat on the bench dressed in a business suit, a stiff collar, a tie and a hat. He moved outfielders and infielders with subtle waves of his scorecard. Griffith was no longer managing, but was the Senators' president and so sharp a judge of talent that he was called "the Old Fox."

Mack and Griffith came from poor families. Mack's real name was Cornelius McGillicuddy; he was one of seven children born to an Irish immigrant couple in East Brookfield, Massachusetts. When Mack was born in 1862, his father was off with the Union Army, fighting in the Civil War. At nine, Connie started spending summers working 12-hour shifts in a cotton mill. He quit school at 16 to work in a shoe factory, but was forced to look for other

A true student of the game, Connie Mack (opposite) guided the Philadelphia Athletics with a slow but steady hand for 50 years. "I have never known a day when I didn't learn something new about this game," he said.

Connie Mack (above, second row, center) earned a shot as player-manager with the Pittsburgh Pirates in 1894 partly because, according to one Mack biographer, "of his reputation as a tricky catcher who distracted hitters by talking and tipping their bats." He guided the team to a 149–134 won-lost record in a little over two seasons.

employment when the New England shoe industry fell on hard times, costing Connie his job. He chose baseball, an activity that had filled his leisure hours, and was signed by Meriden of the Connecticut State League.

Thanks to limited space in newspaper box scores, "McGillicuddy" quickly became "Mack." Standing 6′ 1″ and weighing barely 150 pounds, he didn't look the part of a ballplayer. But he was a superb catcher, using his long reach to snare foul tips that would have eluded other catchers. He later began wearing a thin glove and a natural padding: a small steak, cut to size daily and slipped inside the glove.

Mack made the major leagues in 1886. Eight years later, he got his first managing job. Ban Johnson, one of baseball's pioneering executives, was then president of the Western League, a top minor circuit; Johnson was impressed by Mack's ability. In 1900 Johnson changed the Western League's name to the American League, declared it a major league, and in 1901 awarded the new Philadelphia franchise to Mack and Benjamin F. Shibe, a Philadelphia businessman and partner in the Reach Sporting Goods Company, a manufacturer of baseballs.

The upstart American League challenged the National League's monopoly. The NL had a salary ceiling of $2,400, and Mack was among the AL executives who lured several stars away from the NL by paying them for their skills.

A shrewd manager, Mack knew how to find and develop promising young players. His Philadelphia Athletics won pennants in 1902, 1905, 1910, 1911, 1913 and 1914, with world championships in 1910, 1911 and 1913. He developed stars such as Eddie Collins and Frank "Home Run" Baker, stalwarts in what was known as Mack's "$100,000 infield."

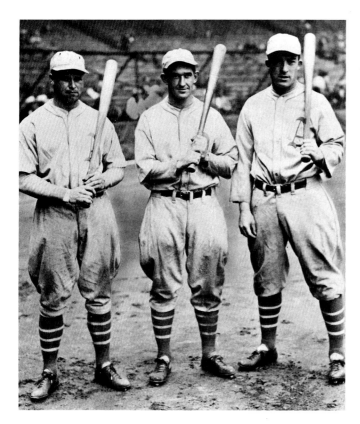

In 1929 facing the heart of the Athletics' lineup was enough to strike terror in the heart of any AL pitcher. First baseman Jimmie Foxx (far left), catcher Mickey Cochrane (center) and left fielder Al Simmons (right) combined for 74 home runs, 369 RBI and hit a collective .350, leading the A's to 104 wins.

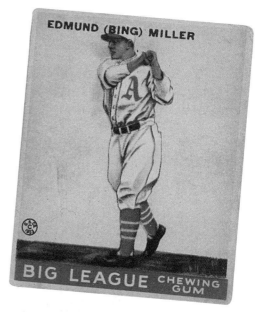

EDMUND (BING) MILLER

BIG LEAGUE CHEWING GUM

Outfielder Bing Miller would have been a star on most teams, but on the Athletics he was just another great bat. Hitting behind Cochrane, Simmons and Foxx, Miller batted .335 in 1929, with a 28-game hitting streak. He followed it up with a .303 average and 100 RBI in 1930.

Ironically, Mack fell victim to another interleague bidding war. In 1914 James A. Gilmore, a Chicago businessman who headed a minor circuit called the Federal League, did just what Ban Johnson had done 13 years before. He declared the Federal League a major league and offered higher salaries to lure stars from the National and American Leagues.

Mack couldn't keep up with the bidding. "We tore up some contracts in midseason, wrote new ones, entered into three-year agreements with Eddie Collins, Frank Baker, and other key players," he later told his biographer, Frederick G. Lieb. "Still the Feds kept raising their offers, and my players were dissatisfied."

Embittered and short of cash, Mack sold Collins to the Chicago White Sox for $50,000. His three star pitchers, all veterans, were released, too: Chief Bender, Eddie Plank and Jack Coombs. He sold two young pitchers who would later star for the Yankees—Herb Pennock and Bob Shawkey. He let other players go, and the Athletics plummeted from first place in 1914 to last place in 1915 and went on to finish last seven straight years.

But Connie Mack rebuilt. Farm systems were still in their infancy; most minor league teams were independently owned and could hang on to star players until they got the right price. In 1924 Mack bought a minor league outfielder whose name had been changed by a sportswriter from Aloys Szymanski to Al Simmons, for the same reason McGillicuddy's name had been changed to Mack. The price was moderate because other major league teams were leery of Simmons' unusual "foot-in-the-bucket" batting stance.

Connie Mack usually drew a crowd when he was offering a class on the finer points of pitching. Mack—whose pitchers included Rube Waddell and Lefty Grove—was the first to claim that pitching is 70 percent of the game.

Portland of the Pacific Coast League didn't want to sell its superb young catcher, Mickey Cochrane, so Mack bought the Portland franchise and promoted Cochrane to Philadelphia. Baltimore, then of the International League, was winning pennants regularly behind pitcher Lefty Grove; in 1925 Mack bought Grove for $100,600, a stunning price in its day, especially considering that Baltimore owner Jack Dunn had acquired Grove from the Martinsburg, West Virginia, team of the Blue Ridge League for $3,000. Martinsburg, it seemed, needed a new outfield fence and was short of cash.

Jimmie Foxx came cheaper. In 1924 Foxx, a muscular farm boy only 16 years old, got a penny postcard from Frank "Home Run" Baker, who was then managing in the minor leagues and had spotted Foxx. "Would you be interested in being a professional ballplayer?" Baker wrote in pencil. "If you are, contact me." Foxx did, and the next year Baker sold Foxx to the Athletics.

In 1928 Mack bought another pitching standout from Baltimore, George Earnshaw, and purchased center fielder Mule Haas from Atlanta, then a minor league team. The Athletics had quite a club, but they needed every man; to win the pennant, they had to edge the New York Yankee team that most authorities consider the greatest in history—the "Murderers' Row" club of Babe Ruth, Lou Gehrig, Bob Meusel, Tony Lazzeri and Earle Combs.

But the Yankees won their third straight pennant in 1928, edging the A's by 2½ games. In 1929, however, Mack's crew decimated the league, leaving the Yankees in second place by 18 games. The Athletics beat the Cubs in the 1929 World Series and then won repeat pennants in 1930 and 1931.

Rarely in history have two competing teams boasted such devastating punch as the Athletics and Yankees of that era. In late May of 1930, the A's

and Yanks played three doubleheaders in four days and scored a total of 99 runs. The Yanks swept two of the three twin bills, while the A's swept the other. Ruth hit eight homers—three of them in one game. Gehrig hit three in another of the slugfests, while Foxx hit two.

The A's got their toughest fight that season from Griffith's Senators, who were managed by Walter Johnson, the former pitching great. Johnson had something that most teams lacked in 1930: a pretty good pitching staff. The staff consisted of 16-game-winner Lloyd Brown and four 15-game winners: Sad Sam Jones; Alvin "General" Crowder, acquired early in the season from the St. Louis Browns; Bump Hadley, whose 8.4 hits per game was a league low in that Year of the Hitter; and Firpo Marberry, a relief expert who posted a .750 winning percentage.

Nevertheless, on Memorial Day, 1930, the Washington pitchers played supporting roles while Al Simmons took the lead. With two out in the Philadelphia ninth, Simmons hit a three-run homer to tie the game. He doubled in the 15th inning and scored the winning run on a single by Eric McNair.

But Simmons wrenched his knee on the basepaths and couldn't start the holiday's second game. By the seventh, Washington led, 7–4, but the A's loaded the bases. Mack sent Simmons up to pinch-hit, and he homered to put the A's ahead for good, 8–7.

Simmons hit .365, .381 and .390 in the Athletics' three championship seasons, averaging 31 homers and 150 RBI. Foxx and Cochrane weren't far behind. Mickey Cochrane, still considered one of history's finest catchers, peaked in 1930 with a .357 average. Foxx's best years were ahead of him. He intimidated pitchers with his physique and his long drives, hitting 58 homers in 1932 to threaten Ruth's record. Foxx cut off his sleeves to show off his

Continued on page 30

The 1931 World Series was the only one that Athletics shortstop Dib Williams (above, center, with second baseman Max Bishop) ever played in, and he made the most of it. Although his A's lost to the Cards in seven games, Williams hit .320 and handled 31 chances without an error. The A's didn't win another pennant until 1972.

Shibe Park

n April 12, 1909, baseball entered a new era, and it happened in the Swampoodle section of north Philadelphia. Some said the new stadium—the first ever made of concrete and steel—was too big and too far from the center of the city. But it was built by a pair of dreamers, Athletics owners Ben Shibe and Connie Mack—who also managed the team. In baseball, dreamers are right more often than skeptics.

Until Shibe Park opened, baseball stadiums were essentially grandstands with roofs, built of wood, and rarely held more than 15,000 fans. But the Phillies' Huntingdon Grounds burned down in 1894, and after 12 people were killed when a balcony in the reconstructed stadium collapsed in 1903, Shibe decided that it was time for a change. He believed that his A's could fill the 20,000-seat park, and on Opening Day he was proved right. More than 30,000 fans showed up to watch the A's beat the Red Sox, 8–1. Attendance hit 674,915 that season, and other team owners took notice. Within five years, ten new concrete-and-steel stadiums were built. But none of them hosted better baseball than Shibe Park.

The Athletics in the early 1910s were awesome, and won four pennants and three world titles from 1910 to 1914. Mack's second dynasty arose in the late 1920s, and Shibe Park was ready. A second deck had been added in 1925, increasing the seating capacity to 33,608. With a Hall of Fame quartet—pitcher Lefty Grove, catcher Mickey Cochrane, first baseman Jimmie Foxx and left fielder Al Simmons—the 1929 A's won their first of three straight pennants. A 2,500-seat mezzanine section was added in 1929, and in 1930 the grandstand roof was raised to add another 3,000 seats.

But Mack was hit hard by the Depression and had to sell off his stars. He made at least one other unpopular decision. For its first 25 years, Shibe Park featured a 12-foot wall in right field, affording a good view for fans on the rooftops of buildings across 20th Street. By 1935 Mack decided he was losing too much money, so he raised the wall to 50 feet, 13 feet higher than Fenway Park's Green Monster. Money dictated another drastic change at Shibe Park. On July 4, 1938, the Phillies abandoned a dilapidated Baker Bowl and moved in with the A's, providing much-needed revenue. In 1939 Shibe hosted the AL's first night game, but by then the Athletics' glory days in Philadelphia were over. The Phillies won their first pennant in 1950, the year Mack retired. Shibe Park was renamed Connie Mack Stadium in 1953, but the A's moved to Kansas City after the 1954 season.

By 1970 the area around the stadium had become cramped and economically depressed, and attendance was lagging, so the Phillies moved to newly built Veterans Stadium. But Shibe Park had seen a lot of magic in its 61 years. It hosted nine no-hitters, but most of its memorable moments started at the plate. Lou Gehrig hit four home runs there on June 3, 1932, and might have had five if not for a great catch by Al Simmons. Four years later another Yankee, Tony Lazzeri, had a big day, including two grand slams and an AL-record 11 RBI. On the last day of the 1941 season, Boston's Ted Williams went 6 for 8 in a doubleheader to become the last player ever to top .400.

Connie Mack Stadium closed on October 1, 1970, ending its reign as baseball's longest continuously occupied ballpark. Ironically, the stadium—built with water outlets throughout the stands for fire hoses that were never used—was heavily damaged by fire in 1971 and was torn down in 1976.

Rooftops on 20th Street (right) were gold plated in 1929, as Athletics' fans paid $6 each for a view of the World Series across the street at Shibe Park.

Philadelphia's Shibe Park played a graceful host to the World Series in 1929 (above). One of the park's most unusual features was the domed tower (far left) that housed Connie Mack's office.

Shibe Park

Lehigh Avenue and
   21st Street
Philadelphia, Pennsylvania

Built 1909
Demolished 1976

Philadelphia Athletics, AL
   1909–1954
Philadelphia Phillies, NL
   1938–1970

Seating Capacity
33,608

Style
Major league classic

Height of Outfield Fences
Left: 12 feet
Center: 20 feet
Right: 32 feet

Dugouts
Home: 3rd base
Visitor: 1st base

Bullpens
Foul territory
Home: 3rd base
Visitor: 1st base

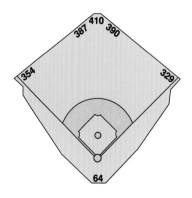

Luck contributed less to the unprecedented success of Athletics ace Lefty Grove (above) than did his wicked fastball. Winner of a record nine ERA titles, Grove could "throw a lamb chop past a wolf," according to sportswriter Bugs Baer.

muscles, and he was called "the Beast" even though he was gentle by nature. Foxx came up one day against Lefty Gomez, the witty Yankee pitching ace. Gomez shook off a half-dozen signs from his catcher, Bill Dickey, who called time and walked to the mound.

"What the hell, Lefty," Dickey said, "what do you want to throw?"

"To tell you the truth, Bill," replied Gomez, "I'd rather not throw the ball at all. Maybe he'll get tired and go back to the bench and sit down."

The Athletics' power was more than matched by that of the Yankees, who scored 1,067 runs in 1931 and 1,062 in 1930—the first and third highest totals in this century, even though the season was expanded from 154 to 162 games in 1961. The Yankees also have the second highest total—1,065 runs in 1936. By comparison, the 1988 Boston Red Sox led the major leagues in runs with a mere 813.

But the Yankees' pitching couldn't match that of the A's, who boasted the great Lefty Grove. Like Walter Johnson, Grove threw virtually nothing but fastballs. He was fast enough to lead the AL in winning percentage and ERA in all three of Philadelphia's championship years, at a time when baseball was decidedly a hitter's game. Moreover, he got better each year: 20–6, 2.81 ERA in 1929; 28–5, 2.54 in 1930; 31–4, 2.06 in 1931.

Thirty-one and four, and he still wasn't satisfied. Grove won 16 straight games in 1931, tying a 1912 record set by both Walter Johnson of the Senators and Smoky Joe Wood of the Red Sox. He then went after his 17th straight against the Browns in St. Louis. With two out in the Browns' third, a fly ball dropped behind Jim Moore, who was playing left field in place of Simmons, who had taken a day off. A run scored, and Grove lost the game, 1–0.

Mack emptied his pockets to Jack Dunn— owner of the minor league Baltimore Orioles—for some of his biggest stars, including pitchers Lefty Grove (above, left) and George Earnshaw (above, right). In the Athletics' three pennant-winning seasons, 1929 through 1931, the pair compiled an amazing 146–43 record for a .772 winning percentage.

Grove never took losing with aplomb, and this time he stormed into the club-house and wrecked the place, cursing Simmons—who fortunately wasn't there. "I didn't say anything to Jim Moore, 'cause he was just a young guy just come to the team and he never played in St. Louis," Grove told author Donald Honig. "It was Simmons' fault. He's the one I blame for it."

Grove is still in the record book as one of four AL pitchers with 16 straight wins in a season, and he followed that 1–0 heartbreaker in 1931 with another half-dozen straight wins. But he might have won 23 in a row—and he never forgot it.

Grove's father and four brothers were coal miners. Grove himself had to quit high school and go to work, typical for ballplayers of that era. The Athletics' other pitching ace, George Earnshaw, was an exception. His father owned a shipping business; George had attended prep school and graduated from Swarthmore College. But like Grove, Earnshaw was tough. Connie Mack was not one to baby his pitchers; he started his aces in rotation and used them in relief, too. In 1931 Earnshaw won 21 games and saved 6; Grove won 31 and saved 5; Rube Walberg won 20 and saved 3. Walberg led the American League in innings pitched; Grove was second, and Earnshaw, third.

In 1930 Grove led the league in wins with 28 and in saves with 9. Together, Grove and Earnshaw pitched 44 of the 52 innings of the 1930 World Series, winning two games apiece as the Athletics bested the Cardinals, four games to two. A year later the Cardinals won in seven games, with Grove and Earnshaw pitching 50 of the 61 innings.

Mack was riding high, but the Depression ruined his dynasty. Mack invested heavily in stocks, reportedly on Ty Cobb's advice, and the 1929

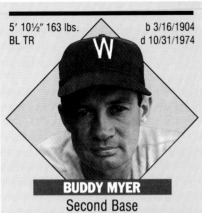

5' 10½" 163 lbs.
BL TR

b 3/16/1904
d 10/31/1974

BUDDY MYER
Second Base

In 1927 Washington Senators owner Clark Griffith swapped shortstops with Boston, giving up Buddy Myer for Topper Rigney. Myer had hit .304 in 1926, but he also committed 40 errors.

By the end of 1928 Myer had another .300 season and an AL stolen base title under his belt, while Rigney had played his last game. Griffith wanted Myer back, and gave up five players to get him. It was worth it. Myer moved to second base, and developed a solid glove to go with his consistent bat. He hit .300 or better seven times in the next 11 years. Underappreciated in an era of power hitters, Myer also had to put up with flurries of anti-Semitism from opponents. But in 1935 he had a season most second basemen only dream about.

Myer hit .349, scored 115 runs and drove in 100. He had 311 combined hits and walks, a total topped by only ten other AL players in history. Myer also turned 138 double plays, the third highest total ever for AL second basemen. And Myer won the batting title because the league leader, Cleveland's Joe Vosmik, and the Indians panicked. Vosmik led Myer by four points at the start of the season's final day and decided to sit out the Indians' doubleheader. But Myer went 4 for 5 in his final game, and when the news of Myer's performance reached the Indians, Vosmik was rushed into the lineup for the second game. He went 1 for 4, and dropped a point behind Myer. Ironically, had Vosmik stayed on the bench, he would have wound up tied with Myer at 215 hits in 616 at-bats.

Former pitcher Clark Griffith turned the Senators around in his first season as manager. They had finished seventh in 1911, allowing 5.0 runs a game. In 1912—under Griffith—they were second, allowing only 3.8 runs a game.

market crash cost him dearly. As if that were not bad enough, the A's fell victim to a Yankee renaissance in 1932. The hard-hitting Yanks finally put together a pitching staff—Lefty Gomez, Red Ruffing, Johnny Allen, George Pipgras—and won the pennant by 13 games.

As the Great Depression took its toll on the American economy, baseball fans had less and less money to spend on tickets. Even as the Athletics continued to win, their home attendance declined from 839,176 in 1929 to 721,663 in 1930 and 627,464 in 1931. With the team out of the race in 1932, the bottom dropped out; only 405,500 paid their way into Shibe Park.

Mack needed revenue, just as he had 15 years before. This time he sold Al Simmons, Jimmy Dykes and Mule Haas to the Chicago White Sox for $100,000. The A's, of course, got weaker. Attendance continued to decline, and Mack continued to sell players: Earnshaw to the White Sox for $20,000; Grove, Rube Walberg and Max Bishop to the Red Sox for $125,000; Foxx to the Red Sox for $150,000. In 1935 the Athletics dropped to last place, and from 1935 through 1946, they finished last nine times. Mack never had another contender, much less a pennant-winner.

Clark Griffith rivaled Mack as a bootstrap baseball operator, and his origins were at least as humble. Griffith's parents moved to Missouri in a covered wagon, and Clark was born in 1869 in a log cabin. When he was two, his father was killed in a hunting accident, and by the time he was ten, Griffith was trapping animals and selling their furs to help his mother support the family. He worked as a cowpuncher, a card dealer and a singer. Although only 5' 6½" tall, Griffith was an outstanding young pitcher and broke into professional baseball with Bloomington, Illinois, in 1888. In 1891

he made the major leagues with St. Louis of the American Association; when not pitching, he collected tickets at the gate.

Griffith was a frequent 20-game winner in the 1890s. Like Mack, he jumped to the brand-new American League in 1901, managing the White Sox and then the New York Highlanders, who later became the Yankees. In 1911 Griffith mortgaged his Montana ranch to buy a part interest in the Washington Senators, and he became their manager. In 1921 he gave up managing and took over the team's presidency. Griffith was the patriarch of an extended family, and his Senators employed many of its members. He adopted his niece, Mildred Robertson, who worked as his secretary. In 1934 she married his shortstop and playing manager, Joe Cronin.

The Depression pinched Griffith just as it pinched Mack. Although the Senators played well, finishing second in 1930 and third in 1931 and 1932, attendance in Washington declined from 614,474 in 1930 to 492,657 in 1931 and 371,396 in 1932. Griffith fired his manager, Walter Johnson, and replaced him with Joe Cronin, the Senators' star shortstop and, at 26, the youngest player in the lineup. Johnson had been making $20,000; Cronin was given a raise of $2,500. That saved the team $17,500, which in 1933 was a lot of money—more, for example, than any of the players earned, Cronin included.

Griffith's choosing the young shortstop to be player-manager was not capricious. The Senators had won their only pennants, in 1924 and 1925, with second baseman Bucky Harris at the helm. Harris was 27 in 1924. They called him "the Boy Manager," and Griffith thought lightning might strike again with Cronin in charge. He was right, thanks largely to the team that Griffith painstakingly assembled. In a startling series of trades between the 1932 and 1933 seasons, the Senators acquired pitchers Earl Whitehill, Walter

Selling relatives can be touchy, but when Senators owner Clark Griffith (above, right) was offered a whopping $250,000 for his shortstop, manager and son-in-law Joe Cronin (above, left) in 1934, he couldn't resist. Besides, Griffith was selling Cronin to Red Sox owner Tom Yawkey, who could afford to pay Cronin a lot more than Griffith could.

Continued on page 36

Joe Cronin

A skinny kid from a poor Irish family in San Francisco, Joe Cronin combined self-reliance and hard work to become a Hall of Fame shortstop, a winning manager and a league executive. Often he was compared to the rags-to-riches characters in Horatio Alger stories.

But Cronin was nearly finished before he got started. His tryout with the Pittsburgh Pirates in 1926 and 1927 produced mediocre results, and in 1927, after hitting .227 as a part-time player, he was sent to the minors in Kansas City. After 74 games with Kansas City, Cronin was about to be demoted to a Western League team in Wichita. But before he arrived in Wichita, he was rescued by Washington. The Senators, who needed someone to replace their ailing shortstop, bought his contract in the middle of the 1928 season and made him a starter.

Fortune often smiled on Cronin that way. "There are those who think he is the luckiest man in the world," Ed Linn wrote in *Sport* magazine in 1956. The truth was, Linn added, "no man ever worked at any profession any harder."

Cronin, at 6', 152 pounds, worked at batting and at building muscles. He used rainy days for extra batting practice so often that showers became known as "Cronin weather." He spent the winter of 1929 running and chopping wood. At spring training he emerged a muscular 180 pounds, and the results that season were a .346 average, 13 homers and 126 RBI. Cronin was also a fine defensive player. In the 1930s only Luke Appling rivaled him at short. "Joe was really a great fielder, had a lot more range than Appling, and was what I'd call more agile," said his teammate Ossie Bluege.

In 1933, the 25-year-old Cronin became the Senators' player-manager, replacing Walter Johnson as the team's leader. That year he became the youngest manager to win a pennant. But Cronin performed under some novel pressures. His boss, Senators owner Clark Griffith, was his future father-in-law. Griffith avoided family conflict by trading Cronin to Boston after the 1934 season—and during Cronin's honeymoon. Red Sox owner Tom Yawkey gave up a shortstop *and* paid Griffith a then-exorbitant $250,000 for Cronin.

Overeager to play up to his price tag, Cronin started booting easy plays. To compensate he began to drop to one knee to pick up grounders; Red Sox players called it "the $250,000 squat." But Cronin recovered from his fielding slump, and made the All-Star team seven times during the decade—every year from its start in 1933 through 1939. Cronin remained player-manager with the Sox through the war years, into 1945, then managed for two more years. In 1946 he led the team to a first-place finish with a 104–50 record. He retired in 1947 after a 15-year managing career with a .540 winning percentage.

In 1959 Cronin was named president of the American League. "He always had the ball players at heart," said league secretary Bob Holbrook. "Whenever there was a disagreement between management and players, he would always ask me, 'Bob, is it good for the players?' " Cronin also advocated divisional play to complement the expansion of the 1960s. "You can't sell a 12th-place team," he said.

When Cronin died in 1984, retired Yankee catcher Ralph Houk said, "To me, Joe Cronin meant baseball. It's a shame there aren't more baseball men like him."

As the Red Sox player-manager from 1935 through 1945, Joe Cronin got the most out of his players—including himself. Late in his playing career he evolved into baseball's finest pinch hitter, and in 1943 he hit .429 with five pinch-hit home runs—an AL record that still stands.

JOE CRONIN

Shortstop
Pittsburgh Pirates 1926–1927
Washington Senators 1928–1934
Boston Red Sox 1935–1945
Hall of Fame 1956

GAMES	2,124
AT-BATS	7,579
BATTING AVERAGE	
Career	.301
Season High	.346
SLUGGING AVERAGE	
Career	.468
Season High	.536
HITS	
Career	2,285
Season High	203
DOUBLES	
Career	515
Season High	51
TRIPLES	
Career	118
Season High	18
HOME RUNS	
Career	170
Season High	24
TOTAL BASES	3,546
EXTRA-BASE HITS	803
RUNS BATTED IN	
Career	1,424
Season High	126
RUNS	
Career	1,233
Season High	127
WORLD SERIES	1933

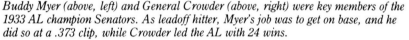

Buddy Myer (above, left) and General Crowder (above, right) were key members of the 1933 AL champion Senators. As leadoff hitter, Myer's job was to get on base, and he did so at a .373 clip, while Crowder led the AL with 24 wins.

Stewart and Jack Russell, catcher Luke Sewell, and outfielders Goose Goslin and Fred Schulte. The choices were shrewd and deliberate. Whitehill and Stewart had winning records against the Yankees. Russell seemed to always beat the Senators; it would be good to have him on their side. Likewise with Goslin, who had played on the Senator championship teams in 1924 and 1925, and had pleaded with Griffith to buy him back from the purgatory of the St. Louis Browns. "You've never won a pennant without me," the Goose reminded Griffith.

Goslin was a ferocious hitter, as was Heinie Manush, the Senators' glowering left fielder. Goslin and Manush batted left-handed and were slow in the field; Schulte was acquired because he batted right and played center field with speed and abandon. "Before that season," Schulte recalled, "Cronin told me, 'I want you to catch every ball you can in the outfield.'" Cronin had the right man. Schulte had played alongside Goslin in St. Louis, and once collided with his slower teammate so hard that both ended up in the hospital—Schulte with a broken jaw and missing several teeth.

Sewell was a wise, veteran catcher, and he gave the Senators the most intellectual catching crew in baseball. The son of a country doctor in Titus, Alabama, Sewell attended a one-room schoolhouse. By simply listening as the older students took their lessons, he learned quickly, jumped grades and enrolled at the University of Alabama at 15. The Senators' reserve catcher, Moe Berg, graduated from Princeton and the Sorbonne, spoke many languages—some accounts say seven, some as many as ten—and wrote a thesis on Sanskrit.

The new President of the United States, Franklin Delano Roosevelt, threw out the first ball of the 1933 season and cheered the Senators to a 4–1

victory over the Athletics. But the Yankees looked invincible that year. They had eight future members of the Hall of Fame: Ruth and Combs in the outfield; Gehrig at first base; Joe Sewell at third; Bill Dickey catching; and Gomez, Ruffing and Herb Pennock pitching.

The Senators and Yankees banged heads repeatedly that season. On April 23, Earl Whitehill beaned Gehrig so squarely that the ball bounced twenty feet into the infield. Players didn't wear helmets back then, and Gehrig fell like a dead man. But the trainer rubbed Gehrig's neck, sat him up and gave him a glass of water. The Iron Horse stood, tested his legs and trotted to first. The Senators won that game with a rally in the ninth, won the next day, 11–10, and brawled with the Yanks the following day, 300 Washington fans pouring onto the field to join in. But it didn't help; the Yankees won, 16–0.

On July 4 the Senators swept the Yankees in a doubleheader, disappointing a record Yankee Stadium crowd of 77,365. The Senators clinched the pennant September 21 before an enthusiastic Ladies' Day crowd in Washington. Cronin tried to escape the adoring throng after the game, but a crowd, mostly women, pursued and caught him. He smiled, said thank you, and trotted away, the hero of what would be Washington's last pennant.

Connie Mack and Clark Griffith didn't know the future would be so bleak. Neither quit trying, though their corner-store style didn't offer them much chance against wealthier competitors. The Athletics, like the Senators, were a family operation, so in 1946 Mack turned his share of the team over to his sons, but stayed on as manager. His sons finally persuaded him to retire after the 1950 season; he was 87, and more than once during games had called out the names of players long since retired.

Washington's Heinie Manush slid in ahead of the tag by Giants third baseman Travis Jackson in the sixth inning of Game 5 of the 1933 World Series. Manush had gone to third on a single by Joe Cronin, then scored on Fred Schulte's game-tying three-run homer. But the homer merely kept the Senators alive a few innings longer, as the Giants won the game and the Series on a tenth-inning homer by Mel Ott.

Everyone was off and running on Joe Kuhel's bases-loaded grounder in the ninth inning of Game 1 of the 1933 World Series. Kuhel's bouncer scored Heinie Manush to cut the Giants' lead over the Senators to 4–2, but Carl Hubbell fanned Ossie Bluege and got Joe Sewell on a ground out to end the threat and the game.

After the Athletics had an abysmal season in 1954, the Mack family sold the team to Arnold Johnson, who moved it to Kansas City. Mack died two years later at the age of 93.

The Kansas City A's never contended for a pennant, but in 1968 they moved to Oakland, and by 1972 they had won their first pennant for the city. By the late 1980s, the A's were again at the top of their league.

Clark Griffith died in 1955 at 85, still president of the Washington Senators. His son Calvin succeeded him and moved the Senators to Minnesota in 1961, despite protests from members of Congress and from President Eisenhower himself. The old Senators won their first pennant as the new Twins in 1965.

Things have changed; modern club owners lack neither wealth nor sophistication, but they cannot match the color that characters like Clark Griffith and Connie Mack brought the game of baseball. After all, who among today's owners was born in a log cabin, or used raw steak to pad a catcher's mitt? ◗

Clark Griffith (opposite, with Yankee manager Frank Chance) was all baseball. During World War I he raised enough money to send 3,100 baseball kits—gloves, bats, balls, bases, scorecards and rule books—to American soldiers in Europe. According to General Black Jack Pershing, playing baseball made American soldiers more proficient at throwing grenades.

Al Simmons

Al Simmons had a saying about pitchers: "I wanted them dead." And he made sure they knew it. Before facing a pitcher, Simmons would work himself into a murderous rage, then step to the plate with an intensity few hitters have ever matched. "You gotta hate those pitchers," he said. "They're trying to take the bread and butter right out of your mouth." He turned his rage into results, and murdered American League pitching for the better part of 20 years, putting up numbers that were startling even in the era of the lively ball.

Even more startling than Simmons' statistics was his batting stance, which earned him an unwanted nickname: "Bucketfoot Al." Simmons, a right-handed hitter, stood in the batter's box with his left foot pointed down the third-base line, a practice known as hitting with your foot in the bucket. It wasn't pretty, and it certainly didn't hasten Simmons' trip to the majors. But players with major flaws in their swings don't hit .334 lifetime, and Simmons himself said it always looked worse than it was. "I've studied movies of myself," he said. "Although my left foot would stab out toward third base, the rest of me, from the belt up, especially my wrists, arms and shoulders, was swinging in a proper line over the plate." Fortunately for Simmons, most scouts and managers looked past his stance to his swing. One minor league manager, upon seeing Simmons' unusual posture, told him he'd never make it as a hitter. Simmons hit .360 that season.

He was born Aloys Szymanski, the son of Polish immigrants who settled in Milwaukee, and was playing sandlot ball in 1920 when an umpire recommended him to Eddie Bodus, manager of the Juneau, Wisconsin, semipro team. Bodus paid Simmons' train fare to Juneau, and was paid back immediately, as the 18-year-old homered in his first at-bat. Simmons used a long bat to compensate for his bucketfoot style, and Bodus quickly gave up trying to change him. "He loved to hit," Bodus said, "especially high, outside pitches."

Simmons' hometown Milwaukee Brewers of the American Association signed him in 1922 and farmed him to Aberdeen, South Dakota, where full-time lawyer and part-time manager E. B. Harkin left well enough alone. "I never thought about changing Simmons' batting stance," Harkin said. "He had tremendous power, and his drives used to handcuff the opposing infielders. I was glad to have a man who could hit a baseball like that, and it never entered my mind to correct him." Simmons hit .365 for Aberdeen, then .360 and .398 in stints with Shreveport and Milwaukee in 1923.

In 1924 Simmons was invited to his first major league training camp, and his stance was greeted with laughter from just about everyone except Athletics manager Connie Mack. "You can hold the bat in your teeth," Mack told the rookie, "provided you hit safely and often." Simmons did exactly that, and wound up opening the season as the team's start-

In 1930 Al Simmons won the AL batting title and his Athletics won the pennant. In the spring of 1931 manager Connie Mack told Simmons, "A man is never a real champion unless he repeats." Simmons did and so did the Athletics.

ing center fielder, ahead of Paul Strand, who had hit .394 with 187 RBI in the Pacific Coast League and cost Mack $70,000. Simmons was very good as a rookie, hitting .308 with 102 RBI, but he was sensational in his second year. With a better lineup around him in 1925, including rookie catcher Mickey Cochrane, Simmons exploded for a .384 average, 24 homers, 43 doubles, 129 RBI and 122 runs scored. His 253 hits and 392 total bases led the major leagues, and the Athletics came in second, their highest finish since 1914. Simmons stayed busy, hitting .392 in 1927 to finish second to Detroit's Harry Heilmann, then found himself sharing the outfield with 40-year-old Tris Speaker and 41-year-old Ty Cobb in 1928. "If this keeps up, by the end of the season I'll be an old man myself," Simmons said.

But the arrival of Jimmie Foxx in the starting lineup in 1928 gave the A's a devastating threesome that rivaled the Yankees' trio of Babe Ruth, Lou Gehrig and Bob Meusel, and kept Simmons young and productive. With Foxx and Cochrane hitting around him, Simmons became a run-producing machine. In Philadelphia's pennant years, 1929 through 1931, Simmons hit .378, slugged .664, and *averaged* 208 hits, 40 doubles, 13 triples, 31 home runs, 124 runs scored and 150 RBI, while the A's averaged 104 wins. Bucketfoot Al hit .333 in three World Series with the A's, including six homers, 17 RBI and 14 runs scored in 18 games. And it wasn't just Simmons' bat that helped the A's win. Despite nagging rheumatism in his ankles, he was a better than average outfielder, and the aggressiveness and competitive fire of players like Simmons and pitcher Lefty Grove kept the A's razor sharp. "I was a fighting, snarling player on the field," Simmons said. "I am proud, not ashamed, of that reputation. I played to win."

His intensity made him one of the game's finest clutch hitters. In 1930, for example, Senators owner Clark Griffith discovered that 14 of Simmons' 36 home runs came in eighth or ninth innings. And he didn't need much time to get ready to hit, either. Simmons held out for all of spring training in 1931, and didn't sign his contract until hours before the A's opener. He homered on the first pitch he saw that season and won the first of two straight batting titles, which helped to earn him a three-year $100,000 contract in 1931. Simmons had another outstanding season in 1932, including a leaping catch that robbed Lou Gehrig of a five-homer day, but the big contract had

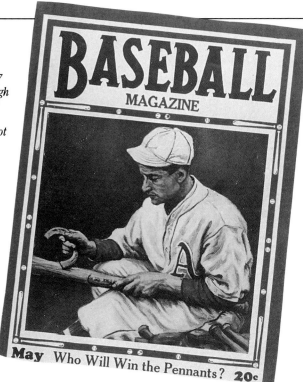

Al Simmons played and coached for Athletics manager Connie Mack (opposite) for a total of 17 seasons from 1924 through 1949. In 1944 he said of Mack, "I only wish he were 50 instead of 80. Not that he is less keen now, but we would have him with us longer."

BASEBALL
MAGAZINE

May Who Will Win the Pennants? 20¢

AL SIMMONS

Outfield
Philadelphia Athletics 1924–1932,
    1940–1941, 1944
Chicago White Sox 1933–1935
Detroit Tigers 1936
Washington Senators 1937–1938
Boston Braves 1939
Cincinnati Reds 1939
Boston Red Sox 1943
Hall of Fame 1953

GAMES	2,215
AT-BATS	8,761
BATTING AVERAGE	
Career	.334
Season High	.392
SLUGGING AVERAGE	
Career	.535
Season High	.708
BATTING TITLES	1930, 1931
HITS	
Career	2,927
Season High *(4th all time)*	253
DOUBLES	
Career	539
Season High	53
TRIPLES	
Career	149
Season High	16
HOME RUNS	
Career	307
Season High	36
TOTAL BASES	4,685
EXTRA-BASE HITS	995
RUNS BATTED IN	
Career	1,827
Season High	165
RUNS	
Career	1,507
Season High	152
WORLD SERIES	1929–1931, 1939

changed him. "When I finally decided I had it made, I was never again the ballplayer I was when I was hungry," he said. In September 1932, Simmons became part of Mack's white sale and was peddled to Chicago along with third baseman Jimmy Dykes and center fielder Mule Haas.

Simmons was one of the few bright lights on the also-ran White Sox, and played in each of baseball's first three All-Star games, hitting .462 with three doubles. Although he continued to hit well, Simmons was sold four times from 1935 through 1939, and wound up back with the Athletics as a player-coach in the early 1940s. In 1945 he became the A's full-time third-base coach, and helped Mack, now in his eighties, manage the team. "When [Mack] signals for a wrong move these days," wrote Bob Considine in 1948, "Al Simmons turns his back a bit sadly on the old man, as if he did not detect the signal, and calls for the right move."

But Mack had made a lot more right than wrong moves in his career, and even in 1949, at the age of 86, he remembered one of his best. When asked by a reporter what he thought his team needed, Mack replied, "I wish we had nine men named Al Simmons."

Hard Times

The Great Depression took a severe toll on baseball. Nationwide unemployment reached 25 percent, and a ticket to the ballgame became an unaffordable luxury for many fans. Major league attendance declined from 10.1 million in 1930 to 6.3 million in 1933. The drop in attendance prompted sportswriters and baseball executives to wonder whether something had gone wrong with the game. Judge Kenesaw Mountain Landis, baseball's commissioner, correctly diagnosed baseball's ills: "Steel, factories, railroads, newspapers, agriculture, baseball—we rode down together, and we'll ride back together," Landis said in late 1933. "A man can't go to a baseball game when he hasn't any money. He won't have money as long as he doesn't have a job. The American people love baseball. Many of them now peer over the fence or through it, and they will return as paying customers as soon as they have money."

Government policy contributed to baseball's woes. The economic dogma of the time led Congress to balance the federal budget by raising taxes—the very opposite of today's practice. In 1932 the federal government imposed a 10 percent sales tax on sporting goods and another tax on tickets that cost more than 40 cents. The ticket tax cut into purchases of the more expensive—and profitable—seats, taking a disproportionate toll on baseball profits. According to figures provided to a congressional subcommittee in 1953, major league teams, in total, earned a healthy profit

During the Depression, baseball refused to change its policy of selling World Series tickets only in three-game blocks. As a result (opposite), fewer fans than ever lined up to get into Yankee Stadium for Game 1 of the 1932 Series leaving 20,000 empty seats.

A ballgame and a box lunch were a little bit of heaven for John Karl Jr. as he set himself for a game in the 1936 World Series. Karl came over from Maplewood, New Jersey, to watch the renewal of the Subway Series between the Giants and the Yankees. The Yankees won in six games.

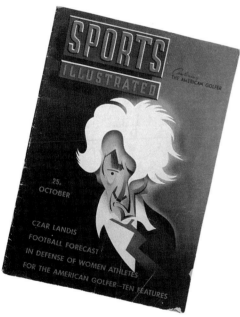

By 1937 baseball—and the U.S. economy—was on its way back, and Commissioner Kenesaw Mountain Landis had seen the game through another crisis. Attendance had climbed back to almost nine million, and Landis was featured on the cover of Sports Illustrated and the American Golfer (above), a short-lived magazine whose name was adopted in the early 1950s by the current Sports Illustrated magazine.

of $1,462,000 in 1930. In 1931 profits dropped to $217,000, and in 1932 baseball plunged into the red, losing $1,201,000. Losses increased to $1,651,000 in 1933 before a gradual recovery began. In 1934 net losses came to $290,000; in 1935 baseball edged back into the black with profits of $565,906. The recovery was slow; not until after World War II did profits exceed those of 1930.

Pay cuts were the rule. In a symbolic gesture, Commissioner Landis and John A. Heydler, president of the National League, voluntarily cut their own pay following the 1932 season. Involuntarily, Babe Ruth suffered cuts from $80,000 in 1930 and 1931 to $70,000 in 1932, $52,000 in 1933, $35,000 in 1934 and $25,000 in 1935, his final season.

Mel Harder, a fine young pitcher with the Cleveland Indians, remembered those hard times: "Because of the Depression, your best friends were out pushing a rake somewhere for the WPA," Harder said, referring to a government make-work program. "So you didn't squabble about salaries so much . . . Back in 1933 we all took a 10 percent pay cut in Cleveland. The club wasn't making any money."

According to historian David Quentin Voigt, the average salary of a major league player declined from $7,500 in 1929 to $6,009 in 1933; by 1939 the average was up, but only to $7,306. Not that the citizenry took pity; the average industrial worker made $1,421 in 1929, $1,064 in 1933 and $1,269 in 1939.

Despite the pay cuts, some observers criticized the players of the 1930s as soft and overpaid, just as they do in every era. Sportswriter John E. Wray wrote in a July 1934 edition of the St. Louis Post-Dispatch: "There isn't much

doubt that the ball player of today is far more mercenary than he was 30 or even 20 years ago . . . you will have a hard time convincing some observers that present day players are working wholeheartedly."

In another money-saving move, club owners in 1931 reduced the maximum number of players on a team from 25 to 23 and became devout advocates of player-managers, thereby saving themselves yet another name on the payroll. In 1932 the Chicago Cubs used two playing managers—Rogers Hornsby followed by Charlie Grimm—and won the pennant. In the 1933 World Series, first baseman Bill Terry's New York Giants defeated shortstop Joe Cronin's Washington Senators. A year later, second baseman Frankie Frisch's St. Louis Cardinals edged catcher Mickey Cochrane's Detroit Tigers; the pennant winners were only two of ten teams managed by active players that year. Bill Terry's final season as a player was 1936; he hit .310 and managed the Giants to another pennant. In 1938 the Cubs fired Grimm—then a player in name only—and replaced him with catcher Gabby Hartnett. Hartnett not only called the pitches, he called the shots well enough to lead the team to another pennant.

Ballpark maintenance suffered throughout the Depression, just as salaries and team rosters did. With the help of federal money, Cleveland Public Municipal Stadium was built in 1931, partly to provide jobs for the city's unemployed. No other big league ballparks were built during the decade. None were built in the 1940s, or, except to accommodate teams that moved, in the 1950s. Largely a result of the Depression and World War II, many ballparks saw extraordinarily long periods of service. As a result, many fans developed sentimental attachments to old ballparks; the

Tiger outfielder Jo-Jo White (25) used his head in Game 2 of the 1935 World Series to deflect a throw from Cub reliever Fabian Kowalik (24). White was safe at first, but then was thrown out trying to reach second. Still, Detroit won the game, 8–3, and, in a matchup between teams that had each lost their last four Series, won the championship four games to two.

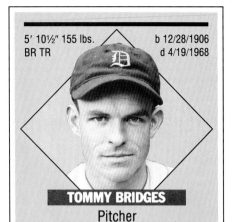

5' 10½" 155 lbs.   b 12/28/1906
BR TR   d 4/19/1968

TOMMY BRIDGES
Pitcher

When Tommy Bridges joined Detroit in 1930, people felt sorry for him. He was skinny and frail-looking, and some thought he wasn't strong enough to last the season. Bridges, who weighed just 145 pounds when he joined the majors, inspired such paternal concern that when he took the mound for the first time and threw a couple of wild warm-up pitches, umpire Bill McGowan called a time out to calm the little guy.

But Bridges threw everyone a curve. In his first inning as a major league pitcher, Bridges got past the Yankees' biggest guns—Babe Ruth, Tony Lazzeri and Lou Gehrig—without allowing a run. He even retired Gehrig on strikes, which was a preview of things to come.

An amazing curveball enabled Bridges to lead AL pitchers in strikeouts two years in a row. His curve, coupled with a good fastball, helped him post more than 20 wins three years in a row, from 1934 through 1936, with a league-leading 23 wins in 1936.

Ironically, it was a curveball that robbed Bridges of a spot in the history books. On August 5, 1932, Bridges was within one out of a perfect game when he served up a curve to Washington pinch hitter Dave Harris, who slammed it to left for a base hit.

After 16 years in the majors, all with the Tigers, Bridges retired in 1946 with 194 wins and 138 losses. But his curve was not forgotten. Beau Bell, a curveball hitter who topped .300 for the St. Louis Browns in 1936 and 1937 said, "I never saw a better curve than the one Tommy Bridges had."

The Yankees were a powerhouse on the field and at the box office, so owner Jake Ruppert didn't suffer much during the Depression. Ruppert, whose family owned a successful brewery, fought against profit sharing among owners. "There is no charity in baseball," he said.

images of Dodger fans carrying off bits and pieces of Ebbets Field after the last game there attest to that.

Few teams of the 1930s were bankrolled by multimillionaires or big corporations, as many of today's teams are. So the Depression hit hard—and separated relatively prosperous teams from the poor ones—the "haves" from the "have-nots." The Yankees and Cubs made money, fielding consistent contenders in the nation's two biggest cities. The Detroit Tigers and New York Giants fared pretty well. The Cardinals stayed in the black, not because they drew well—the fabled Gashouse Gang champions of 1934 attracted only 334,863 home fans—but because they sold lots of players. Branch Rickey's big farm system enabled the club to sell stars like Chick Hafey, Dizzy Dean and Joe Medwick for substantial prices—and obscure minor leaguers for as little as $100 each.

Poorer teams became destitute. The St. Louis Browns, consistent losers, drew only 1.2 million fans for the whole *decade*—an average of 120,000 a season, or 1,558 a game. The Philadelphia Phillies didn't do much better—on the field or at the box office. To pass time, Philadelphia sportswriters used to throw peanuts at each other. One day they began throwing paper cups of water, some of which leaked through the rotted floor of the press box and trickled into the stands. Gerry Nugent, the Phils' president, charged into the press box and expressed outrage. "Don't you realize we have patrons downstairs?" he yelled. Al Horwits of the *Philadelphia Ledger* jumped to his feet in feigned surprise. "My God, what a story!" he shouted.

Boston had two threadbare teams, and the Depression pushed the Braves even deeper into baseball's cellar. The Red Sox had finished last nine times from 1922 to 1932, but were rescued by Thomas A. Yawkey, a young

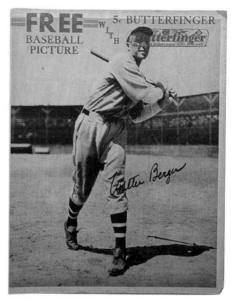

Brothers Rick (left) and Wes Ferrell (right) were reunited in 1934 thanks to the deep pockets of Red Sox owner Tom Yawkey. Wes won 20 or more games twice and Rick hit .300 twice in their first three years with the Red Sox, but Boston finished no better than fourth. So in 1937 Yawkey traded the brothers to Washington.

Wally Berger's picture may have been free, but his bat cost the Giants plenty when they traded for him in 1937. Two years earlier, Berger, despite playing for the last-place Braves, had led the NL in home runs and RBI, so the Giants gave up reliever Frank Gabler and $35,000 to get him. But the honeymoon was short, and after 16 games and a .188 average in 1938, Berger was traded to the Reds.

sportsman who bought the Bosox in 1933. Yawkey's father had made his fortune in mining and lumber and owned the Detroit Tigers for a few years early in the century. He bequeathed that fortune to his nephew and adopted son, Tom, who descended on the American League like a half-starved prospector just in from the hills with a poke of gold.

Yawkey wanted to buy; Connie Mack and Clark Griffith needed to sell. In a few years, Yawkey plundered the Athletics and Senators for more than $1 million in star players, and that was back when a million was a *million*. Yawkey didn't confine his spending to the A's and Senators. From the Cleveland Indians he bought pitcher Wes Ferrell, who was 26 years old and had already won 20 or more games in each of four seasons.

The Red Sox—who a decade before had helped build the Yankee dynasty by selling Babe Ruth, Carl Mays, Herb Pennock and other stars to the New Yorkers—now were spending in pursuit of their own dynasty. Rarely, if ever, has a team bought more big-name stars in such a short period of time. Of future Hall of Famers alone, Yawkey acquired pitcher Lefty Grove; catcher Rick Ferrell, Wes' brother; first baseman Jimmie Foxx; shortstop Joe Cronin and outfielder Heinie Manush.

The Cronin deal symbolized the Depression. He was the manager and star shortstop of the Washington Senators, having led them to the 1933 pennant. The Senators sank to seventh place in 1934. Cronin's team was in decline, but his love life was blooming, and after the 1934 season he married Mildred Griffith, the niece and adopted daughter of the Senators' owner, Clark Griffith. Joe and Mildred embarked on their honeymoon, and upon arriving in San Francisco, they found a message from Griffith. Cronin called, and his father-in-law asked him what he would think of moving to the

Continued on page 52

Floyd Vaughan, present Pirate Short Stop, and Coach Hans Wagner, who was one of the game's greatest

Arky Vaughan

Arky Vaughan was one of baseball's "quiet men": a dignified, no-nonsense shortstop whose powerful bat and talented glove earned him the admiration and respect of his fans and teammates but little space in the sports pages. At the time of his death, one writer noted, "More has been written about the colorful Willie Mays in one year than was said of Vaughan in a lifetime."

While Vaughan had little to say off the field, his prodigious baseball talents spoke for him on the field. Born in the tiny town of Clifty, Arkansas, Joseph Floyd Vaughan was nicknamed after his home state. He was signed by the Pittsburgh Pirates in 1931, and after a year in the minors at Wichita, the 20-year-old became the Pirates' starting shortstop. He hit .318 his rookie year and never looked back. For the next nine years Vaughan hit over .300, and in 1935 he hit .385—an average no National Leaguer has equaled since.

Over his 14-year career Vaughan racked up a .318 average, leading the league in triples and in runs scored three years each. He stole a league-leading 20 bases in 1943. Not only did he have speed and power, he also had a great eye, and he struck out only 276 times in 6,622 at-bats. And his defensive stats are impressive; he led NL shortstops in putouts and assists three times.

Vaughan played in seven All-Star games between 1934 and 1942, and lent his potent bat to the NL cause. In the 1935 game, Vaughan doubled and then scored the NL's only run on Bill Terry's single.

In the 1941 game, Vaughan, who hit only six homers in the regular season, came to the plate in the seventh inning and slugged a homer with a man on to give the NL a 3–2 lead. In the eighth, Vaughan repeated with another two-run homer to increase the lead to 5–2. But the AL, led by Joe DiMaggio and Ted Williams, picked up a run in the bottom of the eighth, then scored four runs in the ninth to win the game, 7–5. Despite his team's defeat, Vaughan made history as the first player ever to hit two home runs in a single All-Star game.

Even though Vaughan was quiet, he expressed his loyalty to his friends. Vaughan was traded to Brooklyn in 1942, and the next season, when Dodger manager Leo Durocher suspended pitcher Bobo Newsom, Vaughan, in support of Newsom, refused to suit up for a game. The incident opened a rift between Vaughan and Durocher, and after the 1943 season, Vaughan retired at the age of 31. When Durocher was suspended in 1947, Vaughan returned to the Dodgers and averaged .325 over 64 games. He retired for good after the 1948 season, and in 1952 died in a swimming accident.

Even though Vaughan was one of the game's great all-around players, he was long denied a place in the Hall of Fame. When another great shortstop, Pee Wee Reese, was elected in 1984, he was asked why he got the votes instead of Vaughan. Reese said he didn't know, but felt "surely Arky deserved recognition by now." Arky finally got that recognition, and was elected to the Hall of Fame in 1985.

Arky Vaughan was a pitcher's nightmare. A notorious first-ball hitter, Vaughan also had a great eye at the plate and tied an NL record by leading the league in walks for three straight years, 1934 through 1936. He also shredded the AL's best pitching, as he hit .364 in seven All-Star games, including two homers in 1941.

ARKY VAUGHAN

Shortstop, Third Base
Pittsburgh Pirates 1932–1941
Brooklyn Dodgers 1942–1943,
  1947–1948
Hall of Fame 1985

GAMES	**1,817**
AT-BATS	**6,622**
BATTING AVERAGE	
Career	**.318**
Season High	**.385**
SLUGGING AVERAGE	
Career	**.453**
Season High	**.607**
BATTING TITLE	**1935**
HITS	
Career	**2,103**
Season High	**192**
DOUBLES	
Career	**356**
Season High	**41**
TRIPLES	
Career	**128**
Season High	**19**
HOME RUNS	
Career	**96**
Season High	**19**
TOTAL BASES	**3,003**
EXTRA-BASE HITS	**580**
RUNS BATTED IN	
Career	**926**
Season High	**99**
RUNS	
Career	**1,173**
Season High	**122**
WORLD SERIES	**1947**

No Fans, No Fortune

As the Great Depression deepened, baseball fans worried more about putting food on their tables than getting to the ballpark. Team owners scampered to lower their expenses and bring in customers with gimmicks like night games and ladies' days. Meanwhile, players watched helplessly as their own gravy train ground to a halt and salaries never regained pre–1930 levels during the decade.

$8,000 —
6,000 —
4,000 —
2,000 —

1925
1930
1935
1940

10.0
8.0
6.0
4.0
2.0

Major league attendance (in millions)

Player's average annual salary in the 1930s

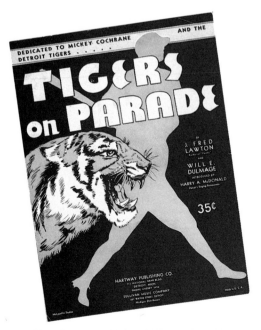

Tiger fans were singing their team's praises in 1934, as player-manager Mickey Cochrane led Detroit to its first pennant in a quarter century. Attendance nearly tripled, from 320,972 in 1933 to 919,161.

Red Sox. It was good news, and not just because Cronin escaped the delicate situation of having Griffith as his father-in-law and boss rolled into one. To be sure, it sounds callous for one man to sell his son-in-law to a rival. But Griffith had struck an excellent deal. Yawkey paid Griffith $250,000 for Cronin and agreed to give his new manager and shortstop a lucrative five-year contract. Griffith was glad to get the $250,000—a record price for a baseball player back then, the equivalent of roughly $1.75 million today. He was just as glad to secure the financial future of his daughter and son-in-law.

Cronin felt the same way. Good jobs were hard to come by during the Depression, even in baseball. Yawkey, however, did not get the pennant he was trying to buy. Even with their expensive lineup, the Red Sox didn't reach second place until 1938 and didn't win a pennant until 1946.

Frank Navin, president of the Detroit Tigers, had better luck. In late 1933 Connie Mack offered Mickey Cochrane, the Athletics' star catcher, for $100,000. The Tigers needed a catcher and a manager, too. Cochrane was a fine candidate—a superb player, a fiery competitor, and an intelligent, high-strung man who had been a star football player at Boston University before pursuing a career in baseball. Trouble was, the Depression had strapped the Tigers, too. Navin had borrowed $25,000 just to cover spring training expenses in 1932. But he had a wealthy partner in Walter Briggs, who had made millions in the auto business. Briggs agreed to put up the $100,000, and Cochrane joined the Tigers in 1934 as player and manager. Although player sales were rife during the Depression, Detroit's purchase of Mickey Cochrane was the first that bought a pennant. In fact, it bought two.

Not that Cochrane was a one-man team. At the same time, the Tigers acquired Goose Goslin, a veteran slugger, from Washington. Cochrane and Goslin were future Hall of Famers, and the Tigers already had two other players of the same caliber: second baseman Charlie Gehringer and Hank Greenberg, the first baseman.

Gehringer was a Michigan farmboy who in 1924 had impressed Ty Cobb, then the Tiger manager. He was a consistently superior hitter and fielder, and he made baseball look easy. "You wind him up opening day and forget him," one teammate said. That comment led to Gehringer's nickname. They called him "the Mechanical Man."

Greenberg grew up in the Bronx. He was the Jewish slugger the Yankees had always wanted to draw fans from New York's large Jewish population. In 1929 the Yanks' ace scout, Paul Krichell, escorted young Greenberg to a front-row box beside the Yankee dugout. Lou Gehrig stepped out of the dugout and kneeled in the on-deck circle. Krichell leaned over and whispered to Greenberg, "He's all washed up. In a few years you'll be the Yankees' first baseman." But Greenberg was awed by Gehrig. He recalled that incident in his autobiography: "His shoulders were a yard wide and his legs looked like mighty oak trees," Greenberg wrote. "I'd never seen such brute strength. 'No way I'm going to sign with this team,' I said to myself, 'not with him playing first base.' " So Greenberg turned down the Yankees and accepted an offer from the Tigers instead. He stood 6' 3½", weighed 210 pounds, and could hit the ball a mile. As a rookie in 1933, he batted .301 and hit 12 homers—a harbinger of better seasons ahead.

The 1930s were marked by high batting averages, and the 1934 Tigers were among the best, batting .300 as a team and getting an astounding

The Tigers' infield—from left, third baseman Marv Owen, shortstop Billy Rogell, second baseman Charlie Gehringer and first baseman Hank Greenberg—was one of the most intimidating offensive infields in history but could also play the field. In 1935 the quartet averaged 105 RBI each and helped the Tigers limit their errors to 128, lowest in the majors that season.

"WE WANT BEER!"

In 1931 the country was in the midst of the Depression, and Prohibition was still in effect. The President, Herbert Hoover, who favored Prohibition, took time off to attend Game 3 of the World Series between St. Louis and Philadelphia at Shibe Park on October 5.

When the President's party arrived, the Athletics' Lefty Grove and the Cards' Burleigh Grimes stopped their warm-up in deference to Hoover. As the President and Mrs. Hoover took their seats, there was a smattering of applause. But then someone started booing. Pretty soon it seemed almost everybody in the park was booing. Then the boos changed to a chant: "We want beer! We want beer!"

If Hoover was surprised or resentful he gave no sign. He sat with his hands folded and looked straight out on the field. Mrs. Hoover seemed to be studying a scorecard.

The crowd settled down as the game began. Grimes was pitching well, and at the end of eight, with the Cards ahead 4–0, a voice crackled through the amplifiers: "Silence. Silence, please." The President was leaving.

As the President, holding Mrs. Hoover's arm, walked slowly past the Athletics' dugout, the booing broke out anew and rocked the stands, finally yielding to the chant, "We want beer! We want beer!"

But the chant fell on deaf ears; Prohibition remained until Hoover was gone and President Franklin Roosevelt gave the people what they wanted on December 5, 1933.

Detroit's Marv Owen was 0 for 19 in the 1935 World Series when he came up in the sixth inning of Game 6, but he came through with a game-tying single that scored Billy Rogell (above). The Tigers won the Series in the ninth on an RBI hit by Goose Goslin.

462 RBI from the four infielders: Greenberg, 139; Gehringer, 127; shortstop Billy Rogell, 100; and third baseman Marv Owen, 96. As for the Tiger pitchers, Schoolboy Rowe won 16 straight games and wound up the season at 24–8. Tommy Bridges was 22–11, and Firpo Marberry and Eldon Auker—who pitched underhand—won 15 games apiece.

In the 1934 pennant race, the Tigers faced tough competition in the Yankees—it was Babe Ruth's last season in pinstripes—but Detroit won by seven games.

They won again in 1935. Greenberg, a relentlessly hard worker, was 24 and getting better. He hit a league-leading 36 homers, drove in 170 runs and was unanimously chosen MVP. But as baseball's first Jewish star, he endured cruel insults from rival bench jockeys. The Cubs were particularly harsh in the 1935 World Series. "Throw him a pork chop, he'll never hit it!" yelled Billy Jurges. That was clean; the anti-Semitic taunts became vulgar enough to incur a warning from umpire George Moriarty.

The Cubs won the Series opener, 3–0, Lon Warneke outduelling Schoolboy Rowe. Greenberg hit a two-run homer in the second game—won by the Tigers, 8–3—but in the seventh inning he broke his left wrist in a collision at home plate with catcher Gabby Hartnett. The Tigers nevertheless won the Series in Game 6 as Goslin, the old pro, singled home the winning run with two outs in the ninth.

Greenberg's wrist was re-injured early in the 1936 season, and he missed most of the season. The Tigers were plagued by other injuries—and by the Yankees, who now had Joe DiMaggio to bat in front of Lou Gehrig. Cochrane suffered a nervous breakdown in June and was sent to a Wyoming ranch to recover.

Mickey Cochrane's career ended abruptly on May 25, 1937, when he was beaned by a pitch from the Yankees' Bump Hadley. Cochrane had homered off Hadley earlier in the game, but refused to blame the Yankee pitcher, admitting that he was crowding the plate in an attempt to pull the ball behind the runner at first.

Pennants—and admirers—seemed to follow Goose Goslin wherever he went. In 1933 he helped the Senators win a pennant, then was traded to Detroit. When he returned to Washington's Griffith Stadium in late August of 1934 (above), the Senators were headed for seventh place and the Tigers were on their way to a pennant.

He came back, led the Tigers into a close race with the Yankees in 1937, and then suffered a severe injury. At Yankee Stadium on May 25, Cochrane hit a homer in the third inning off Bump Hadley, a fastballer who once pitched for the St. Louis Browns. Cochrane came up again in the fifth. The count went to 3 and 1. Hadley threw a fastball. It sailed and hit Cochrane in the head; batting helmets were unknown back then. Bill Dickey, the Yankee catcher, described the scene: "The ball dropped in front of the plate and Mike almost fell on top of it, right on his face. Then he rolled over on his back and said, 'Good God almighty.' "

Cochrane's skull was fractured in three places. He nearly died. He never played again—he was 34—and after resuming the managership, he continued to suffer seizures and night sweats. The Tigers, no longer contending, fired him in 1938.

Gehringer and Greenberg continued to excel. In 1937 Gehringer batted .371 to lead the league, and Greenberg drove in 183 runs, just one short of Gehrig's American League record, set in 1931. A year later, Greenberg chased Ruth's record of 60 homers. He wound up with 58, giving the fourth-place Tigers a badly needed boost in attendance. In reward, the Tigers sent him a 1939 contract calling for the same amount he had received the year before—$35,000. Greenberg was a shrewd and hard-nosed salary negotiator and talked the Tigers into a $5,000 raise—big stuff back then. At $40,000, Greenberg was probably baseball's highest-paid player. After all, times were hard.

Baseball was still strictly segregated and times were harder yet in the Negro leagues, which temporarily went out of business in 1931. Satchel Paige, the great black pitcher, played in Venezuela during the winter of 1933

Continued on page 58

"CHARLEY" GEHRINGER

Charlie Gehringer

harlie Gehringer was a pretty quiet guy. Once he was having breakfast with Tiger teammate Chief Hogsett, who also rarely spoke. Hogsett broke the silence, asking Gehringer to "pass the salt, please." Gehringer obliged, but added, "You might have pointed."

The Tiger second baseman preferred to let his bat and his glove do the talking, and from 1926 through 1940 he was arguably baseball's most consistent all-around performer. "Charlie Gehringer is in a rut," Yankee pitcher Lefty Gomez once said. "He hits .350 on Opening Day and stays there all season." They called Gehringer "the Mechanical Man" for his flawless style at bat and in the field, and for his seeming ability to excel without effort. He hit over .300 thirteen seasons, scored more than 100 runs twelve seasons and had more than 100 RBI seven seasons. The finest defensive second baseman of his era, he led the AL seven times each in fielding percentage and assists. And while Gehringer said little, others were vocal—and unanimous—in his praise. For years former AL batting champ Lew Fonseca filmed the swings of great hitters, and called Gehringer's "as close to being perfect as any we have ever taken on film. He had great hand action, and the bat was level coming into the ball at any height."

Detroit first baseman Hank Greenberg, who played alongside Gehringer for seven years, said, "He made everything look so simple it used to make me mad. He had this terrific ability to play the hitters just right. He'd be where the ball was hit—practically before the batter even swung."

Gehringer started his career as the best ballplayer in Fowlerville, Michigan, and kept raising his level of play to match the competition. Discovered by a hunting partner of former Detroit star Bobby Veach, Gehringer signed with the Tigers in 1923, and by 1926 was their starting second baseman. He cracked the .300 barrier in 1927, and dipped below it just once in the next 13 years. In 1929 he had his first star-quality season, hitting .339 and leading the AL in hits, doubles, triples, runs scored and stolen bases. By 1934 the Tigers had ripened into contenders, and Gehringer responded with his best season yet—a .356 average with 50 doubles, 134 runs scored, 127 RBI and 99 walks. He hit .379 in the Tigers' loss to the Cardinals in the World Series, then in the 1935 Series hit .375 in their win over the Cubs.

In his midthirties and supposedly past his prime, Gehringer kept getting better. In 1936 he hit .354 with 60 doubles and 144 runs scored. In 1937 he won his first batting title with a career-high .371 average, and in 1938 he banged a career-high 20 home runs.

He entered the Navy in 1942, and rose to the rank of lieutenant commander, but by the time the war ended he was too old to return to the field. He joined the Tigers as general manager in 1951, and was vice president from 1953 through 1959. "It wasn't near as much fun as playing," he said.

Had Gehringer been more outgoing, he might be more quickly and fairly remembered as one of the four or five greatest second basemen ever. But his style was very much his own, and is perhaps best captured in an incident described by Greenberg. "One day I'm circling under one of those towering pop-ups, falling all over my feet, and the ball drops in back of me for a hit," Greenberg said. "I turn around, sore as blazes, and there's Charlie. 'I'd have caught it,' he says very quietly, 'if you'd asked me to.'"

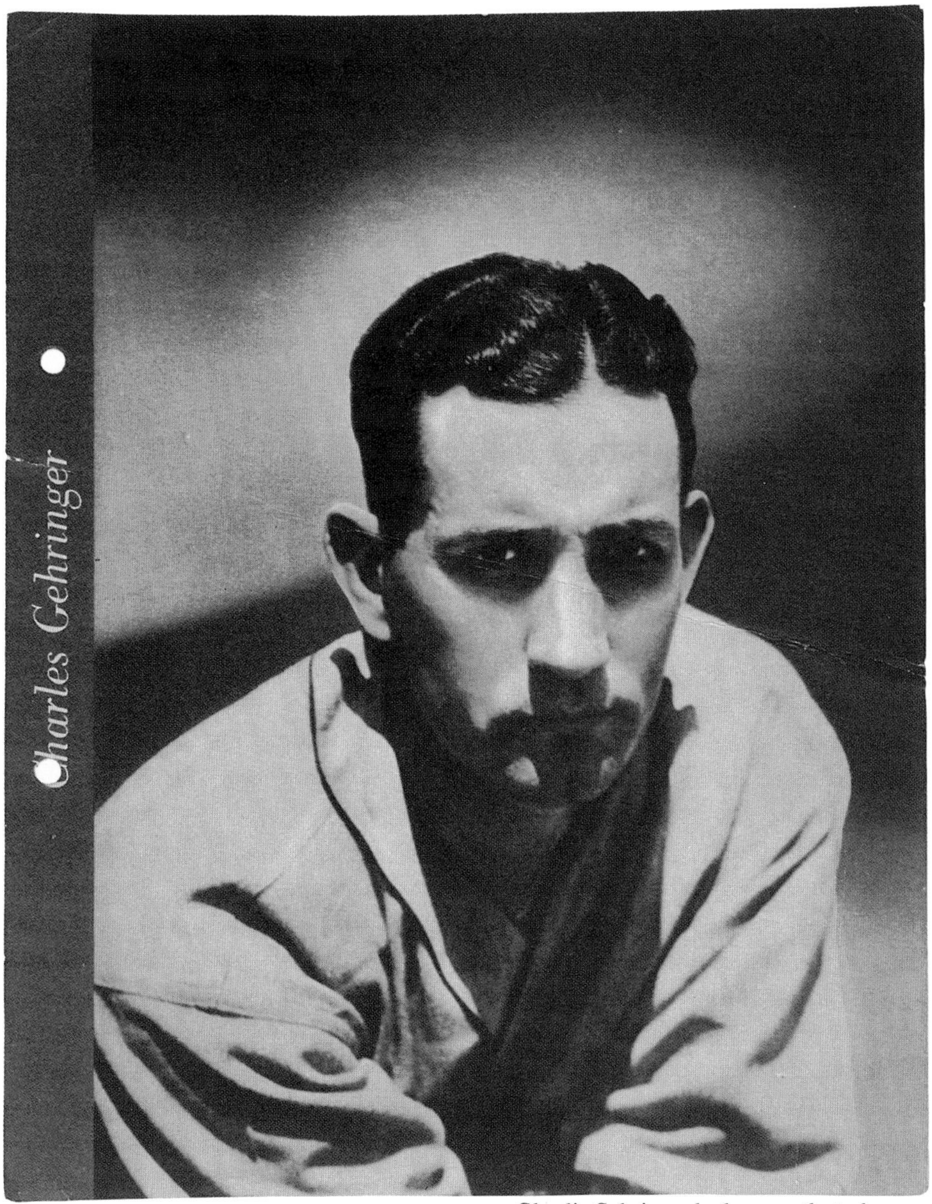

Charlie Gehringer had a smooth stroke, a great eye and an amazing ability to get his hits no matter what the count. "I honestly believe," said Tiger manager Del Baker, "Charlie could spot a pitcher two strikes all season and still hit within 15 points of his regular average."

CHARLIE GEHRINGER

Second Base
Detroit Tigers 1924–1942
Hall of Fame 1949

GAMES	**2,323**
AT-BATS	**8,860**
BATTING AVERAGE	
Career	**.320**
Season High	**.371**
SLUGGING AVERAGE	
Career	**.480**
Season High	**.555**
BATTING TITLE	**1937**
HITS	
Career	**2,839**
Season High	**227**
DOUBLES	
Career *(10th all time)*	**574**
Season High *(6th all time)*	**60**
TRIPLES	
Career	**146**
Season High	**19**
HOME RUNS	
Career	**184**
Season High	**20**
TOTAL BASES	**4,257**
EXTRA-BASE HITS	**904**
RUNS BATTED IN	
Career	**1,427**
Season High	**127**
RUNS	
Career	**1,774**
Season High	**144**
WORLD SERIES	**1934–1935, 1940**
MOST VALUABLE PLAYER	**1937**

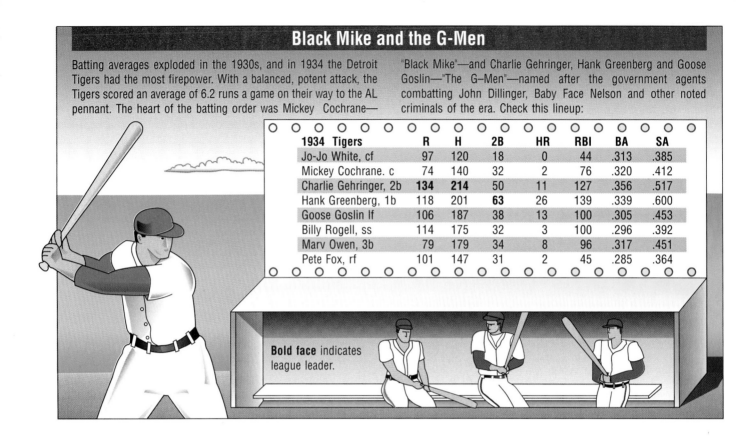

Black Mike and the G-Men

Batting averages exploded in the 1930s, and in 1934 the Detroit Tigers had the most firepower. With a balanced, potent attack, the Tigers scored an average of 6.2 runs a game on their way to the AL pennant. The heart of the batting order was Mickey Cochrane— "Black Mike"—and Charlie Gehringer, Hank Greenberg and Goose Goslin—"The G-Men"—named after the government agents combatting John Dillinger, Baby Face Nelson and other noted criminals of the era. Check this lineup:

1934 Tigers	R	H	2B	HR	RBI	BA	SA
Jo-Jo White, cf	97	120	18	0	44	.313	.385
Mickey Cochrane. c	74	140	32	2	76	.320	.412
Charlie Gehringer, 2b	**134**	**214**	50	11	127	.356	.517
Hank Greenberg, 1b	118	201	**63**	26	139	.339	.600
Goose Goslin lf	106	187	38	13	100	.305	.453
Billy Rogell, ss	114	175	32	3	100	.296	.392
Marv Owen, 3b	79	179	34	8	96	.317	.451
Pete Fox, rf	101	147	31	2	45	.285	.364

Bold face indicates league leader.

because, he said, "I didn't have a topcoat." The Negro leagues revived in 1933, but Paige and other black stars of the 1930s rarely caught the attention of white fans. Since the late 1880s, the major leagues had consisted of all-white teams. Among whites, in and out of baseball, the color ban was rarely discussed; segregation was taken for granted in virtually every area of American life. Black baseball stars played in their own leagues, earning a fraction of what white players earned. The most prominent of the all-black circuits was the Negro National League, with teams in the bigger eastern and midwestern cities. And while few segments of American society suffered as much as urban blacks did in the 1930s, the NNL enjoyed a lively following in the black community. White newspapers, from *The New York Times* on down, largely ignored the Negro leagues, but there were occasional exceptions. The *Cleveland Plain Dealer* carried this item on page 1, October 22, 1934: "Mr. Dizzy Dean is so dizzy that nearly 12,000 fans turned out yesterday on a threatening day to see him and his brother, Daffy, and, incidentally, Mistuh Leroy Satchel Paige, the colored pitcher for the Pittsburgh Crawfords."

Only "incidentally" did Satchel Paige and other black stars of the 1930s catch the attention of white fans, and it took someone like Dizzy Dean to change that custom, even temporarily. After pitching the Cardinal Gashouse Gang to the 1934 world championship, Dizzy and Paul Dean were news wherever they went. As was the custom back then, the Deans barnstormed for several weeks after the World Series, playing against various teams. Their schedule included three games against the Pittsburgh Crawfords, a Negro league powerhouse that included 5 of the 11 Negro league players later elected to the Baseball Hall of Fame. Besides Paige, the future Hall of

Eldon Auker's submarine-style delivery earned him 18 wins in 1935, making him third on the Tiger staff—behind Schoolboy Rowe and Tommy Bridges. But Auker lost just seven games and led the AL with a .720 winning percentage.

Famers were James "Cool Papa" Bell in center field; Oscar Charleston at first base; Josh Gibson, the legendary slugger, catching; and William "Judy" Johnson at third base. The Deans were there to draw fans, and from the promoters' standpoint, it didn't much matter who played alongside them.

It certainly didn't matter to Paige, who, like Diz, was expected to pitch at least a few innings of every game. The series opened in Cleveland on October 21, with the Deans playing with a Class A championship team called the Cleveland Rosenblums. Paul Dean played the outfield. Dizzy did his job, pitching three innings and yielding four hits and one run. Paige did his job, too. He pitched six innings and retired all 18 men he faced, striking out 13 of them. The Crawfords won, 4–1.

The series moved on to Columbus, Ohio, where chilly weather held the crowd to 1,650. The Deans were teamed with white professionals—a few journeyman major leaguers, coupled with good minor leaguers. Dizzy and Paul pitched two innings each and yielded one run apiece. Josh Gibson hit a two-run homer off Bob Kline, who pitched for the Philadelphia Athletics and Washington Senators in 1934. Paige pitched three innings. He walked the first man he faced and struck out the next three. He yielded two singles in the second inning, but stranded both men on base as he struck out the side. In the third, he walked the bases loaded with none out, then struck out the side once again. That was it for Paige—three innings, no runs, nine strikeouts. The Crawfords won, 5–3.

There were no days off in this series, so the third game, played in Pittsburgh, marked the third straight day of pitching for both Dizzy and Satchel. Diz pitched two shutout innings. *The Pittsburgh Press* didn't bother to mention Paige, and box scores back then didn't include pitchers' lines, so

The Pittsburgh Crawfords were a powerhouse of Negro baseball in the 1930s. The 1932 Crawfords (above) boasted five future Hall of Famers on their roster—pitcher Satchel Paige (back row, fourth from left), catcher Josh Gibson (back row, center, wearing jacket), outfielder Oscar Charleston (back row, second from right), and third baseman Judy Johnson and outfielder Cool Papa Bell (not pictured).

the record is a little cloudy. What is known is that Paige started and didn't bat, so he probably only pitched an inning or two. The white team scored one run in the first and another in the second. Paige fanned three and walked one. Gibson hit another homer. The Crawfords won, 4–3, to sweep the series.

Satchel Paige is best remembered for his colorful style, his pitching guile, and his "hesitation pitch," all of which delighted major league fans who saw him pitch for the Cleveland Indians in 1948 and 1949, and for the St. Louis Browns from 1951 through 1953. But Paige was 42 when he finally got into the major leagues, one year after Jackie Robinson broke the color barrier in 1947.

In 1934 Paige was 28 and in his prime. He threw a fastball and not much else. Still, the Deans had a few things to say about him. According to Paul, "that guy must have something. Yeah, he's got a helluva fast ball. Yes, sir, he's got a fast ball." Dizzy, usually staunch in his belief that only Paul could throw as hard as Dizzy himself, said this of Paige: "If you think I'm fast, you should see him." On yet another occasion, Paige aroused this evaluation from Dizzy: "A bunch of the fellows get in a barber session the other day and they start to arguefy about the best pitcher they ever see. Some says Lefty Grove and Lefty Gomez and Walter Johnson and old Pete Alexander and Dazzy Vance. And they mention Lonnie Warneke and Van Mungo and Carl Hubbell, and Johnny Corriden tells us about Matty and he sure must of been great and some of the boys even say Old Diz is the best they ever see. But I see all them fellows but Matty and Johnson and I know who's the best pitcher I ever see and it's old Satchel Paige, that big lanky colored boy."

Walter Johnson, the great Washington pitcher who managed first the Senators and then the Cleveland Indians in the 1930s, had observed another black star, Josh Gibson, and was equally impressed: "There is a catcher that any big league club would like to buy for $200,000. His name is Gibson . . . he can do everything. He hits the ball a mile. And he catches so easy he might as well be in a rocking chair. Throws like a rifle. Bill Dickey isn't as good a catcher. Too bad this Gibson is a colored fellow."

Too bad. Gibson, "the Babe Ruth of the Negro Leagues," died from a brain tumor in January 1947, just three months before Jackie Robinson played his first game for the Brooklyn Dodgers. Gibson was 35.

During the major leagues' winter meetings following the 1937 season, several black newspapermen sent this telegram to Pie Traynor, manager of the Pittsburgh Pirates: "KNOW YOUR CLUB NEEDS PLAYERS STOP HAVE ANSWERS TO YOUR PRAYERS RIGHT HERE IN PITTSBURGH STOP JOSH GIBSON CATCHER B. LEONARD FIRST BASE AND RAY BROWN PITCHER OF HOMESTEAD GRAYS AND S. PAIGE PITCHER COOL PAPA BELL OF PITTSBURGH CRAWFORDS ALL AVAILABLE AT REASONABLE FIGURES STOP WOULD MAKE PIRATES FORMIDABLE PENNANT CONTENDERS STOP WHAT IS YOUR ATTITUDE? WIRE ANSWER." Traynor didn't reply. Of the five Negro league stars recommended to the Pirate manager, only Paige made it to the major leagues. With any one of them, the Pirates probably would have won the 1938 pennant; as it was, they missed by two games. Too bad. ◖◗

Big Bill Foster—brother of Negro league pioneer Rube Foster—was the ace of the Chicago American Giants, one of the best Negro league teams in the 1930s. But his brightest moment came in the 1926 Negro National League playoff between the Giants and the Kansas City Monarchs. The Giants trailed four games to three in the best-of-nine series, but Foster shut out the Monarchs in both ends of a doubleheader, 1–0 and 5–0, to give the Giants the title.

COCHRANE
PHILA. "ATHLETICS"
28

Mickey Cochrane

To the fans, he was "Mickey." To the players, he was "Black Mike." The players had it right. Their nickname was a perfect fit for Gordon Stanley Cochrane, even though at first it was meant only to describe his raven black hair. Quickly, he became Black Mike, a fierce, brawling rogue whose high-test personality ignited his teammates just as it intimidated his opponents. Ultimately, he became the prototype for generations of firebrand catchers who inspired their teammates. He led his teams to pennants in Philadelphia and then in Detroit, where he not only lifted the Tigers to their first American League championship in 25 years, but also helped rouse the city out of the depths of the Depression. Black Mike had that effect on people.

It became clear when he was in college that Cochrane was not just another talented athlete. At Boston University, he was a one-man football team, running, kicking, passing and single-handedly keeping his squad in games against much stronger opponents. In practice he would take kickoffs and see if he could run through the whole team without the help of any blockers. He could box, and was as tough as he was fast. In one college match, he knocked out a fighter who was at least a foot taller and 100 pounds heavier than he was.

To make money during the summer, Cochrane played baseball for a team in Dover, Delaware, starting out as an infielder but switching to catcher when that was the only spot open. He was not a pretty sight behind the plate, looking particularly ugly on pop fouls. But his aggressive bat drew the attention of a Pacific Coast League team in Portland, Oregon, where he played in 1924, then of Connie Mack, the wily owner and manager of the Philadelphia Athletics. In 1924 Mack bought the Portland team and turned Cochrane over to Cy Perkins, the A's regular catcher, for training. Perkins drilled Cochrane, and the next season, when Mack sent Cochrane into a game, Perkins knew what was happening. "There goes my job," he announced.

He was right, of course. Almost immediately Cochrane began driving the team, catching 133 games and finishing his rookie year with a .331 average. In the next eight seasons, he never caught fewer than 115 games, and he hit over .300 five more times. In 1928 he was chosen the American League's Most Valuable Player and when the Athletics won the World Series in 1929 and 1930 and another pennant in 1931, Cochrane, according to Connie Mack himself, was the main reason. This, on a team with Jimmie Foxx, Al Simmons and Lefty Grove.

Two years later, though, a Depression-drained Connie Mack, desperate for money, sold his star to the Tigers. It was one of the biggest deals of the decade; with Cochrane as player-manager, the Ty Cobb style of baseball came back to Detroit. Cochrane played with a fury, cursing foes, scowling at teammates and pushing himself harder than ever. He batted second in the Tigers' powerful lineup, an unusual spot for a catcher, but Cochrane was unusually fast for a catcher. Still, by the end of the 1934 season, he was so drained he sometimes slept in hos-

Mickey Cochrane was an all-around threat at the plate. A patient, high-average hitter with good power, Cochrane was one of only two players to hit for the cycle twice in the 1930s. Lou Gehrig was the other.

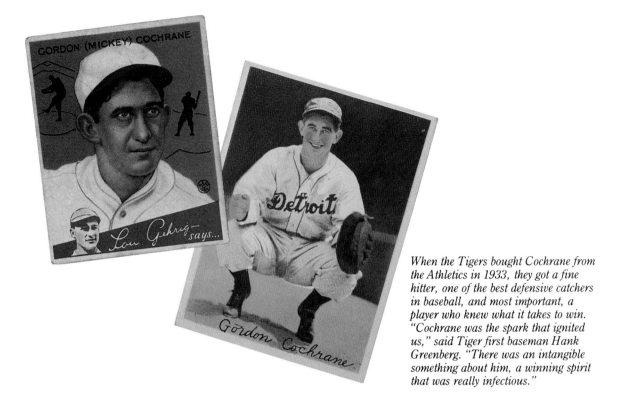

When the Tigers bought Cochrane from the Athletics in 1933, they got a fine hitter, one of the best defensive catchers in baseball, and most important, a player who knew what it takes to win. "Cochrane was the spark that ignited us," said Tiger first baseman Hank Greenberg. "There was an intangible something about him, a winning spirit that was really infectious."

pitals between games. Despite his exhaustion, he wouldn't miss a game. "So long as I can limp behind the plate," he said, "I'll play ball." Cochrane limped through the Series, which the St. Louis Cardinals' Gashouse Gang won, four games to three. After the Tigers lost the Series, Cochrane promised a Detroit championship the following year. True to his word, the team edged the Yankees for the pennant in 1935, then beat the Cubs in the Series. Naturally, Black Mike scored the winning run, capping off what he called "my greatest day in baseball."

But the team suffered a slump the next season, something that literally drove the high-strung Cochrane to a nervous breakdown. After ten days in the hospital and two weeks at a friend's dude ranch, he returned to the dugout and led the team on a late-season surge that earned them second place. Cochrane was confident the Tigers would come back in 1937. By May, the team was battling the Yankees for first place and Cochrane was hitting .306. On May 25, Cochrane was at the plate with a 3–1 count when Yankee Bump Hadley threw a high fastball. Cochrane

lost sight of the ball and the pitch struck him on the right temple, cracking his skull in three places. After ten days in a coma, he regained consciousness. He told the first person to interview him, "I don't think I'll ever catch again." Doctors warned that another head injury could be fatal. And after such a close brush with death, the team decided his playing days were over.

He returned as manager, but removed from the heat of battle, he lost some of his rage. The team wilted, and midway through the 1938 season, he was fired. When a crowd of fans gathered at the airport to say good-bye and wish him well, Black Mike broke down and cried.

Cochrane joined the Naval Reserves during World War II and became athletic director, training baseball players, football players, basketball players and boxers. He was elected to the Hall of Fame in 1947 and returned to the major leagues for one season as general manager of the A's in 1950. In 1961 he became vice president of the Detroit Tigers. He died in 1962.

MICKEY COCHRANE

Catcher
Philadelphia Athletics 1925–1933
Detroit Tigers 1934–1937
Hall of Fame 1947

GAMES	**1,482**
AT-BATS	**5,169**
BATTING AVERAGE	
Career	**.320**
Season High	**.357**
SLUGGING AVERAGE	
Career	**.478**
Season High	**.553**
HITS	
Career	**1,652**
Season High	**174**
DOUBLES	
Career	**333**
Season High	**42**
TRIPLES	
Career	**64**
Season High	**12**
HOME RUNS	
Career	**119**
Season High	**23**
TOTAL BASES	**2,470**
EXTRA-BASE HITS	**516**
RUNS BATTED IN	
Career	**832**
Season High	**112**
RUNS	
Career	**1,041**
Season High	**118**
WORLD SERIES	**1929–1931,**
	1934–1935
MOST VALUABLE PLAYER	**1928,**
	1934

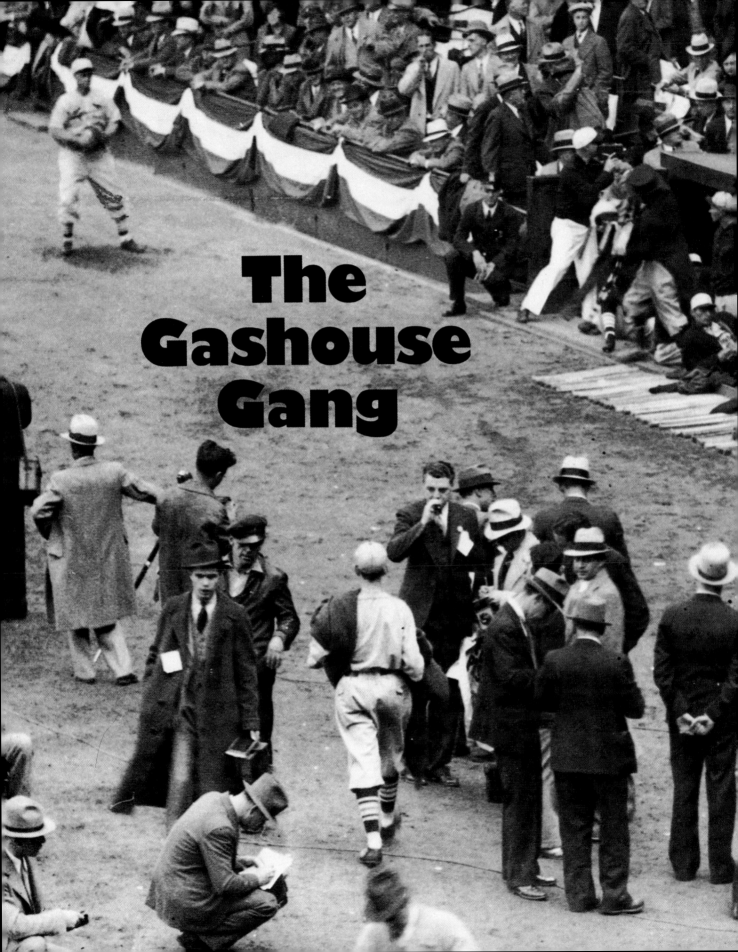

The Gashouse Gang

In the spring of 1934, both Dizzy (above, right) and Paul Dean were coming off 20-win seasons. Dizzy had won 20 for St. Louis, Paul 22 for Class AA Columbus. By mid-October they had 53 wins, 373 strikeouts and a pair of world championship rings.

All eyes—and a lot of camera lenses—were on Cardinal right-hander Dizzy Dean (preceding page) as he warmed up prior to Game 1 of the 1934 World Series. Five years earlier, a scout's trained eye picked the 18-year-old Dean (above) from a semipro team in San Antonio, Texas.

Dizzy Dean growed up poor, as he would put it, but he was never humble. Take his name—or rather, his names. Jay Hanna Dean was born January 16, 1911, in Lucas, Arkansas. His father was a cotton sharecropper. As a child, Dizzy made fifty cents a day picking cotton; with that kind of wage, who needed school? So after fourth grade, Dizzy quit. About that time his playmate died, and Diz was moved to an act of charity. Here's how he described it to sportswriter J. Roy Stockton: "My name, in the first place, was Jay Hanner Dean and this boy's was Jerome Herman something or other. I was named after some big shot in Wall Street, or he was named after me, I don't know which. Anyhow, this boy Jerome Herman took sick and died, and we sure did feel sorry for his dad. He just moped around and didn't care for nothin' no more. So I went to him and told him I thought so much of him that I was goin' to take the name of Jerome Herman, and I've been Jerome Herman ever since. He perked up right away, and I guess wherever he is he's mighty proud."

At 17, Diz joined the Army and got "the first pair of shoes I ever owned." He also got his enduring nickname. Pitching for an Army team in an exhibition game against major leaguers, Dean was mowin' 'em down. In frustration, the opposing manager exhorted his players. "Don't let that dizzy kid beat you!" he said. Dizzy it was.

Back then, a soldier could buy his way out of the army. Diz's little brother, Paul, saved $120 from his cotton-field earnings and bought Diz back to civilian life in 1929. Diz then got a job in San Antonio, Texas. Pitching for a company team, he caught the eye of Don Curtis, one of Branch Rickey's far-flung Cardinal scouts. The Cardinals signed Dean in late 1929, and in

There was little deception involved in Dizzy Dean's pitching. He threw hard—and often. "He never tried to hide what was coming next," said veteran NL shortstop Dick Bartell. "He'd tell you if you asked, or even if you didn't. And he'd still strike you out."

The Cardinals did manage to win a few games before the Dean brothers arrived and the Gashouse Gang got its name. In 1931 they won their fourth NL pennant and second world championship in six years.

1930, at the age of 19, Dizzy Dean made his professional debut with St. Joseph, Missouri, of the Western Association.

The team was weak, but Diz was sensational. He won 17 games and became the darling of the fans. Civilization was new to him. He learned to check into hotels but not to check out, so he kept rooms at the YMCA and two hotels, enabling him to sleep wherever he had the urge to. When his clothes got dirty, he stuffed them in a drawer and bought new ones. When threatened with a bill, Diz had it sent to the team's business manager.

The Cardinals promoted Dean to Houston of the Texas League. He won his first start, 12–1, and apologized to the team president, Fred Ankenman. "Can you imagine them bums gettin' a run off me?" Diz asked. He won eight games for Houston, bringing his total for the season to 25.

The Cardinals had just clinched the pennant after a harrowing 1930 pennant race and brought up Dean to watch a few games and pitch the season finale. He stopped the Pirates on three hits, two of them by Pie Traynor, and won, 3–1. Dean thought it unfortunate that he had come up too late to be eligible for the World Series. "Gee, I'll bet a lot of St. Louis people wish I was pitching every game," he said.

The season over, Dean—still just 19—returned to St. Joseph and gave local sportswriters a modest analysis of his prospects, which he had already confided to the Cardinal manager, Gabby Street. "I don't recall seeing any better than myself," Dean said of the National League's pitchers. "I told Gabby I could win him 20 or 30 games next year. And to tell the truth I don't think I will be beaten." He said he knew only one pitcher who could throw the ball harder, a precocious 17-year-old named Paul. Paul Dean.

Cardinal team captain and second baseman
Frankie Frisch (above, center) was named the
league's Most Valuable Player in 1931—the
first year the award was made by the Baseball
Writers Association of America. Frisch
earned the award with a .311 average, 24
doubles, 96 runs scored, a league-leading 28
stolen bases and just 13 strikeouts.

Diz came to spring training in 1931, drove poor Gabby Street up the
wall and found himself back in Houston, where he won 26 games. In 1932 he
made the Cardinals' roster, won 18 games, led the NL in strikeouts for the
first of four consecutive seasons and persuaded the Cardinals to sign his little
brother, Paul. By 1934 Diz was the best pitcher in baseball, Paul was ready
for the big leagues and the Cardinals had put together the rough, rowdy, colorful team that has gone down in history as "the Gashouse Gang."

Its manager, oddly enough, was a college man. Frankie Frisch grew
up in a well-to-do New York family. He attended Fordham University,
where he captained the football, basketball and baseball teams. He was a
good enough halfback to earn second-team All-American honors, and his alma
mater gave some sportswriter the inspiration for Frisch's enduring nickname. He was "the Fordham Flash," and in 1934, at 35, he was still the NL's
best second baseman.

Frisch came to the Cardinals in one of history's most startling trades.
He broke in with the New York Giants in 1919 and by 1921 was a star on
John McGraw's world-champion team, batting .341 and leading the league in
stolen bases with 49. But no one would have called him the league's best infielder back then because the league's best player, Rogers Hornsby, played
second for the Cardinals.

Many authorities consider Hornsby the greatest right-handed hitter
in history. Over five seasons—1921 through 1925—he batted .397, .401,
.384, .424 and .403. Match *that,* Ty Cobb. Hornsby led the league in
batting and slugging all five of those seasons, and in home runs for two. As
playing manager, he led the Cardinals to their first pennant in 1926, and in

Rogers Hornsby played for the Cardinals from 1915 through 1926 and managed them to a world championship in 1926. "The Rajah" was a stupendous hitter, but an ornery man whose abrasiveness made him tough to play for. "Hornsby didn't coax or coddle anybody," said shortstop Dick Bartell. "He had no feelings and didn't think anybody else did, either."

the World Series he tagged Babe Ruth for the final out as the Cards won in seven games.

Hornsby was the toast of St. Louis. He owned stock in the Cardinals. He demanded a big salary for 1927, and he spoke rudely to Sam Breadon, the Cardinals' owner, accusing him of scheduling too many exhibition games. "You're money hungry," Hornsby told Breadon. Enraged, Breadon ordered his general manager, Branch Rickey, to get rid of the ungrateful Hornsby. Rickey swapped Hornsby to the Giants for Frisch and a journeyman pitcher, Jimmy Ring.

The St. Louis fans were outraged. The mayor protested the trade, the Chamber of Commerce condemned it by proclamation, and many of Breadon's acquaintances stopped speaking to him. Frisch was greeted as an interloper, but he played so well and with such abandon that he gradually won the fans over, particularly when the Cardinals won pennants in 1928, 1930 and 1931.

Frisch was named manager midway through the 1933 season. He inherited a happy-go-lucky team and quickly imposed the disciplined system that he had learned under McGraw. The Cardinal players grumbled, and the team finished fifth in 1933. No one picked the Cards to win in 1934, but they were loaded with talent, thanks to Branch Rickey's fertile farm system.

Rickey had a superb eye for young talent, and he was merciless. The Cardinals couldn't afford to pay good salaries—they didn't draw nearly as well as the Giants, Dodgers or Cubs—so Rickey sold or traded star players and replaced them with hungry youngsters developed within the Cardinal farm system. Other big league teams were just catching on to the idea of

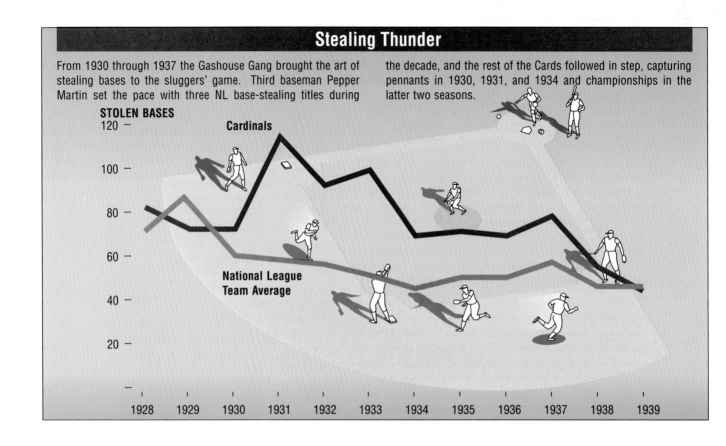

Stealing Thunder

From 1930 through 1937 the Gashouse Gang brought the art of stealing bases to the sluggers' game. Third baseman Pepper Martin set the pace with three NL base-stealing titles during the decade, and the rest of the Cards followed in step, capturing pennants in 1930, 1931, and 1934 and championships in the latter two seasons.

STOLEN BASES

Cardinals

National League Team Average

120 — 100 — 80 — 60 — 40 — 20 —

1928 1929 1930 1931 1932 1933 1934 1935 1936 1937 1938 1939

developing players through a chain of minor league affiliates. Commissioner Landis opposed the farm-system concept, saying it impeded the progress of young players and deprived minor league towns of their independence. But the farm system worked, and from the early 1920s until the mid to late 1930s, it was virtually a Cardinal monopoly. At one minor league convention, Rickey and his party occupied 27 hotel rooms. In the spring of 1934 more than 450 rookies reported to Cardinal training camps. That summer, another 1,000 found their way to Cardinal tryout camps—another Rickey innovation. Rickey himself worked practically around the clock. He signed players, sold players, traded players without hesitating. He lent money to threadbare minor league teams in exchange for the right to pick their best players at season's end.

With so much talent waiting in the wings, even Cardinal veterans looked over their shoulders. Two future Hall of Famers—outfielder Chick Hafey and first baseman Jim Bottomley—found themselves traded to last-place Cincinnati after helping the Cardinals win back-to-back pennants in 1930 and 1931, and hitting a combined .333 in the process. Bottomley's replacement was Ripper Collins, who earned his way with a pretty good season at Rochester in 1930, when he hit .376 with 40 homers and 180 RBI. Hafey was later replaced by Joe Medwick, up from a .354 season at Houston in 1932 and a future Hall of Famer himself. Collins proceeded to tie Mel Ott of the Giants for the 1934 home-run crown, while batting .333 and driving in 128 runs. Medwick, then only 22 years old, hit .319 and drove in 106 runs. Medwick was called "Ducky" or "Ducky Wucky" because a fan once remarked that he walked like a duck. He hated the nickname. "It makes me want to fwow up," he said.

Cardinal third baseman Pepper Martin had an unusual way of looking at things. For example, he claimed that chewing tobacco— Martin used Beech-Nut (left)—made him a smarter player. "When your jaws work you can't talk, and when you can't talk you must think," he reasoned.

Pepper Martin hunted in the off-season and offered Cardinal executive Branch Rickey a package of venison after they finished negotiating his contract in 1938. Rickey was the Cardinal vice president for all but one of Martin's 13 major league seasons.

Pepper Martin played third base for the "Gang," and he was almost as colorful as Dizzy Dean. From Oklahoma, he was every bit as much a farm boy, and he could *run*. They said Martin hunted rabbits back home by running alongside them, feeling their ribs and tossing the fat ones in his sack. In the 1931 World Series Martin stole five bases off the best catcher in baseball, Mickey Cochrane. He also batted .500, scorching Lefty Grove and George Earnshaw, as the Cardinals beat the Athletics, 4–3.

His full name was Johnny Leonard Roosevelt Martin. Everyone called him Pepper, and sportswriters gave him a beautiful nickname—"the Wild Hoss of the Osage." Martin was all smiles, dirt and hustle. He led the NL in stolen bases three times and batted around .300 year after year. He and Diz liked to cut up together. Passing time on a road trip, they dressed themselves in overalls one day, found ladders and other equipment, and walked loudly into a convention at Philadelphia's Bellevue-Stratford Hotel. They knocked down chairs, moved tables, climbed ladders, talked about the renovations they were beginning, and finally feigned a fight, Dean collapsing from a ferocious pantomimed right from Martin. Someone recognized the great Dizzy Dean, and the conventioneers were delighted.

When exhibition play took the Cardinals to an out-of-the-way community, Dean and Martin put on a street-corner act to give the town its money's worth. This was before television, and celebrities were not recognized as readily as they are today. Martin would stroll to one corner, Dean to another a block away. "Hey there, Dizzy Dean!" Martin would yell. "Hey, Pepper Martin!" Dean would reply, and the townsfolk would come running.

With the temperature over 100 degrees, as it often was on sultry afternoons at St. Louis' Sportsman's Park, Dean and Martin lit a bonfire in front of

Continued on page 76

JOE DUCKY MEDWICK, Cards

Joe Medwick

Hitters are inspired by all kinds of things: team pride, personal glory, the challenge of facing a great pitcher. Joe Medwick, left fielder for St. Louis' Gashouse Gang, was inspired by money. His creed was simple: "If I get the base hits, I will get the buckerinos."

And it worked: he set a National League record for most doubles in a season with 64 in 1936, won the Triple Crown in 1937 and led the NL in RBI from 1936 through 1938. For that he was paid $19,000 a year, at a time when major league salaries averaged about $6,000.

In his 17 years in the majors, Medwick batted .300 or better 13 times. Not bad for a notorious bad-ball hitter, who was known to jump after pitches well outside the strike zone.

Medwick didn't achieve those numbers without being aggressive. Known as "Muscles" to his teammates, he cut off his sleeves, baring his powerful arms in an attempt to intimidate pitchers. That worked, too. Dodger reliever Dutch Leonard described the prevailing attitude among NL pitchers: "I think the league should forbid his carrying a bat to the plate. Make Medwick use his fist to swing against us. Then he'd only smack out singles."

Pitchers on his own team could vouch for the power of his fists. When Ed Heusser complained in the dugout that Medwick had slacked off in the outfield, Medwick knocked him out. Tex Carleton, another St. Louis hurler, took a punch from Medwick after they disagreed over who should take batting practice first. Dizzy Dean, the team's most colorful pitcher, said, "Durndest man I ever seen. Before you even get to do enough talking and get mad enough to fight, Joe whops you and the fight's over."

Medwick's aggressive play caused a celebrated incident in the 1934 World Series against Detroit. As Medwick slid hard into third base, Tiger Marvin Owen stepped on top of him. Medwick turned and kicked at Owen with his spikes. The Detroit fans were outraged, and when Medwick returned to his position in left field, he felt their resentment. As the *New York Daily News* described it, "A single red apple flew from the crowd and rolled at his feet, and Medwick fielded it lazily and gracefully. . . . The next moment the air was full of flying fruit—apples, oranges, bananas—and beer and pop bottles, the fruit squashing and breaking into little bits, the . . . bottles striking the turf and rolling over and over." Commissioner Landis had to remove Medwick from the game to stop the shower and allow the game to continue.

Despite his abrasiveness, Medwick was a popular player, especially among women fans. While he was playing for Houston of the Texas League, a woman in the stands commented that he walked like a duck, referring to him as her "little Ducky Wucky." The name stuck, and although Medwick hated it, he was willing to live with it when a local candy company offered him royalties if they could market a candy bar by the same name. Anything for money.

Years later, after Medwick had retired, he was approached by a writer who wanted to interview him about his days with the Cardinals. "I'm not going to talk to you about the Gashouse Gang," Medwick said, "unless I'm paid. I want fifteen hundred dollars or I won't answer questions." But either age had softened him, or he was softer than he seemed all along: they eventually settled on $250.

Extremely aggressive, Ducky Medwick led the NL at one time or another in every hitting category except walks. In the 1934 All-Star Game he hit a three-run homer off a pitch from Lefty Gomez that was so high that catcher Bill Dickey admitted he could never have caught it.

JOE
MEDWICK

Outfield
St. Louis Cardinals 1932–1940, 1947–1948
Brooklyn Dodgers 1940–1943, 1946
New York Giants 1943–1945
Boston Braves 1945
Hall of Fame 1968

GAMES	1,984
AT-BATS	7,635
BATTING AVERAGE	
Career	.324
Season High	.374
SLUGGING AVERAGE	
Career	.505
Season High	.641
BATTING TITLE	1937
HITS	
Career	2,471
Season High	237
DOUBLES	
Career	540
Season High *(2nd all time)*	64
TRIPLES	
Career	113
Season High	18
HOME RUNS	
Career	205
Season High	31
TOTAL BASES	3,852
EXTRA-BASE HITS	858
RUNS BATTED IN	
Career	1,383
Season High	154
RUNS	
Career	1,198
Season High	132
WORLD SERIES	1934, 1941
MOST VALUABLE PLAYER	1937

The 1934 Cardinals could beat you at every phase of the game. They led the NL in runs scored, doubles, batting, slugging, stolen bases, double plays, complete games, strikeouts and shutouts. The cast included, from left, pitcher Paul Dean, shortstop Leo Durocher, pitchers Tex Carleton and Wild Bill Hallahan, outfielder Chick Fullis, infielder Whitey Whitehead, catcher Spud Davis and pitchers Bill Walker and Jim Mooney.

the dugout one day, wrapped themselves in blankets and squatted by the blaze. The fans, of course, loved it.

In 1932 in the off-season, the Cardinals lost their superb shortstop, Charley Gelbert, who accidentally shot himself in the foot while hunting. So Rickey traded an excellent pitcher, Paul Derringer, to the Reds for a scrappy veteran shortstop who added a new shade to the Gashouse palette. He played a sharp game of billiards, dressed like a dandy, talked out of the side of his mouth Damon Runyon-style, and was called "C-note" because he often ran out of money and asked for a salary advance by saying, "Gimme a C-note," although he usually had to settle for a twenty. He wasn't much of a hitter, so they also called him "the All-American Out." He was a big talker, a genuine loudmouth, and for that he earned the nickname that endures—"the Lip." But Leo Durocher played shortstop very well, and with his fiery personality he was right at home with Martin, Frisch, Medwick and Dean.

Legend has it that the Cardinals came to be known as the Gashouse Gang after taking the field in New York one day in filthy, wrinkled uniforms. In fact, dirty uniforms were the norm back then; after a game, clubhouse attendants merely brushed the heavy, hot, flannel uniforms and hung them up for wear the next day. Laundering uniforms was an occasional thing anyway, but the Cardinals somehow got dirtier, sweatier and sometimes bloodier than their opponents. New York had a dangerous slum called the Gas House district. According to *The Dickson Baseball Dictionary,* a sportswriter told Leo Durocher one day that the Cardinals were good enough to play in the American League, which was then regarded as superior to the National. Durocher replied, "They wouldn't let us play in the American

League. They'd say we were just a lot of gashouse players." In his autobiography, Durocher recalled a newspaper cartoon by the great sports cartoonist, Willard Mullin. "It showed two big gas tanks on the wrong side of the railroad track, and some ballplayers crossing over to the good part of town carrying clubs over their shoulders instead of bats. And the title read: 'The Gas House Gang.'"

In 1934 the New York Giants were defending world champions, favored to repeat. Bill Terry, the Giant manager and first baseman, made no secret of his optimism. "Anybody want to bet a hat that we don't win again?" he asked a bunch of sportswriters. One of the assembled writers covered the Dodgers, who had finished sixth in 1933. "Do you fear Brooklyn?" the writer asked.

"Is Brooklyn still in the league?" Terry replied.

Terry's flip remark outraged Dodger fans, and the new Dodger manager, a former outfielder named Charles Dillon "Casey" Stengel, seized upon it as a rallying cry. "The first thing I want to say is that the Dodgers are still in the National League," Stengel told the writers. "Tell that to Bill Terry. And I don't care what you fellows call my club—the Daffiness Boys, the Screwy Scrubs, or anything, so long as they hustle."

Out in St. Louis, Dizzy Dean predicted that he'd break the major league strikeout record. Brother Paul was up after a 22–7 season at Columbus, and briefly held out for a higher salary. Paul was quiet; Diz spoke for him. "The club offered him a raise over what he got at Columbus, but it wasn't enough for a man of his skill," Diz explained. "It was the same salary the club offered other young pitchers, and Paul ain't an ordinary pitcher. He's a great pitcher. He's even greater than I am, if that's possible."

Although the rowdier members of the Gashouse Gang got most of the ink, first baseman Ripper Collins (above, sliding) was hands down the team's best hitter in 1934. Thirty-five home runs tied him with Mel Ott for the NL lead, and he added 40 doubles and 12 triples for a league-high .615 slugging percentage.

Pennant Poetry

oems—mostly doggerel—once graced the sports pages of American newspapers. Before the 1934 season, Bill Terry, the New York Giants' manager, asked, "Is Brooklyn still in the league?" As the 1934 pennant race between the Giants and the St. Louis Cardinals ground down to its final two games, sportswriter John Kieran penned this masterpiece for *The New York Times* to remind Bill Terry of his flippant question. Kieran's verse was prophetic: the sixth-place Dodgers—managed by Casey Stengel—were spoilers, winning both games from the Giants and allowing St. Louis to slip past New York and win the National League pennant.

Casey Stengel

BALLAD OF BITTER WORDS

Why, Mister Terry, oh! why did you ever
Chortle the query that made Brooklyn hot?
Just for the crack that you thought was so clever,
Now you stand teetering right on the spot!
Vain was your hope they forgave or forgot;
Now that you're weary and bowed with fatigue,
Here is the drama and this is the plot:
Brooklyn, dear fellow, is still in the league.

Sir, if they can they will blithely dissever
Giants in segments unequal or not.
Homicide, Bill, is their plan and endeavor;
Starting on Ryan and Jackson and Ott,
You they expect to reduce to a blot.
La guerre a la mort! (Or in German *"Der Krieg!"*)
Vengeance they want to the ultimate jot:
Brooklyn, dear fellow, is still in the league.

Detroit awaits you? Says Lopez: "Ah, never!"
Pennant for Terry? Says Casey: "What rot!"
Using your scorn as a club or a lever,
Brooklyn will labor and chisel and swat.
Prize in the bag—now it may go to pot!
(Furnish sad music by Haydn or Grieg),
Bill, you won't like it a bit or a lot;
Brooklyn, dear fellow, is still in the league.

Bill, get out the bandages; set up the cot;
Trouble looms up in this bitter intrigue.
Stengel is handing out powder and shot:
Brooklyn, dear fellow, is still in the league.

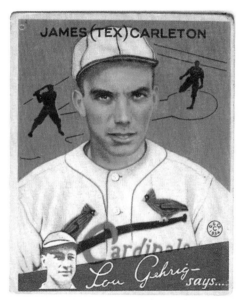

Although Dizzy and Paul Dean often mangled the English language, they were popular enough in 1935 to appear on the cover of a composition notebook. Their combined career totals with the Cardinals include 180 wins, 105 losses and a .632 winning percentage.

As a starter in the same rotation as the Dean brothers, Tex Carleton got little attention despite 16 wins in 1934. Carleton was traded to the Cubs at the end of the 1934 season for pitchers Bud Tinning and Dick Ward. Tinning and Ward never won a game for the Cards, while Carleton went 51–35 in four seasons with Chicago, then pitched a no-hitter for Brooklyn in 1940.

Paul signed a week later, and Diz reassured Cardinal owner Sam Breadon that he would get his money's worth. "If we don't win 40 or 45 games between us, we'll give the money back to you, Mr. Breadon," he said. It wasn't exactly a bet, but if it had been, the Deans would have won. Not that Dizzy and Paul got big money from Breadon and Rickey. Diz was paid $7,500, the same salary he earned in 1933, when he won 20 games for a fifth-place club. Paul got $3,000. That was lousy pay, but not as lousy as it sounds. After holding out, Jimmie Foxx signed with the Athletics for about $18,000; he was coming off a 1933 season in which his .356 average, 48 homers and 163 RBI earned him the Triple Crown.

Branch Rickey told Ernie "Showboat" Orsatti, the Cards' regular center fielder, that he'd have to take a 25 percent salary cut, and when Orsatti threatened to give up baseball for a career in Hollywood, Rickey called his bluff, saying, "If Orsatti's prospects in the movies are as encouraging as he outlined to me, he would be foolish not to quit baseball." Orsatti signed, although he really *did* have an off-season job as a Hollywood stunt man; he stood in for Buster Keaton, among others, in dangerous scenes.

To save money, the Cardinals went with a 21-man roster. The brothers Dean shouldered extra burdens from the start, starting in rotation and also working in relief. Their pitching was no more sophisticated than their talk; both Deans threw *hard*. Paul was almost as good as Diz said he was, and so was Diz himself. On May 9, 1934, Diz shut out the Giants, 4–0. Two days later, Paul beat Carl Hubbell, the Giant ace, 3–2, in ten innings. Nine days later, the Cards routed Hubbell again, as Collins and Medwick homered, and Frisch tripled home three runs. Blessed with a big lead, Diz taunted the

Giants, chatted with the umpires, strutted around the pitcher's mound and put on a show for 40,000 New York fans.

On May 30 the Cardinals swept a doubleheader in Cincinnati, Medwick contributing five hits in the nightcap. But through the summer the Giants held first place and looked secure. The Cardinals had four good pitchers: the Deans, Tex Carleton and Bill Walker. But Diz didn't credit Carleton or Walker, much less the team's weaker pitchers, and his comments were not always designed for team harmony. Diz was standing with three other Cardinal pitchers one day, when a writer asked him his opinion of Frisch. "I think Frisch is the most wonderful manager in the world," Diz replied. The writer asked why, and Diz said, "because he's the only man who could keep a club in a pennant fight with only two pitchers."

"Who are the two pitchers, Dizzy?"

"Me and Paul."

In August "Me and Paul" skipped a trip to Detroit, where the Tigers had sold 40,000 tickets for an exhibition game against the Cards; Diz and Paul were supposed to man the coaching lines. The Cardinals fined Diz $100 and Paul $50, whereupon the brothers refused to play in the Cardinals' next game. They were suspended without pay. Diz, in a rage, tore up his uniforms. The Cards deducted $36 from his paycheck to pay for them. The team was left with 19 players, and Frisch said Pepper Martin might pitch.

Deanless, the Cardinals won three straight from the Phillies. Paul ate crow, was reinstated, and beat the Phils, 12–2, for his 13th victory. Diz sought a hearing before Commissioner Landis, who traveled to St. Louis and opened the transom above his office door so writers could hear the testimony. Frisch summarized the resentment against Diz. "There are 10 million

Ducky Medwick had a sweet swing, and in 1937 he could do little wrong. Not only did he win the Triple Crown, he set a record with four hits in the All-Star Game. Medwick's All-Star mark was later tied by a pair of Red Sox—Ted Williams in 1946 and Carl Yastrzemski in 1970—but never bettered.

Pepper Martin shocked the baseball world with his hitting and hustle in the 1931 World Series, and in the 1934 World Series picked up right where he left off. Against Detroit, Martin scored eight runs— including one in a four-run rally in an 8–3 Cardinal win in Game 1 (opposite)—drove in three, stole two bases and hit .355.

Spud Davis (above, left) and Bill Delancey shared the catching duties for the Cardinals in 1934. They combined for 22 home runs, 105 RBI and a .307 average. Davis came up with the Cards in 1928 but played only two games before being traded to the Phillies for catcher Jimmie Wilson. Wilson had three good years for St. Louis, then slumped and was traded back to the Phils—for Davis.

people out of work in this country, yet Dizzy Dean is willing to sacrifice a daily income of approximately $50 to fill the role of a playboy," the Cardinal manager said. Landis ruled in the Cardinals' favor, and Diz capitulated. "I can't afford to lose any more money," he said. "It costs me $50 a day to be idle, and so far I've lost $486—a $100 fine, $36 for two uniforms I destroyed, and $350 for seven days under suspension." Then as now, there was big money being thrown around in baseball.

Diz returned, shut out the Giants, and stole his only base of the season. His demeanor was appropriately subdued, and he resumed his remarkable pace. But the Giants were playing better ball. On Labor Day, the Cardinals lost a doubleheader to the Pirates; the next day, the Giants swept a doubleheader and pulled seven games ahead. The Giants had 24 games to play, 20 of them at the Polo Grounds. "I guess we couldn't ask for much more," said Bill Terry. The New York manager began discussing whether he would start Carl Hubbell or Hal Schumacher in the first game of the World Series.

Suddenly the Cardinals got hot. On September 16 the biggest crowd in NL history, 62,573 fans, poured into the Polo Grounds to watch the Giants tackle the Deans in a doubleheader. Paul had beaten them three days before, pitching 12 innings to outduel Freddie Fitzsimmons, 2–0. This time Diz won the opener, 5–3, with help from Tex Carleton. Paul, pitching on two days' rest, fought Hubbell to a 1–1 tie through ten innings. Darkness was setting in, and umpire Bill Klem almost called the game, but he decided to let it go one more inning. Pepper Martin homered to lead off the St. Louis eleventh. Paul then set down the Giants in the home half for the victory.

Five days later, the Deans were scheduled to pitch a doubleheader at Ebbets Field—Diz working the first game, Paul the second. Frisch knew the

Dodger hitters and was giving advice: "Keep the ball high and outside for [Sam] Leslie. He'll hit it over the fence if you get it inside."

"That ain't how I pitch to him," Diz replied. "I give him nothin' but low and inside stuff, and he ain't got a hit off me yet."

Tony Cuccinello was next up in the discussion. "Nothing but curves for Tony," said Frisch. "Tony'll slap a fastball into the left-field lumber every time you give him one."

"That's mighty funny," said Diz. "I never have bothered to dish him up a curve yet, and he's still trying for his first loud foul off old Diz."

On it went, Diz countering Frisch's advice for every Brooklyn hitter. Finally, Diz said, "This is a silly business, Frank. I've win 26 games already this season and it don't look exactly right for an infielder like you to be tellin' a star like me how I should pitch."

Frisch exploded. He told Dean to pitch any way he liked and suffer the consequences. Diz dismissed the suggestion that he might lose. He won, 13–0, yielding just three hits. Paul pitched a no-hitter. "If I'd a knowed Paul was gonna throw a no-hitter I'da throwed one too," Diz complained.

The Cards played another doubleheader two days later. Paul relieved in one game, Diz in both. They split. So did the Giants, whose 2½-game lead prompted this headline in the *New York Post:* "GIANTS REST UP FOR WORLD SERIES."

The Cardinals proceeded to win four of their next five games, while the Giants lost two and suffered through three idle days. With two games to play in the season, St. Louis and New York were tied for the lead. Both teams were at home, the Cardinals hosting last-place Cincinnati, and the Giants taking on the sixth-place Dodgers—and thousands of Dodger fans, who

To the victor go the spoils, even if they have to be ripped from the ground in hostile territory. Jubilant Cardinals fans made off with home plate from Detroit's Navin Field after St. Louis hammered the Tigers, 11–0, in Game 7 of the 1934 World Series.

5′ 11″ 180 lbs.
BR TR

b 8/12/1912

HARLOND CLIFT
Third Base

Harlond Clift was one of the best third basemen in baseball in the 1930s. Unfortunately, there was hardly anybody around to notice.

Clift was the shining star of the St. Louis Browns—baseball's black hole in the 1930s. During Clift's tenure with the team, from 1934 through 1943, the Browns drew an average of 2,000 fans per game. Twice they drew fewer than 100,000 in a season, and twice they lost more than 100 games. They languished in the shadow of the more successful Cardinals, and sportswriter Jim Baker likened playing third base for the Browns in the 1930s to "teaching astronomy at the Colorado School of Mining."

But Clift was a star, and among the first of a new breed of power-hitting third basemen. In 1937 he set a record for third basemen by hitting 29 home runs, then broke it the following year with 34. He drove in 118 runs each of those seasons, scored more than 100 runs seven times and had at least 100 walks six times. Clift was also a fine fielder, and playing behind a pitching staff whose ERA was 6.00 or higher three times in the decade, he worked overtime. He handled 603 chances cleanly in 1937, still a major league record, and his 405 assists and 50 double plays set records that lasted until Graig Nettles broke both in 1971.

Clift toiled in St. Louis obscurity until August of 1943, when he was traded to Washington. A year later, the Browns won their first and only pennant. The Senators finished last.

By 1936 the Cards had slipped to third, but their farm system kept producing great talent. First baseman Johnny Mize (right) became one of the game's finest power hitters, while Terry Moore established himself as the NL's best defensive center fielder.

remembered Bill Terry's preseason put-down. The Brooklyn fans carried homemade banners proclaiming, "YEP, WE'RE STILL IN THE LEAGUE." They rang cowbells, jeered Terry and the other Giants, and cheered the eccentric Dodger pitching ace, Van Lingle Mungo. Mungo pitched a five-hitter and got two key hits himself.

In St. Louis, Paul Dean, working on two days' rest, let Cincinnati scatter 11 hits for a single run. This time the headline of the day graced the front page of the *Brooklyn Times-Union*: "BROOKLYN DODGERS 5; NEW YORK GIANTS 1. ST. LOUIS CARDINALS 6; CINCINNATI 1. YES, INDEED, MR. TERRY, THE DODGERS STILL ARE IN THE LEAGUE."

With one game to go, the Giants could tie the race if they won and the Cards lost. The Giants scored four runs in the first inning, but the Dodgers pecked away, and the game went into the tenth. In St. Louis, the Cardinals were breezing behind Diz. They led, 9–0, but in the top of the ninth, the Reds loaded the bases with no outs. Diz fanned the next batter. He had two strikes on the following batter, when the St. Louis crowd of 37,402 erupted; the scoreboard had posted the final score in New York—Brooklyn over the Giants, 8–5. Diz proceeded to finish his shutout—and his 30th win of the season, to go with Paul's 19.

The World Series opened in Detroit, but the visiting Dean brothers were the center of attention. Fans and reporters followed them everywhere. Diz started the first game on two days' rest. Mickey Cochrane, Detroit's catcher-manager, countered with Alvin "General" Crowder, his third-best starter. The Tigers were tense, and their fielding misplays helped the Cardinals win, 8–3. Dean was invited to a radio studio to give a firsthand account of the game for Admiral Richard Byrd, who at the time was questing for the

South Pole. "Howdy there, Dick Byrd, down at the South Pole," Diz said. "Well, it was a hard-pitched game. I didn't have anything on my ball. That's why I had to work so hard. I finally staggered through. But it was a lousy, tick-flea and chigger-bit ball game. I'd be tickled plumb pink to pitch tomorrow again," Diz continued. "I'd have my stuff I know and I'd shut Detroit out. If they'd let me pitch all the games, I think I could probably win all four."

In fact, Diz *lost* a game. With the Series tied at two games each, Tommy Bridges outdueled the elder Dean, 3–1. Diz was lucky to be pitching. The day before, he had been called in as a pinch-runner for Spud Davis at first base. Pepper Martin, the next batter, hit a double-play grounder to Charlie Gehringer at second base, who flipped the ball to Billy Rogell, the Tiger shortstop. Protocol called for Diz to slide, but instead he ran straight up at Rogell, whose throw to first conked Diz squarely in the head. Dean fell like a dead man; the ball bounced into right field. "The blow that floored Dizzy would have knocked down two elephants," Grantland Rice wrote in the *New York Sun.* Diz was carried from the field. He spent the night in a hospital, but pitched well the next day in a losing cause.

Back came Paul to win the sixth game, 4–3, over the Tiger ace, Schoolboy Rowe. The Cardinal bench loudly reminded Rowe of his bumpkin line to his sweetheart while he was starring in a radio show. "How'm I doing, Edna?" Rowe had said and regretted it ever since.

With the Series tied at three games each, Frisch debated his pitching choice for the seventh game. Logic led him to consider Bill Hallahan, who had pitched well in two previous World Series. Dizzy Dean, his best pitcher, had only had one day of rest. Diz nominated himself and suggested that Paul be waiting in the bullpen. "This is a family matter," Diz said.

It wasn't exactly the way Dizzy Dean envisioned himself being carried from the field in the 1934 World Series, but it was his own fault. Appearing as a pinch runner, Dean failed to duck under a throw from Tiger shortstop Billy Rogell in Game 4 and got beaned. Manager Frankie Frisch took the heat for using his star pitcher to pinch-run, but Dean came back. He started Game 5 and lost, 3–1, but two days later pitched a shutout to win Game 7.

Commissioner Kenesaw Mountain Landis (right) told Cardinal manager Frankie Frisch (3) that Ducky Medwick (center) would have to leave Game 7 of the 1934 World Series for his own safety. Medwick slid hard into Tiger third baseman Marv Owen in the sixth inning, leading to a mild scuffle, and frustrated Tiger fans—with their team behind by nine runs—showered Medwick with fruit, garbage and pop bottles when he took his position in left. Medwick's unusual ejection hardly mattered, however, as the Cards won, 11–0.

He got the call, and before the game he walked over to watch Eldon Auker warm up for the Tigers. Auker, a fine pitcher, threw almost underhand. Diz laughed at him. "You don't expect to get anyone out with that stuff, do you, podner?" he asked. Auker didn't retire many. The Cardinals knocked him out in the middle of a seven-run rally in the third inning. Dean started it with a double, came up again with the bases loaded and beat out an infield hit to drive in a run. Frisch drove in three runs with a double of his own. In the Cardinal sixth, Martin singled. With two out, Medwick tripled. Taking the throw into third behind Medwick, Owen, the Tiger third baseman, stepped on Ducky—perhaps by accident. Medwick, still on the ground from his slide, kicked at Owen, causing an uproar in the stands. For the moment, Medwick escaped the heat by scoring on the fourth straight hit by Ripper Collins.

Diz had the Tigers shut out, and with the Cards ahead, 9–0, the game was all but over. But not for the Detroit fans; they took out their frustration on Medwick, throwing fruit, vegetables and soda bottles at him as he took his position in left field. He stayed out of range and played an idle game of catch with Pepper Martin, the third baseman. Three times Medwick tried to take his position. The fans continued to throw at him, littering the field. "Take him out! Take him out!" they shouted. Commissioner Landis beckoned Medwick, Frisch, Marv Owen and umpire Bill Klem to his box seat. Over Frisch's objection, Landis ordered Medwick removed from the game for his own safety. Chick Fullis trotted out to take his place. Diz finished his shutout, a six-hitter, and the Cardinals won, 11–0. Appropriately enough, Diz and Paul had each won two World Series games. They had shared 49 victories during the regular season. The world

President Franklin Delano Roosevelt threw out the first ball for the 1937 All-Star Game at Griffith Stadium, but the ball remembered most from that game was the one hit by Earl Averill that broke Dizzy Dean's toe. Dean, just 26, was never the same after the injury. "I got over 2,000 hits in my career," Averill said years later, "but the thing I'll always be most remembered for is breaking a guy's toe."

championship provided a big Depression payday for the Cardinals, who took home shares of $5,821.19 each.

The Gashouse Gang never won another pennant, although they came close in 1935, when Diz won 28 games and Paul won 19, and in 1936, when Diz won 24. Paul, 22 years old, developed a sore arm that year and won only five games. He hung around a few more years, but never regained his form.

Diz started strong in 1937. In the All-Star Game he blanked the AL for two innings, and retired the first two men he faced in the next frame. Then Joe DiMaggio singled and Lou Gehrig homered. Earl Averill, the Cleveland slugger, lined a shot off Dean's left toe.

"Your big toe is fractured," the doctor told Dean.

"No it ain't," Dean replied. "It's broke."

After the All-Star break, the Cardinals were still in the pennant race, and Dean continued to pitch. Favoring his left foot, he was forced to adopt an unnatural motion. His arm got sore and never recovered. In 1938 the Cardinals dealt him to the Chicago Cubs for three players and $185,000. He never again won as many as ten games, and he closed his career with 150 wins, the fewest of any pitcher in the Hall of Fame.

But he gave baseball a heckuva ride. After his playing days, he became the nation's most popular baseball broadcaster, thanks to his cheerful and colorful patter. His grammar was so bad that a schoolteachers' organization tried to get him fired, but the fans rallied to his side. They always did, and Diz always left 'em laughing. ◐

Inside the Park

I f you could put together the price of a ticket—anywhere from about 50 cents for a bleacher seat to around $2 for a box seat—and actually get through the turnstiles of a ballpark in the 1930s, you were in for a treat. Baseball had embraced power, with all its allure and excitement. And while the bunt, run and steal strategy of the early 20th century was largely gone, aggressive, combative baseball was still in style. Rough-hewn country boys brought farm-bred muscles to the big cities, and pounded balls over fences—or into catchers' mitts—at an unprecedented pace. Great rivalries produced the kind of intensity that's always good for the game. The Dodgers hated the Giants, the Cardinals hated the Cubs, and everybody hated the Yankees. It was a decade-long roller-coaster ride around the bases, and although few could predict what would happen next, everyone knew it would be exciting.

New York's Polo Grounds was a great place to be in the 1930s, as Giants fans (above) cheered their heroes on to three pennants in the decade. Even exhibition games were hotly contested, as Cleveland's Ken Keltner (right) slid safely into second with a steal and Giants shortstop Billy Jurges leaped in vain for a wild throw from catcher Ken O'Dea.

The pressure of the World Series got to Giants first baseman Johnny McCarthy in 1937, and he was charged with two errors on the same play in the fifth inning of Game 3. McCarthy (right) first booted a grounder hit by the Yankees' George Selkirk (3), then made a bad throw to pitcher Hal Schumacher (17). Selkirk went to second and later scored the final run in a 5–1 Yankee win. The Yankees won the Series in five.

Pittsburgh's Adam Comorosky was severely outnumbered in this rundown in 1931, chased by Giants catcher Bob O'Farrell toward third baseman Johnny Vergez, with shortstop Travis Jackson covering third. The whole year was like that for Comorosky, who had hit .313 and had an NL-high 23 triples in 1930, then plunged to .243 in 1931.

The Phillies had a hard time scoring runs in 1939, when they managed to lose 106 games. But center fielder Herschel Martin (left) came home safely on the back end of a double steal on May 13. Martin eluded the tag of Giants catcher Harry Danning, and umpire Larry Goetz made the call.

By Popular Demand

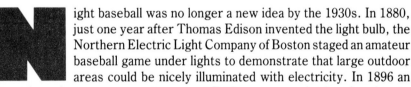

Night baseball was no longer a new idea by the 1930s. In 1880, just one year after Thomas Edison invented the light bulb, the Northern Electric Light Company of Boston staged an amateur baseball game under lights to demonstrate that large outdoor areas could be nicely illuminated with electricity. In 1896 an up-and-coming young promoter named Ed Barrow organized a minor league exhibition game under the lights; among the players was Honus Wagner, who later had more than a few good days in the sun. George F. Cahill, a Massachusetts inventor, came up with a portable lighting system in 1909 and hauled it around the country, staging successful demonstrations at minor league fields and even at Chicago's brand-new White Sox Park, later renamed Comiskey Park.

The lights worked and fans turned out for such curiosities, but the major leagues didn't give night baseball the time of day. Then came the Depression. In 1929 Des Moines of the Class A Western League announced that it would open its 1930 home season under the lights. The Independence, Kansas, Producers of the Class C Western Association staged organized baseball's first night game on April 28, 1930, beating Des Moines. On the same night, the first Negro league night game was played in Enid, Oklahoma.

Four nights later, an overflow crowd of more than 10,000 turned out to watch the Des Moines Demons shine under six brand-new light towers. The proceeds were more than enough to pay the electric bill, reported by

The night sky over Cincinnati's Crosley Field was never so bright as on May 24, 1935, when night baseball burst upon the big leagues. But some were skeptical, including Senators owner Clark Griffith, who said, "High-class baseball cannot be played under artificial light."

Night baseball was dubbed "MacPhail's Madness," after its major league originator, Reds general manager Larry MacPhail. But former Reds president Garry Herrmann liked what he saw, as the Reds beat the Phillies in baseball's first night game (above). "Night baseball has come to stay," he said.

The Sporting News to be $25. Players said they noticed little difference, if any, in the playing conditions. The dam had broken, and night baseball swept through the minor leagues, saving a number of franchises from Depression bankruptcy.

This example was not lost on Sam Breadon, owner of the St. Louis Cardinals, a team that was drawing poorly despite a fine record. In August 1930 Breadon threw a picnic for New York and St. Louis sportswriters at his farm outside St. Louis, and used the occasion to sing the praises of night baseball. "It makes every day a Sunday," Breadon said. He got nowhere. Two years later he offered to pay for installing lights at Sportsman's Park, which the Cardinals rented from the Browns. Phil Ball, the Browns' owner, rejected the offer.

The breakthrough was achieved by Larry MacPhail, general manager of the Cincinnati Reds, who had seen the success of night baseball firsthand as general manager of an American Association franchise in Columbus, Ohio. By the mid-1930s, the Reds desperately needed a boost. They were the dregs of the National League, finishing last in 1931, 1932, 1933 and 1934. Fans stayed home in droves; in 1934 Cincinnati's home attendance sank to 206,773, an average of fewer than 3,000 fans a game.

At the National League's annual meeting in December 1934, MacPhail asked permission to play night games at Crosley Field, the Reds' home grounds. Most club owners and sportswriters considered night games not only a break with tradition, but a downright sacrilege. But the Depression had cut deeply into attendance, plunging most teams into the red, and the success of night ball in the minor leagues indicated that fans would turn out to see

games played under the lights. Of course they would; most people work in the daytime and pursue leisure and recreation in the evening. Movie theatres had grasped this obvious fact from the beginning, but baseball resisted until pushed to the wall by economic pressures.

Reluctantly, with distaste and apology, the major leagues allowed night baseball to begin in 1935. NL owners voted to let the Reds play seven night games that year—one against each visiting team, although any team had the right to refuse. Doubt and apprehension accompanied the decision. "Night baseball is not to be compared to day baseball," reported baseball's own organ, the *Spalding Official Baseball Guide*. "It is entirely different, although masquerading under the same name."

MacPhail was a showman, and he was not about to back down. The first major league night game was staged May 24, 1935. President Franklin D. Roosevelt pushed a button in the White House to turn on Crosley Field's 632 lights. Ford Frick, president of the National League, threw out the first ball. With 20,422 fans on hand, the Reds beat the Phillies, 2–1, behind the strong pitching of Paul Derringer.

The Reds drew 130,000 fans to their handful of night games in 1935, yet other teams continued to spurn the practice. "Baseball is made to be played in God's own sunshine," proclaimed Clark Griffith, owner of the Washington Senators. Not until 1938 did a second team install lights, and again the perpetrator was Larry MacPhail, who had moved from the Reds to the Brooklyn Dodgers. MacPhail lit up Ebbets Field, and 38,748 fans turned out on June 15, 1938, for New York City's first big league night game. They got their money's worth, as Cincinnati's Johnny Vander Meer pitched the second of his two consecutive no-hit games.

Larry MacPhail was convinced he was right about baseball under the lights—even if no other baseball executive agreed with him—so when he moved from Cincinnati to Brooklyn in 1938, he put lights in Ebbets Field (above). Brooklyn's first night game was a memorable one: Cincinnati's Johnny Vander Meer, who had pitched under the lights at Crosley Field, tossed his second consecutive no-hitter, despite walking eight, including three in the ninth.

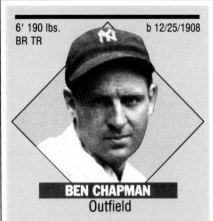

6' 190 lbs.
BR TR

b 12/25/1908

BEN CHAPMAN
Outfield

With a flash of spikes and a cloud of dust, Ben Chapman slid into the major leagues in 1930. And by reviving the lost art of base stealing, the Yankee rookie made himself a fan favorite.

"The crowd would rather see Chapman steal second than to see me make a homer," observed Babe Ruth. And while that may not have been completely true, Chapman did put on quite a show.

In 1931 fans clamored to see "the next Ty Cobb" steal a league-leading 61 bases—almost twice as many as anyone else. On June 14, 1932, they held their breath as "the fastest man in baseball" scored on a triple steal for a Yankee win over Cleveland. In 1932 and 1933, they watched as Chapman again led the AL in stolen bases. And in 1934, he raced around the basepaths for a league-leading 13 triples.

But despite tremendous speed, a great arm and a lifetime batting average of .302, Chapman never achieved superstar status. A big ego and a bad temper tripped him up, and after several trades, he went back to the minors in 1942. Though he returned to the majors—as a pitcher—for Brooklyn in 1944, he never hit his stride. After pitching 13 games in 1945, he was traded to the Phillies, becoming the team's player-manager. But he antagonized players. He was accused of making racist remarks toward Jackie Robinson and other blacks, and he compiled a losing record over his four years as manager. The Phillies gave him his walking papers in 1948.

A flick of the switch lit up Brooklyn's Ebbets Field on June 15, 1938. It was the second major league stadium to host night baseball.

Connie Mack, by then 76, brought night baseball to the American League in 1939. The inaugural night game at Philadelphia's Shibe Park was played May 16, with the Athletics losing, as usual, this time to the Cleveland Indians. Attendance was 15,109. The Phillies used Shibe Park too, and both Philadelphia teams played seven night games at home in 1939. Fans voted for night baseball with their presence and their ticket money.

Night baseball spread in 1939 to Municipal Stadium in Cleveland, Comiskey Park in Chicago and the Polo Grounds, home of the Giants, in New York. In that year, the St. Louis Browns drew as many fans in 14 night games as they did in 63 day games. Pittsburgh followed in 1940 and Washington in 1941, Clark Griffith having overcome his distaste for nocturnal play. But a few teams, notably the Yankees, still held their noses high. "If night ball is stopped, I will not be the one to cry," said Edward G. Barrow, the general manager of the Yankees. "It's a wart on the nose of the game."

The Chicago Cubs bought a lighting system and planned to install it at Wrigley Field in time for the 1942 season, but instead they donated the entire system to the federal government for defense use after the Japanese bombed Pearl Harbor on December 7, 1941, plunging the United States into World War II. Wrigley Field remained without lights until 1988, when it finally straggled into the fold, the final major league holdout.

Night baseball was not the only innovation viewed with suspicion by baseball men of the 1930s. Another was a newfangled thing called radio. Play-by-play broadcasting began in the 1920s, and by 1930 the World Series was carried on NBC and CBS. Radio equipment was not cheap, but by the 1930s more American families had radios than indoor plumbing and

Lights brought nightlife to the ballpark, and in Brooklyn, Rudy Friml Jr.'s band (above) entertained fans before a 1939 game against the Cardinals.

motorcars. Radio delivered baseball to listeners far from franchise cities, and listening to a game on the radio was cheap compared with buying a ticket.

In that innocent era, radio stations didn't pay the teams for broadcasting rights, as they do today. The question facing baseball teams was whether or not to allow radio men and their equipment into the press boxes. The Chicago Cubs, for one, believed that play-by-play broadcasts would arouse fan interest and increase attendance. They welcomed broadcasters; five Chicago stations carried Cubs' play-by-play. At the other extreme were the three New York teams. They feared that fans would listen at home rather than buy tickets at the park, so all three barred play-by-play broadcasts until 1939.

In Detroit, station WWJ carried Tiger games as a public service, refusing commercial sponsorship until 1934. Three teams—the Cardinals and Browns in St. Louis and the Pirates in Pittsburgh—barred broadcasts on Sundays and holidays. There were, after all, empty seats to fill. By 1936 all big league teams, except those in New York, agreed to have at least some of their games broadcast over the radio.

But not every day. In cities with two teams—Boston, Chicago, Philadelphia and St. Louis—the team playing at home had its game on the air, but the team on the road did not. The feeling was that teams competing for the same public had more to lose from fans' loyalty to one team or the other than they did from radio broadcasts. It wouldn't be fair, went the logic of the day, for the White Sox to lose a ticket sale at Comiskey Park because some Chicagoan sat home listening to the Cubs' away game.

Broadcasters of the 1930s just sat down in the press box and talked. They didn't travel around with crews of producers and directors and technical experts and statisticians. Most of them didn't travel at all. Games on the

Continued on page 106

Wes Ferrell

Wes Ferrell liked to say that his father didn't just raise wheat, corn and tobacco on the family's 150-acre farm in Greensboro, North Carolina. "More than anything else we raised ballplayers," explained Ferrell. Two of his six brothers played professional ball. Brother George played the outfield in the minors for more than 20 years and had a .321 career batting average. Brother Rick, a Hall of Fame catcher, originally signed with the St. Louis Browns, then went to the Boston Red Sox in 1933. The next year, Wes was traded to Boston, and the two became one of the greatest brother batteries of all time. "He was a real classy receiver," Wes said of his brother. "You never saw him lunge for the ball; he never took a strike away from you. He'd get more strikes for a pitcher than anybody I ever saw, because he made catching look easy."

Like countless other pitchers, Wes often dreamed of walking up to the plate and slapping out singles, doubles, triples and even—God willing—home runs. *Unlike* most other pitchers, he realized his dream. Over his 15-year career the 6′ 2″ farm boy hit .280 and set both the single-season and career records for home runs by a pitcher—records that still stand. Some compared Ferrell to Babe Ruth, the game's most famous hard-hitting pitcher. Historian Bill James noted, "As a hitter, I think he would be in the Hall of Fame had he become an outfielder, and he is the one pitcher I would say that about."

Ferrell's blazing fastball made him more valuable on the mound than in the outfield. He won over 20 games in each of his first four full seasons with Cleveland. No other pitcher in either league has ever done that. In 1930 he went 25–13 and in 1931 he pitched a no-hitter. With the Red Sox in 1935 he posted a 25–14 record, and led the AL in wins, starts and completions. He pitched more innings than any other American Leaguer from 1935 through 1937.

While Ferrell's fastball eventually faded, his hair-trigger temper never disappeared. The man sportswriters dubbed "Terrible-tempered Ferrell" regularly flew into rages over salary disputes, bad calls, lost games and more. After giving up six runs in an inning and being knocked out of the box during a 1934 game, he returned to the dugout and took out his revenge—on himself. Ferrell hit himself so hard in the jaw that he went reeling against the dugout wall. Then he doubled up his fist and smacked himself again. Luckily, his teammates came to his aid and stopped the one-man brawl.

Ferrell once explained the method in his madness: "On the field . . . I gave the impression that I was mean. After all, this was my job, my livelihood. So I put an act on. I'd look wild warming up. I'd stomp and storm around there like a bear cat, fight my way through a ball game, fight like the devil, do anything to win. And I got that reputation for being temperamental and mean, and it stuck, even with people who should have known better."

After 15 years in the majors, Ferrell finally realized his dream of becoming a home run king. In 1942 he signed on as manager-second baseman with Lynchburg in the Virginia League. The 34-year-old hit 30 homers that season—a league record. As one sportswriter noted, "It's a rare thing when Heaven rewards a pitcher here on earth with a chance to break home run records. The terrible-tempered Ferrell must have had very good connections above."

Wes Ferrell liked to finish what he started. He led the AL in complete games four times—including the three seasons from 1935 to 1937—and completed 70 percent of his career starts.

WES FERRELL

Right-Handed Pitcher
Cleveland Indians 1927–1933
Boston Red Sox 1934–1937
Washington Senators 1937–1938
New York Yankees 1938–1939
Brooklyn Dodgers 1940
Boston Braves 1941

GAMES	374
INNINGS	
Career	2,623
Season High	322⅓
WINS	
Career	193
Season High	25
LOSSES	
Career	128
Season High	19
WINNING PERCENTAGE	
Career	.601
Season High	.737
ERA	
Career	4.04
Season Low	3.31
GAMES STARTED	
Career	323
Season High	38
COMPLETE GAMES	
Career	227
Season High	31
SHUTOUTS	
Career	17
Season High	3
STRIKEOUTS	
Career	985
Season High	143
WALKS	
Career	1,040
Season High	130
NO-HITTER	1931

By 1932 veteran broadcaster Graham
McNamee (above, second from left) was
calling his tenth World Series, but baseball
on radio was still far from universal. It
wasn't until seven years later that New York
fans were able to tune in to Dodger, Giant
and Yankee games.

road were re-created from a Western Union telegraph wire, not because
broadcasting from a distant city was technically difficult, but simply to
save money. Some stations in cities that lacked a big league team carried
play-by-play broadcasts entirely through the economical process of recreation. One of these was station WHO of Des Moines, which employed
baseball's most famous play-by-play re-creator, a young man with promise
named Dutch Reagan.

In 1934 Judge Kenesaw Mountain Landis, the commissioner of baseball, sat down with Henry Ford and negotiated baseball's first World Series broadcasting contract. Ford paid $400,000 for four years of World
Series broadcasting rights, making his company the first sponsor for
the event.

Landis always selected the announcers for the World Series and
All-Star games, and the commissioner's office retained that right until
the 1960s. In 1935 Landis barred Ted Husing, the star baseball announcer for CBS, because he had criticized the umpiring in the 1934
Series. NBC's original star sports broadcaster, Graham McNamee, faded
out about the same time. McNamee had a reputation for being more colorful than accurate, but he set the tone for celebrity sportscasting. Former
baseball players were still permitted only rare appearances in front of
the microphone.

Younger announcers were coming along, and some became local celebrities: Ty Tyson in Detroit, Bob Elson in Chicago, Fred Hoey in Boston,
Arch McDonald in Washington. Harry Hartman was a favorite of Cincinnati
fans until a young man named Red Barber arrived in 1934 and eclipsed him.
Three Cincinnati stations carried the Reds' games, although Larry MacPhail

limited broadcasts to fewer than 20 games a year. Even MacPhail, the great innovator, was initially suspicious of radio.

By 1938 MacPhail himself had converted to the faith. He took over the Dodgers and announced that Brooklyn would no longer cooperate with the ban on baseball broadcasting in New York. MacPhail sold rights to broadcast home and away games to station WOR in 1939 for $77,000, and brought in Barber as announcer. The Yankees and Giants didn't like it, but they, too, permitted play-by-play broadcasts, with young Mel Allen working as an assistant on Yankee games.

Night baseball and radio! What was baseball coming to? It was coming to television. On May 17, 1939, NBC televised a college game in New York between Columbia and Princeton. The announcer was Bill Stern, a colorful and prominent broadcaster; the audience numbered 400, assuming that every TV set in New York City was tuned in. On August 26, 1939, the same tiny audience got to see the first televised big league game: Cincinnati at Brooklyn, with Red Barber announcing. Ernie Lombardi, the Cincinnati catcher, didn't like it. "I felt as if someone was looking over my shoulder all afternoon," he said.

Lombardi was right; the game was coming closer to the fans. Things on and off the diamond were changing fast. In 1929 baseball's first public-address loudspeaker system was installed at the Polo Grounds in New York. In 1930 fans were suddenly allowed to keep foul balls that were hit into the stands. Uniform numbers, which were quietly introduced in the 1920s, became standard in the majors in 1932. "Blue laws" prohibiting Sunday baseball were abolished in Boston in 1929, and in Philadelphia and Pittsburgh in 1933.

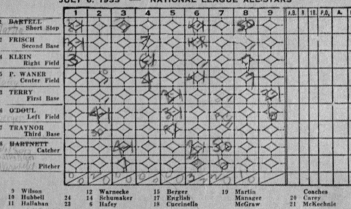

JULY 6, 1933 — NATIONAL LEAGUE ALL-STARS

	1	2	3	4	5	6	7	8	9	A.B.	R	1B.	P.O.	A.	E
1 BARTELL Short Stop															
2 FRISCH Second Base															
4 KLEIN Right Field															
5 P. WANER Center Field															
3 TERRY First Base															
16 O'DOUL Left Field															
7 TRAYNOR Third Base															
8 HARTNETT Catcher															
Pitcher															

9 Wilson	12 Warnecke	15 Berger	19 Martin	Coaches
10 Hubbell	24 14 Schumaker	17 English	Manager	20 Carey
11 Hallahan	23 6 Hafey	18 Cuccinello	McGraw	21 McKechnie

AERZONATORS FOR TOILET ROOM DEODORIZATION FURNISHED BY THE
U. S. SANITARY SPECIALTIES CORPORATION

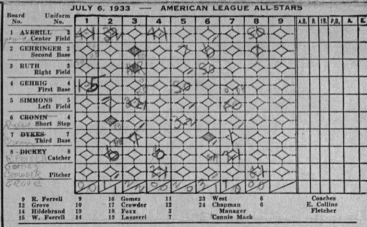

JULY 6, 1933 — AMERICAN LEAGUE ALL-STARS

Board No.	Uniform No.	1	2	3	4	5	6	7	8	9	A.B.	R	1B.	P.O.	A.	E
1 AVERILL	3 Center Field															
2 GEHRINGER	2 Second Base															
3 RUTH	3 Right Field															
4 GEHRIG	4 First Base															
5 SIMMONS	5 Left Field															
6 CRONIN	4 Short Stop															
7 DYKES	7 Third Base															
8 DICKEY	8 Catcher															
Pitcher																

9 R. Ferrell	9	16 Gomez	11	23 West	6	Coaches
12 Grove	10	17 Crowder	12	24 Chapman	6	E. Collins
14 Hildebrand	19	18 Foxx	3	Manager		Fletcher
15 W. Ferrell	14	19 Lazzerri	7	'Connie' Mack		

UMPIRES — AMERICAN, 1-DINEEN, 2-McGOWAN   NATIONAL, 3-KLEM, 4-RIGLER

32 BENTLEY, MURRAY & CO.

What next? Whatever happened to the old verities? Somehow, club owners and sportswriters seemed more averse to change than did the fans. Reluctantly, baseball's insiders yielded sacred ground to those who thought baseball should be more enjoyable to more people. The National Pastime was earning its nickname.

H istory does not always make sense. Given the Depression's effect on baseball attendance, it would be logical to credit farsighted baseball executives with two innovations—or flashes of promotional genius—that yielded baseball a rich harvest of public attention: the All-Star Game and the Baseball Hall of Fame. But that is not the way things happened. A sportswriter named Arch Ward dreamed up the All-Star Game, and a couple of promoters out to bring attention to their hometown of Cooperstown, New York, gave baseball the Hall of Fame on a silver platter. Both were creations of the 1930s, when baseball needed help, and both demonstrated baseball's unique ability to embellish itself with flourishes of self-congratulation—the kind of thing that might seem out of place for other enterprises.

Arch Ward, a popular sports reporter and columnist for the *Chicago Tribune,* promoted the All-Star Game in his columns as an appropriate feature of Chicago's Century of Progress Exposition—or as it was known for short, the World's Fair of 1933. Ward was inspired largely by the hardships of the Depression. He urged that the game's profits be doled out to aged and indigent former ballplayers. The baseball hierarchy reluctantly accepted Ward's proposal, but only on condition that the game be a one-time event. So much for vision.

The Yankees' Ben Chapman (above) batted leadoff for the AL in the inaugural All-Star Game in 1933. Facing St. Louis' Bill Hallahan, Chapman grounded out, with the Giants' Bill Terry taking the throw.

The scorecard from the first All-Star Game (opposite) was jammed with future Hall of Famers, some of whom lived up to their billing. Appropriately, Babe Ruth hit the first home run, while a pair of Leftys—Gomez and Grove—pitched six scoreless innings in a 4–2 AL win. Frankie Frisch homered for the NL.

Continued on page 112

The Game in Print

The themes of the 1930s were deprivation at home and the stirrings of war abroad. But in baseball, every spring brings new hope, and the sport never lost its appeal. Only a lucky few could afford to go to the ballpark, so more than ever before the sports pages became an indispensable diversion.

Sportswriting was in transition. Radio had laid claim to the straightforward play-by-play reporting of games, so columnists became humorists and storytellers in order to attract readers. Take, for example, John Kieran:

They would play. They wouldn't play. They must play. They can't play. Showers in the morning. Fog at noon. Clouds over Harlem. A thin drizzle downtown. Casey Stengel surveyed the thick atmosphere with gloom. Eddie Brannick sank into a coma. But Bill Terry was determined. Playing on the home field of the Giants, Bill was the headman. He could start the game come low or high water. After that it was up to the umpires as to whether the game would sink or swim.

Instead of the crowded arena that fine weather would have furnished, only the dyed-in-the-wool fans, the rainproof rooters, fast afoot with all-weather treads, dashed to Harlem in a last-minute sprint through the mist when word spread that the gates were open and the teams would battle until it was time to take to the lifeboats.

The New York Times,
September 30, 1934

Arch Ward wrote a column called "Talking It Over," composed of curios and trivia. Even though this particular piece was written at the height of the 1935 World Series, Mr. Ward seems determined to talk about everything but *the contest between the Cubs and the Tigers.*

Lon Warneke is anxious for the Cubs to win as quickly as possible so he can return to Arkansas and go a-fishin' and a-huntin'. . . . Charley Grimm intends to go back to his Missouri farm and "unlax". . . . He will forget baseball until the league meetings in December. . . . The home run that Demaree knocked into the right field stands in the second inning was an outside pitch that he caught on the end of his bat. . . . The Cubs made twice as many errors in the first two innings of yesterday's game as they made in the first two games of the series. . . . Pitcher Fabian Kowalik committed the only bobble in Detroit. . . . The special bleachers, reported to have cost $29,000, may not bring back the cost of construction. . . . Demaree's perfect throw from right field to Stan Hack at third base in the third inning brought ahs and ohs from the admirers of strong arm men. . . . The capacity of the Detroit bleachers is 21,000 and Wrigley field 13,500. . . . They were packed both days at Navin field, but there was room for at least 3,000 more sun worshipers at the opening game in Chicago. . . .

Chicago *Daily Tribune,*
October 5, 1935

Stanley Frank found his voice somewhere between the epic style and incomplete sentences. He described the Giants' 17-run rout of the Dodgers from the point of view of the Yankees, who were making the most of a day off by taking in the game at Ebbets Field.

They saw every Giant get at least two hits, with the exception of Mel Ott, who was walked three times. But hits. The first six were two-base knocks and before the horror was done there were two more doubles and a homer. But a homer. It was unloaded by Hank Leiber with the bases full. Di Maggio [*sic*], Gehrig or Dickey never wreaked more havoc with one blow. And few men have hit a ball harder. The slightly flattened spheroid landed halfway up in the upper tier of the left field stands.

The confusion of the gentlemen from the American League was pardonable. They understood that Leiber, who tore off two doubles in addition to his grand slam, is not even a regular. Then what manner of man is this Red Ripple? Ott, whom one and all respect, was given a set of horse-collars. How tough are the Giants when their power-house is hitting?

New York *Evening Post,*
September 18, 1936

Statistics are meat and potatoes to baseball lovers, and Fred Lieb was one of the few writers who rang the dinner bell for a nation of hungry fans.

Regardless of whether the Giants finish first, second or third in this spirited National League pennant battle, the McGraw legion promises to conclude the season with the most robust batting average in the two majors.

The Giants and Phillies both are hitting in the neighborhood of .320, some 10 points better than the Cubs, Yanks and Dodgers. The Yanks lead all clubs of the two majors in piling up runs, as the New York Americans and Athletics are the only teams which have scored more than 700 runs and the Yanks have gone well past 800.

No other team has a two-man punch like Ruth and Gehrig, but the Giants have about as well balanced a batting order as there is in the country. . . . from Leach down to Jackson there is one sturdy .300 hitter after another. And Roettger, hitting eighth in the batting order, is just a few points below .300.

Mel Ott hovers between .340 and .350, but his . . . hitting has not been so timely and he will finish well behind his 151 runs of last year.

New York *Evening Post,*
August 15, 1930

Verse in the sports pages was rare, but not yet extinct. Grantland Rice made his apologies to Rudyard Kipling for a parody he titled, "Dizzy Gunga Dean." Below is the final refrain.

Yes—it's Dean—Dean—Dean—
He's a beggar with a bullet through your spleen.
Though at times some bat has flayed you,
By the Texas sun that made you,
You're a better man than bats are, Dizzy Dean!

New York *Sun,*
July 20, 1934

Al Simmons, Lou Gehrig, Babe Ruth and Jimmie Foxx (above, from left) combined for 2,048 career home runs, but in 1934 none could get even a loud foul off the Giants' Carl Hubbell in the All-Star Game. Hubbell fanned all four—plus Joe Cronin—consecutively.

Trouble was, the idea of an All-Star Game between the two big leagues was too good to stop. John McGraw came out of retirement to manage the National League team in the 1933 All-Star Game, while Connie Mack managed for the American League. The game was played on July 6, drew 47,595 fans to Comiskey Park and raised nearly $45,000 for needy former players. If you were writing the script, you'd want Babe Ruth to star. He did. In fact, he stole the show. Ruth was 38 and past his prime, but he hit a two-run homer in the third inning. In the eighth, he made a superb running catch to rob Chick Hafey of a hit. The AL won, 4–2.

New York made a pitch for one more All-Star Game, arguing that since Chicago and the American League played host once, New York and the National League should get their turn. Several owners opposed it. Speaking on the condition that he not be identified by name, one owner explained why to sportswriter Dan Daniel: "Here we are," the owner said, "breaking into the season with a three-day recess in which we have to pay our players, and in which we get no revenues. It has to be stopped before it gains real impetus."

Daniel disagreed. "It is a disgrace," he wrote, "that the major leagues should have to be urged to stage a publicity benefit for themselves, which also would help old, broken-down members of the diamond fraternity."

The 1934 game drew 48,363 fans to the Polo Grounds, where they witnessed one of history's most memorable pitching feats—Carl Hubbell's consecutive strikeouts of Babe Ruth, Lou Gehrig, Jimmie Foxx, Al Simmons and Joe Cronin. Once Hubbell left the mound for the National League, however, the American League took charge and won, 9–7.

After that, there was no stopping "the Midsummer Classic," as baseball jargonists soon began to call it. The American League won the first three

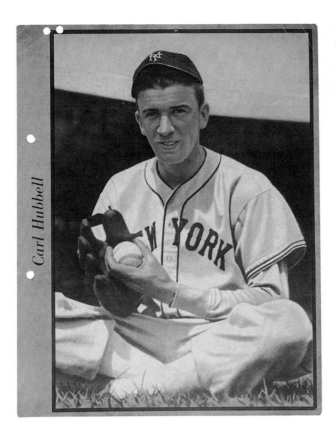

Carl Hubbell

Despite his dazzling performance in the 1934 All-Star Game, Giants ace Carl Hubbell didn't even get a win. The AL pounded three other NL pitchers for nine runs in a 9–7 win. Still, Hubbell claimed he had never had more stuff in his life than on that day.

"LEFTY" GOMEZ

After Carl Hubbell's string of strikeouts in the 1934 All-Star Game was broken at five by Bill Dickey's single, Yankee pitcher Lefty Gomez stepped to the plate. "You are now looking at a man whose batting average is .104," Gomez told catcher Gabby Hartnett. "What the hell am I doing up here?" Gomez struck out.

All-Star games before the NL broke through in 1936, 4–3, behind the pitching of Hubbell, Dizzy Dean and Lon Warneke. Lefty Gomez of the Yankees started five of the first six All-Star games; he was the winning pitcher three times and the loser once. Yankee dominance was showing up in this event as in all others; in 1939 six Yankees were among the starters for the AL. Joe DiMaggio homered, and the Yankees—or rather the American League—won, 3–1.

T he Hall of Fame grew from an imaginative and energetic local promotion scheme by two leading residents of a small town in upstate New York. Small towns are forever trying to promote something unique about themselves. In 1934 Stephen Clark and Alexander Cleland of Cooperstown seized on an old and much discredited report that named Abner Doubleday the father of baseball and Cooperstown, New York, the game's birthplace.

Early in the 20th century, Henry Chadwick, a pioneering sportswriter who invented the box score, among other achievements, wrote an article contending that baseball evolved from the English game of rounders. That didn't sit right with those who considered baseball uniquely American, among them Albert G. Spalding, a pitcher turned sporting goods manufacturer. At Spalding's urging, team owners appointed a commission to determine the game's origins.

The commission was chaired by Colonel A. G. Mills of New York, who had been president of the National League from 1882 to 1884. It boasted a distinguished membership—present and former senators, governors and league presidents—and worked for three years on the question.

Cub center fielder Augie Galan was congratulated by teammate Billy Herman (2) after hitting a home run into the right field bleachers at Braves Field in the 1936 All-Star Game. Red Sox catcher Rick Ferrell looked on as Galan's fifth-inning blast gave the NL a 3–0 lead. The NL won the game, 4–3, for its first All-Star Game victory.

Ladies' Day meant a packed house for the hapless Philadelphia Phillies in 1939 (preceding page). The Phillies had moved from tiny Baker Bowl to spacious Shibe Park midway through the 1938 season, and in 1939 their attendance jumped by more than 100,000. They still finished last.

But the commission didn't work very hard. Mills was swayed by letters from Abner Graves, a Cooperstown native and Doubleday's schoolmate. Graves wrote that he and his playmates used to play "town ball," a game in which a "tosser" hit balls to 20 or 30 or more boys in the field. One day back in about 1839, wrote Graves, Abner Doubleday refined the game by marking out a diamond-shaped field with bases, and installing a pitcher and catcher.

Commission chairman Mills, too, was part of the Doubleday connection; he had served under Union General Doubleday during the Civil War. Perhaps because of this acquaintance, Mills accepted Graves' testimony as gospel. The Mills Commission issued its report December 30, 1907. "The first scheme for playing baseball, according to the best evidence obtainable to date, was devised by Abner Doubleday at Cooperstown, New York, in 1839," the report said.

No one paid much attention, and other researchers traced baseball's origins to other places and earlier times. But in Cooperstown the legend survived. In the 1920s, a ballpark was built on the pasture where Doubleday supposedly marked out the first diamond. In 1934 Clark and Cleland got involved. Clark was an heir to the Singer Sewing Machine fortune, and Cleland was his top aide. Cleland suggested that they set up a museum featuring bats used by famous players, balls thrown out by presidents, "funny old uniforms" and the like.

The perfect icon came their way in 1935 through an accident of attic archaeology. A trunkful of Graves' belongings was found in a farmhouse attic three miles from Cooperstown. Among other things, it yielded an old, homemade baseball, burst at the seams and stuffed with rags. The Doubleday baseball! Clark bought it for five dollars, put it on display in a building

Dedication of the National Baseball Hall of Fame in Cooperstown, New York, in 1939 produced a portrait of immortals—10 of the 13 men who had been inducted. Front row, from left: Eddie Collins, Babe Ruth, Connie Mack, Cy Young. Back row: Honus Wagner, Grover Cleveland Alexander, Tris Speaker, Napoleon Lajoie, George Sisler, Walter Johnson. Christy Mathewson and Willie Keeler had both died before being inducted into the Hall of Fame, and Ty Cobb arrived late and missed the photo.

that now houses the Cooperstown municipal offices, and began lobbying in earnest. With the help of other local leaders, he chartered the National Baseball Museum, Inc., "for the purpose of collecting and preserving pictures and relics reflecting the development of the National Game from the time of its inception, through the ingenuity of Major General Abner Doubleday, in 1839 to the present."

Cleland toured the country, seeking exhibits. The National League donated the original Temple Cup, bestowed upon league champions of the 1880s. More contributions came from Connie Mack, Clark Griffith, the widow of pitcher Christy Mathewson and others.

Clark decided to dedicate the new museum with a celebration in 1939 marking the 100th anniversary of Doubleday's alleged inspiration. Cleland visited Ford Frick, president of the National League, to seek the cooperation of organized baseball. Cleland told Frick that radio stations in the Cooperstown area might ask fans to pick an all-time all-star team. Frick had recently visited the Hall of Fame for Great Americans at New York University, so he took Cleland's proposal one step further, proposing a Baseball Hall of Fame. Frick persuaded other baseball executives to support the idea, although Commissioner Landis grumbled that his office shouldn't get mixed up in a local promotion.

The Baseball Writers Association of America agreed to select candidates for the new Hall of Fame by ballot, with a 75 percent majority required for admission. A special committee selected the standout players of the 19th century. Elections were held in 1936, 1937, 1938 and 1939—a long drumroll leading up to the dedication of the Hall of Fame in June 1939, when the first members were enshrined. A building, appropriately

Thousands of fans helped open baseball's Hall of Fame in 1939 (above), and the U.S. Postal Service gave the Hall its stamp of approval (below).

Only a handful of New Yorkers had TV sets in 1939, so only a handful were watching as Red Barber (opposite) interviewed Dodger manager Leo Durocher before the first telecast of a major league game. The game took place at Ebbets Field on August 26, 1939, and was carried over W2XBS, a local television station.

Georgian in design and made of Williamsburg brick, was constructed to house the museum.

The voting sportswriters were picky. No one was voted in unanimously, not even Ty Cobb, who led the 1936 ballot with 222 out of 226 votes, or Babe Ruth, who got only 215. By dedication day—June 12, 1939—26 men had been selected. Eleven were living, and all of them journeyed to Cooperstown for the ceremony. Commissioner Landis overcame his disdain and gave a rousing dedication speech. "Nowhere else than [baseball's] birthplace could this museum be appropriately situated," he said. The two league presidents were on hand, and so was the postmaster general, James A. Farley, who issued a special stamp commemorating baseball's 100th anniversary.

Ten thousand fans also journeyed to Cooperstown—an out-of-the-way lakeside village of 2,000 residents—for the dedication ceremonies. The Baseball Hall of Fame was a smash hit, and it has grown into something even bigger. Some 300,000 people a year pay $5 each to tour the museum, which has been repeatedly expanded and modernized. With the addition—or enshrinement—of Johnny Bench, Carl Yastrzemski, Red Schoendienst and Al Barlick in 1989, Hall of Fame membership through its first half-century reached 204 players, including major league managers, umpires and a number of Negro league stars who never made the majors. Like almost everything else about baseball, Hall of Fame selections—still made by the BBWAA—are sometimes the subjects of controversy, which only adds to the general interest, both in the Hall of Fame and in the game of baseball itself. ◗

Hank Greenberg

On September 29, 1945, rain turned Sportsman's Park in St. Louis into a swamp. The Browns' scheduled matchup with the Tigers was postponed to be played as part of a doubleheader the following day. But the rain continued into the next afternoon, delaying the start of the opener until there was time for only one game before darkness fell. It was the final day of the season and the American League pennant hung in the balance. A win in either of the season's last two games would clinch it for the Tigers.

St. Louis took a 3–2 lead in the eighth. In the top of the ninth, the Tigers had men on second and third with one out. Brown right-hander Nelson Potter gave an intentional walk to Doc Cramer to load the bases, and up to the plate stepped Hammerin' Hank Greenberg. Just three months out of the military, where he had hardly touched a bat in four years, the two-time All-Star, two-time MVP was feeling the effects of his long layoff and his 34 years. But despite blistered hands, a sore arm, a charley horse and a sprained ankle, he was tearing up the league that September. He took the first pitch for a ball, then drove the second pitch into the left field bleachers. "Only a few months before, I was in India, wondering if the war would ever end," Greenberg said years later, "and now the war was actually over and not only that but I'd just hit a pennant-winning grand-slam home run. I wasn't sure whether I was awake or dreaming."

It was a pretty fair accomplishment for a man who was never accused of possessing much natural ability. "Someone once said I didn't play ball when I was a kid," Greenberg recounted, "I worked at it." The son of Jewish Romanian immigrants, Greenberg grew up in the Bronx; he was a shy boy who reached his full height of 6′ 3½″ at 13. Feeling something of an adolescent freak, he turned to athletics as an escape and excelled in several sports, particularly basketball and, of course, baseball.

By the time he graduated from high school, the hard work was paying off, and he had a number of offers to play professional baseball. Paul Krichell of the Yankees was the first pro scout to take an interest in him, but Greenberg figured Lou Gehrig had the Yankee slot at first base sewn up for a while, so he went looking for other offers. He elected to sign with Detroit for a $9,000 bonus, and in the spring of 1930 he entered the Tigers' farm system. Over the next three years he mastered his batting stroke. In 1932 he burst into the limelight with Beaumont in the Texas League, where he led the circuit with 39 home runs and 123 runs scored and was named league MVP. With a bat in his hands he was a terror to the opposition, but he struck fear into his teammates with his sloppy baserunning and glovework. While his lack of speed proved incurable, his fielding improved steadily throughout his career, culminating in an errorless half-season of 78 games after his return from the Army in 1945.

In 1933 he was brought up to the Tigers, where he spent all but one season of his war-interrupted career. His timing was good, because by the spring of 1934 Detroit had the look of a dynasty. With Charlie

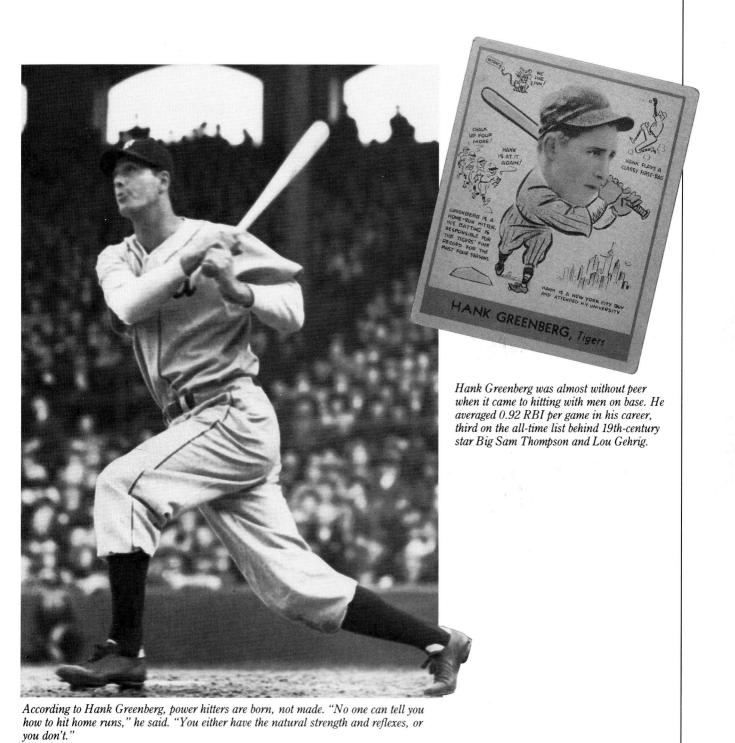

Hank Greenberg was almost without peer when it came to hitting with men on base. He averaged 0.92 RBI per game in his career, third on the all-time list behind 19th-century star Big Sam Thompson and Lou Gehrig.

According to Hank Greenberg, power hitters are born, not made. "No one can tell you how to hit home runs," he said. "You either have the natural strength and reflexes, or you don't."

Greenberg hit two home runs in a single game 35 times in his career. On September 10, 1934, his two homers—the second coming in the bottom of the ninth (above)—provided the only runs in a 2–1 Tiger win over the Red Sox.

Gehringer at second base and Goose Goslin in left field, Billy Rogell at shortstop, Marv Owen at third, and outstanding pitching from Schoolboy Rowe and Tommy Bridges, the Tigers stormed to two consecutive pennants in 1934 and 1935, and won the World Series against the Cubs in 1935.

Greenberg was a team leader and had been instrumental in Detroit's success, but his best years were still to come. He hit 36 home runs in 1935 to win the first of his four home run titles, and in 1938 he set the baseball world on its ear by threatening Ruth's record of 60. He came close—he finished the season with 58—but he was more disappointed in 1937 when he fell one RBI shy of Lou Gehrig's AL record of 184. It was characteristic of Greenberg's team play attitude that RBI were his obsession, not home runs. Charlie Gehringer, who batted ahead of Greenberg, once told him, "I suppose if I hit a double with a man on first, you'd probably trip him if he tried to go past third base." In his seven full seasons of play between 1934 and 1946, Greenberg *averaged* 147 RBI a year.

Off the field Greenberg was the darling of Detroit almost from the moment he arrived. But in the thick of the 1934 pennant race he found himself entangled in controversy over his decision not to play on the Jewish holy day of Yom Kippur. The debate raged in the press and on the streets of Detroit. Then nationally syndicated verse writer Edgar Guest backed him up with a poem, "Speaking of Greenberg." What had been a sprinkle of support turned into a torrent.

After his heroics of 1945, Greenberg had a solid year in 1946, leading the league in homers with 44 and driving in 127 runs. But Detroit put him on waivers, and he was picked up by the Pittsburgh Pirates, who tempted him away from retirement with the NL's first $100,000 contract offer. He hit only .249, but belted 25 home runs—and then retired for good.

At Cleveland president Bill Veeck's bidding, Greenberg moved into the front office of the Indians' organization as a vice president in 1948, beginning a long career in business that made him a wealthy man. Hammerin' Hank was elected to the Hall of Fame in 1956, and died in Beverly Hills, California, in 1986.

HANK GREENBERG

First Base, Outfield
Detroit Tigers 1930, 1933–1941,
  1945–1946
Pittsburgh Pirates 1947
Hall of Fame 1956

GAMES	**1,394**
AT-BATS	**5,193**
BATTING AVERAGE	
Career	**.313**
Season High	**.340**
SLUGGING AVERAGE	
Career *(5th all time)*	**.605**
Season High	**.683**
HITS	
Career	**1,628**
Season High	**203**
DOUBLES	
Career	**379**
Season High *(4th all time)*	**63**
TRIPLES	
Career	**71**
Season High	**16**
HOME RUNS	
Career	**331**
Season High *(4th all time)*	**58**
TOTAL BASES	**3,142**
EXTRA-BASE HITS	**781**
RUNS BATTED IN	
Career	**1,276**
Season High *(3rd all time)*	**183**
RUNS	
Career	**1,051**
Season High	**144**
WORLD SERIES	**1934–1935, 1940, 1945**
MOST VALUABLE PLAYER	**1935, 1940**

Being a star and a member of a minority group at the same time was a situation Greenberg, who was Jewish, could identify with, so the big slugger was one of only a few players to encourage Brooklyn's Jackie Robinson—baseball's first black major leaguer—in 1947. "Hank Greenberg has class," Robinson said. "It stands out all over him."

Bob Feller

Ted Turns Professional

The Changing of the Guard

Early in the century, the Giants, not the Yankees, were the toast of New York and the best team in baseball. They won six pennants before the Yankees won their first, and when the Yanks broke through in 1921 and 1922, the Giants beat them in the first two "Subway" Series. The Giants were synonymous with John McGraw, who managed them for 31 years and won ten pennants—four straight from 1921 through 1924. He finished out of the first division only four times—two of those occasions came in his first and last seasons with the Giants, when he managed less than half the team's games.

McGraw recognized talent. In 1922 he signed first baseman Bill Terry, who was playing for a Standard Oil semi-pro company team in Memphis. In 1925 he granted a tryout to Mel Ott, watched the 16-year-old lift his front leg before every swing, and said of his eccentric batting style, "That's the best natural swing I've seen in years." McGraw signed Ott when he was 17 years old and sat the boy on the Giant bench while teaching him the game. Ott became a Giant regular in 1928. The following year, Ott hit 42 homers; he was 20 years old.

Carl Hubbell signed with the Tigers in 1924, but continued in the minors until 1928. His best pitch was the screwball—a reverse curve thrown with an inside-out twist of the wrist—but Tiger manager Ty Cobb told him the unusual pitch would hurt his arm and ordered him to stop throwing it. Without the "scroogie," Hubbell couldn't make the Tigers. He didn't make the majors until he was 25, and he might never have made it had he continued to heed Cobb's advice and had the Democrats not held their 1928 national convention in Houston. In 1928 Hubbell was pitching for Beaumont in the Texas League, who happened to be playing at Houston

In 1936 Joe DiMaggio (opposite, right) was the AL's best rookie, Lou Gehrig (left) was its MVP, and they combined to lead the Yankees to their first of four straight world championships. By 1939 Gehrig was gone and DiMaggio was the league's MVP.

Four months after signing his contract for the 1932 season, Giants first baseman Bill Terry (above, right) was called into manager John McGraw's office. Terry, who had feuded with McGraw (above, left) in the past, expected to be told he had been traded. Instead, McGraw said he was retiring, and asked Terry to be his successor. Terry agreed, then led the Giants to a world championship in 1933.

during the Democrats' shindig. An Illinois delegate named Dick Kinsella took an afternoon off from politics to watch a ballgame. Hubbell was throwing his screwball again. He beat Houston and impressed Kinsella, who doubled as a part-time Giants' scout. On Kinsella's recommendation, McGraw bought Hubbell.

Terry, Ott and Hubbell. Thanks to the coincidences that brought these three together, the New York Giants were better equipped to play the new brand of baseball of the 1930s and they became one of the few teams that could celebrate that dusty and depressed decade.

Even though baseball was changing, McGraw was not. He was the master of "scientific inside baseball," as he called it—the bunt-and-run game tailored to the dead-ball era. The Giants had plenty of talent, but even with sluggers like Ott in his lineup, McGraw's heart remained with the game that Babe Ruth had made obsolete.

Some of his players doubted that McGraw had a heart. He was called "Little Napoleon" because he was such a strict disciplinarian. He cursed his players for the slightest mistakes. Terry, his brightest star, stopped speaking to him. Freddie Lindstrom, the Giants' star third baseman, described the generation gap that existed between McGraw and his players: "McGraw was one of those fellows who had managed in an era when it was common practice to abuse ballplayers verbally. Later on you had a different breed of ballplayers—Terry, [Travis] Jackson, myself—who resented being verbally abused. He lost some of his effectiveness doing that."

McGraw called every pitch from the dugout, and he didn't trust fastballs. "The only man who thought you could win with one pitch was

*"The whole art of pitching is in the wrist,"
said Giants ace Carl Hubbell, whose strong
left wrist was the key to his famous screwball,
which broke down and away from right-
handed hitters. In the Giants' pennant-
winning seasons of 1933, 1936 and 1937,
Hubbell won 71 games and lost 26 for a .732
winning percentage.*

John McGraw," Hubbell told writer Bob Oates years later. "McGraw
wanted us to throw a curve on every pitch."

By 1932 the Giant players were open in their dislike of McGraw. Despite their talent, the Giants played poorly. McGraw's health was failing, and
on June 3 he suddenly retired and chose Bill Terry to replace him.

Terry was plenty strict himself, but he respected his players and
listened to their suggestions—something McGraw had never countenanced.
He quickly fired Doc Knowles, the team's trainer, whom the players had tab-
bed as the spy who kept McGraw posted on their private lives. The Giants
finished sixth, and when Terry predicted that his team would finish third or
better in 1933, sportswriters laughed at the idea.

Terry made a few astute trades in the off-season, and the Giants
jumped quickly into first place. In late June the Cardinals challenged them,
winning two of the first three games of a Polo Grounds series. If St. Louis
swept the Sunday doubleheader, they would pull within a game and a half.

Tex Carleton started the opener for St. Louis and pitched 16 scoreless
innings. And inning for inning, Hubbell matched him. Jesse Haines relieved
for the Cards; Hubbell kept pitching. With two out in the bottom of the 18th,
The Giants' Hughie Critz singled home the game's only run. Hubbell, who
had pitched 26 consecutive scoreless innings earlier in the season, had won
an 18-inning shutout, striking out 12 and walking none.

The Giants won both games that day and increased their lead to 5½
games. Blondy Ryan, the Giants' shortstop, suffered a bad spike wound in
the St. Louis series and stayed home as the Giants left on a road trip. When
his doctor told him he could play again, Ryan telegrammed his teammates:
"AM ON MY WAY! THEY CAN'T BEAT US!" In truth, Ryan wasn't such

*For almost all of his 22-year career, Giants
right fielder Mel Ott wielded the NL's most
potent home run bat. He led the league in
home run percentage a remarkable ten times,
with his first—a 1929 mark of 7.7
percent—being his career best.*

Reds first baseman Frank McCormick (above, sliding) didn't get a lot of ink, but he was among the best of a crop of young stars in the late 1930s. McCormick led the NL in hits and drove in at least 106 runs in each of his first three full seasons, 1938 to 1940.

In 1939 "the Kid"—Ted Williams (opposite, left)—and "the Beast"—Jimmie Foxx (opposite, right) trampled AL pitching. The 31-year-old Foxx led the league in home runs and slugging percentage, while Williams, who turned 21 during the season, led the league in total bases and RBI, and was second in walks, doubles and runs scored.

a crucial player, but "THEY CAN'T BEAT US!" became the Giants' rallying cry. They won the pennant by five games.

Hubbell's 18-inning shutout was no aberration. Free to mix his pitches, he pitched ten shutouts in 1933, won the ERA championship and collected 23 wins—his first of five straight 20-win seasons. In the 1934 All-Star Game, he achieved the feat for which he is best remembered: striking out Babe Ruth, Lou Gehrig, Jimmie Foxx, Al Simmons and Joe Cronin consecutively.

The Washington Senators were favored to beat the Giants in the 1933 World Series, which opened on a Depression note: at $1.10 a ticket, 8,000 seats at the Polo Grounds were vacant. Ott hit a two-run homer in the first inning, singled home a run his next time up and finished the day with four hits. Hubbell won it, 4–2. Terry homered in Game 4, and Hubbell won it in 11 innings, 2–1. The fifth and deciding game went ten innings, Ott winning it with a homer. For the first time, the Giants had won a World Series *without* John McGraw.

Nevertheless, McGraw threw a party for the team. "The old guard changes, but never surrenders," McGraw once said. In February 1934, he died at the age of 60.

The dusty, rural St. Louis Gashouse Gang may have best epitomized the 1930s, but the Giants basked in the glow of Broadway. After the 1933 Series, Hubbell went on a vaudeville tour, the 1930s version of a talk-show circuit. Ott and other Giant players were often seen at Toots Shor's and Club 21. Actresses Ethel Barrymore and Tallulah Bankhead were prominent Giant fans; their favorite was second baseman Burgess Urquhart Whitehead, a Phi Beta Kappa from the University of North Carolina.

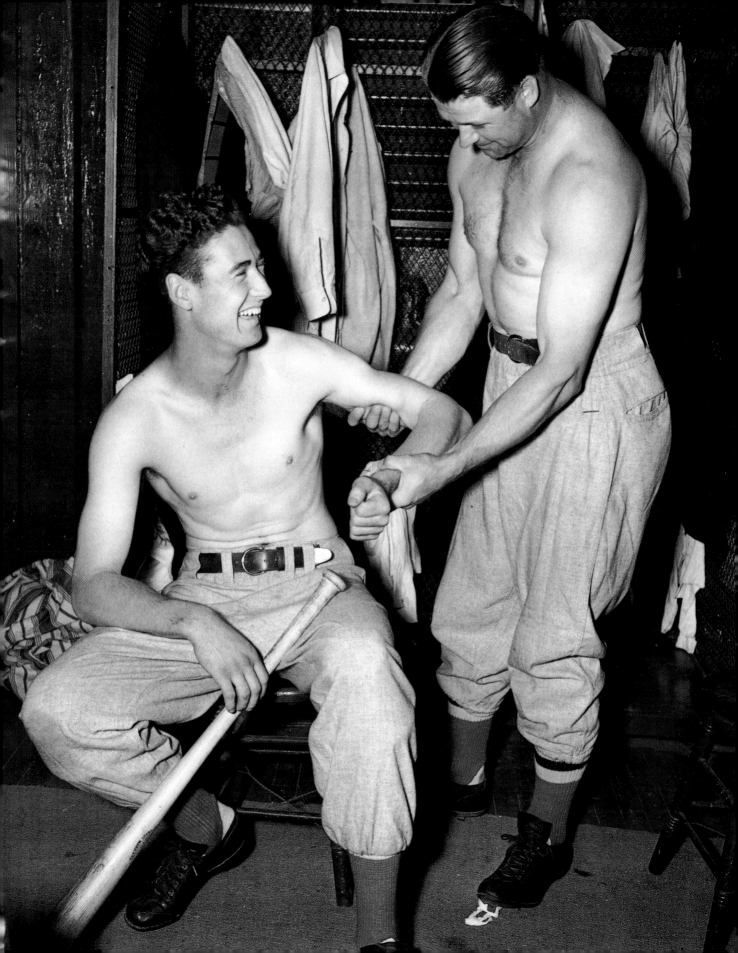

Rookie second baseman Joe "Flash" Gordon added spark to an already explosive Yankee lineup in 1938, then kept getting better. Gordon averaged 27 home runs and 100 RBI his first four seasons in the majors.

The Giants finished second in 1934 and third in 1935. They seemed on their way down, and on July 15, 1936, they were fifth, 11 games behind the league-leading Cubs. Terry was 39, and his doctor had told him to stop playing because of a bad knee. He singled, doubled and tripled that day as the Giants beat the Pirates twice. Ott pulled the Giants from behind the next day with an eighth-inning homer, and Hubbell followed with a shutout.

The Giants inched forward, then won 15 straight. The Pirates broke their streak, but the Giants then swept two from the Cubs, Hubbell winning his 20th of the season and Ott winning the nightcap with a ninth-inning homer, his seventh hit of the day. Hubbell finished the season with 16 straight wins, and Ott won his third National League home run title with 33 as the Giants took the pennant by five games.

In 1937 Terry, no longer playing, moved Ott to third base so he could find a place in the outfield for Hank Leiber, who hit well despite recurring headaches. No one doubted the cause of Leiber's pain; he had been beaned in spring training by an 18-year-old named Bob Feller. Leiber hadn't been wearing a helmet; back then no one did. By late August, the Giants trailed the Cubs by seven games, but once again pulled ahead, winning 9 of 11 games as Ott homered six times. Hubbell won his first eight games of the 1937 season, extending his streak to 24, and wound up with 22 wins. Rookie Cliff "Mountain Music" Melton won 20. Ott earned his fourth NL home run title, and the Giants won their third pennant of the decade. They were good, but no longer could they rival the Yankees, who beat them easily in the Subway Series of 1936 and 1937.

The Giants had moved from the dead-ball era to the power era, but the Yankees had taken yet another step, copying the Cardinals by developing a

A fastball the caliber of Bob Feller's makes managing fairly simple. "Go up and hit what you see," Washington skipper Bucky Harris advised one of his batters. "And if you don't see anything, come on back."

After leading the AL in wins, complete games, innings and strikeouts in both 1939 and 1940, Indians ace Bob Feller deserved to be baseball's highest paid pitcher in 1941—and he was. Feller (center) signed for $30,000 as Indians president Alva Bradley (left) and celebrated scout Cy Slapnicka (right) looked on.

strong farm system that kept them at or near the top until the mid-1960s. The Dodgers soon did the same, and the Giants—for so long the most prominent of New York's three teams—sagged in the standings and fell to third place in local favor. They didn't win again until 1951, when a young player arrived to lead them. The Yankees had passed him up because he was black. His name was Willie Mays.

In the movie *Field of Dreams,* an Iowa farmer builds a baseball diamond and waits for the player of his dreams to appear. A real Iowa farmer built just such a field in 1932, and his dreams came true. The farmer was named Bill Feller. He built the field for his son, Bob.

Bill Feller, a wheat and corn farmer who lived just outside Van Meter, Iowa, started playing ball with his son when Bob was little more than a toddler. When Bob turned ten, his father bought him a glove—a Rogers Hornsby model—a uniform, a bat and baseball shoes. After school and farm chores, Bob and his dad played catch, father teaching son the rudiments of the game. When Bob was 12, his father installed a home generator powered by a windmill—farm country around Van Meter didn't have electrical service in the 1930s. He put in outdoor arc lamps so they could play ball at night.

By the time Bob was 13, he was an overpowering young pitcher, beating teams made up of boys several years older. Bill decided to build the ballfield, organize a team, stage games, sell soda pop and charge admission—not so much to make money as to develop Bob's talents and show them off. He was convinced that his son would pitch in the major leagues.

He was right. When Bob was 16, he and his father were working in the fields one day when they saw a man walking toward them through the wheat.

Continued on page 134

19—THE STADIUM, CLEVELAND, OHIO

Cleveland Stadium

O n July 31, 1932, the first baseball stadium built with public funds made its debut, and the voter turnout was amazing. A crowd of 76,979—the largest to that date to watch a baseball game—jammed the new stadium on the Lake Erie waterfront and watched as the Athletics' Lefty Grove outdueled the Indians' Mel Harder, 1–0.

A referendum to authorize $2.5 million in municipal bonds to build the stadium was held in 1928, and the project was approved by a vote of 112,448 to 76,975. Ground was broken on June 24, 1930, and just 370 days and 3,300,000 bricks later Cleveland Public Municipal Stadium was completed. It was so big that for most of its first 15 years it was used only on special occasions: nights, Sundays and holidays.

In its first decade Cleveland Stadium hosted opera, soccer, football, rodeo, religious events, a jitterbug jamboree and an annual patriotic celebration entitled "The Festival of Freedom," which began in 1939, inspired by the war in Europe. But in between, the Indians played some baseball there. The team played all of its 1933 home games in Cleveland Stadium, but drops in the team's batting average, win total and attendance, as well as high operating costs persuaded management to move the Indians back to the smaller League Park for all but Sunday and holiday games from 1934 to 1939.

The 1935 All-Star Game was played in Cleveland Stadium, and the Indians' Mel Harder pitched three innings of scoreless relief in a 4–1 AL win. The lights went on for baseball at Cleveland Stadium on June 27, 1939, and the Tribe's brightest light—fireballer Bob Feller—tossed a one-hit shutout before 53,305 fans. Two years later at League Park, the Yankees' Joe DiMaggio stretched his hitting streak to 56 games. The next day the Yankees and

the Indians met at Cleveland Stadium, where DiMaggio's legendary streak came to an end, thanks largely to two fine defensive plays by Cleveland third baseman Ken Keltner.

Bill Veeck bought the Indians in 1946 from Alva Bradley and in 1947 moved them permanently into Cleveland Stadium. Veeck also moved in the outfield fences to bring more offense—and more fans—to the park. His flair for promotion coincided with a tremendously talented club in 1948, as a major-league-record 2,620,627 fans came through the turnstiles to watch player-manager Lou Boudreau and the league's best pitching staff carry the Tribe into a one-game playoff with Boston for the AL pennant. Cleveland won, 8–3, then beat Boston's other team, the Braves, in the World Series. The Indians set a Series attendance record in Game 4, as 81,897 watched them win, 2–1, and then broke the record the following day as 86,288 watched them lose, 11–5.

Six years later the Indians broke the Yankees' stranglehold on the AL pennant, as a pitching staff featuring three future Hall of Famers—Bob Lemon, Early Wynn and Bob Feller—led them to 111 wins. On September 12 Cleveland Stadium hosted the largest regular-season crowd in history—84,587—and the Indians rewarded their faithful by sweeping the Yankees in a doubleheader.

Cleveland Stadium has played host to many memorable baseball achievements, but its two proudest moments came 28 years apart, and had little to do with winning. On Independence Day 1947, Larry Doby became the first black to play in the American League. On Opening Day 1975, Frank Robinson became the first black manager in baseball history. Robinson, then a player-manager, homered in his very first at-bat.

What was once the site of a landfill became home to baseball's largest stadium in 1931 as Cleveland Stadium opened on the shores of Lake Erie. It also sported baseball's widest seats—20 inches for box seats, 19 for lower reserved and 18 for the rest.

Cleveland Public Municipal Stadium

Boudreau Boulevard and
  Lake Erie
Cleveland, Ohio

Built 1931

Cleveland Indians, AL
  1932-present

Seating Capacity
77,797

Style
Major league classic

Height of Outfield Fences
8 feet

Dugouts
Home: 1st base
Visitors: 3rd base

Bullpens
Foul territory
Home: right field
Visitors: left field

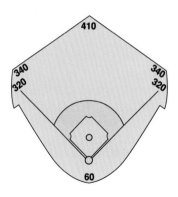

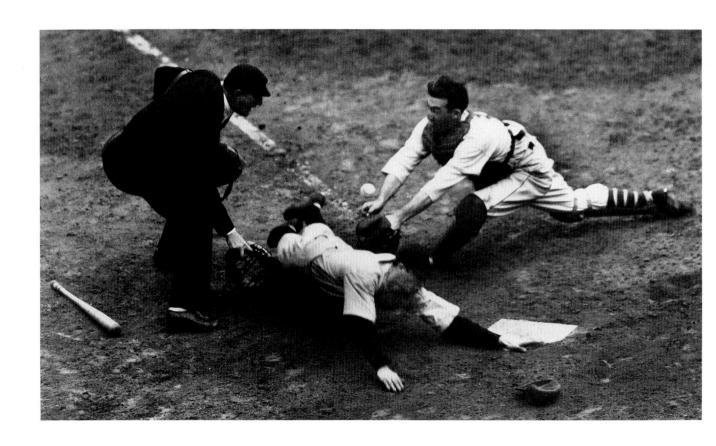

If Yankee rookie Joe DiMaggio felt any pressure in the 1936 World Series against the Giants, it didn't affect his performance. DiMaggio hit .346, with three doubles, three RBI and three runs scored, including one on a headfirst slide during a Series-clinching seven-run rally in Game 6 (above).

He introduced himself as Cy Slapnicka, a scout for the Cleveland Indians, and said he would be there the next time Bob pitched. He was, and that night he signed Bob Feller to a minor league contract.

But Feller never pitched in the minor leagues. In the spring of 1936 he developed a sore arm—perhaps, Bob wrote in his autobiography, from high school basketball or spring plowing. Slapnicka told him to stay home. Feller got better, and Slapnicka invited him to Cleveland so he could work out with the team, get his arm treated by the Indians' trainer and refine his skills by learning how to field his position and hold runners on base.

Feller's arm came back, and the Indians tested him in an exhibition game against the St. Louis Cardinals on July 6, 1936. Feller started the fourth inning. He was fast and wild, and he frightened Leo Durocher, the second batter to face him. "Keep the ball in the park, busher!" Durocher complained. Then he struck out. Feller pitched three innings and fanned eight.

On August 23 he started his first big league game against the weak St. Louis Browns. Feller struck out 15 and won, 4–1. On September 13 he beat the Philadelphia Athletics, 5–2, striking out 17 for a new American League record. Feller was 17 years old, and when the season ended, he returned to the farm for his senior year of high school.

Feller was not the only rookie sensation of 1936. The Yankees had taken a risk on a promising young outfielder. In 1933, when he was 18 years old, Joe DiMaggio hit .340, drove in 169 runs and hit safely in 61 straight games for his hometown team, the San Francisco Seals. Major league baseball hadn't yet expanded to the West Coast; the Seals played in the Pacific Coast League, a top minor league.

In June 1934, DiMaggio's left knee cracked and collapsed as he stepped off a bus. The injury was severe, and DiMaggio's leg had to be splinted from ankle to thigh. Major league scouts had been bidding for DiMaggio, but most of them backed off for fear his knee would never recover. The New York Yankees hired a prominent orthopedic physician to examine DiMaggio. The doctor said the knee would heal, and the Yanks nailed down an unusual deal with the Seals. They sent San Francisco five players and $25,000 for DiMaggio; the young outfielder would play for the Seals in 1935 and take knee treatments all year.

What a deal! The knee never again bothered DiMaggio. He decimated the Pacific Coast League in 1935, hitting 34 homers and batting .398. With Babe Ruth gone, the Yankees were more than ready for him.

In 1936 DiMaggio motored to spring training with two other San Francisco Italians who played for the Yankees: Tony Lazzeri and Frank Crosetti. Lazzeri and Crosetti did the driving, because DiMaggio didn't know how. He came from a poor family and was the eighth of nine children. His parents emigrated from Sicily; his father was a fisherman. Joe dropped out of high school to work in a cannery; he went on to play professional baseball, as did his brothers, Vince and Dominic. Joe was shy and unsophisticated. While he was playing for San Francisco, a sportswriter once asked him for a quote. Joe looked blank; he didn't know what the word meant. "I thought it was some kind of a soft drink," he said, recalling the incident years later.

But young DiMaggio was a natural on the field. He suffered a slight foot injury in his first spring training with the Yankees, and a heat lamp, used by the trainer to help heal the injury, shorted and burned DiMaggio's foot. He missed the first couple of weeks of the 1936 season, but once he made it

A reluctant hero, DiMaggio was nevertheless a media darling by 1938 (above). Joltin' Joe led the Yankees with a .324 average, 32 homers and 140 RBI, and struck out just 21 times all season.

Left fielder Jeff Heath was just one of several fine young hitters the Indians produced in the late 1930s. In 1938, his first full season, Heath hit .343 and led the AL with 18 triples. In 1941 he became the first AL player in history to have at least 20 doubles, triples and homers in a season, with 32, 20 and 24, respectively.

Hard-hitting Reds outfielder Ival Goodman led the NL in triples his first two seasons in the majors, 1935 and 1936, hit 30 homers in 1938, then hit .323 in 1939 to help the Reds win the pennant.

into the lineup, he was an immediate success. He hit safely in 16 straight games and played left field—his first position—with grace and skill. Noting DiMaggio's superior range, the Yankees traded Ben Chapman, their center fielder, and moved DiMaggio to center. He was a superb fielder. Although he never appeared to hurry, he covered ground like no other outfielder in the league. He ran the bases the same way, with a long, seemingly effortless stride that often gained him an extra base.

Joe batted third in the Yankee lineup—the Babe's old spot: behind Frank Crosetti and Red Rolfe, and in front of Lou Gehrig and Bill Dickey. DiMaggio's rookie numbers were outstanding. He hit .323 with 29 homers and 125 RBI. The Yankees had their new star, and after a three-year drought, they won the 1936 pennant with ease. In 1937 they won again. DiMaggio was 22 and better than ever, hitting .346 and leading the AL in homers with 46 and in runs scored with 151.

With DiMaggio on board, the Yankees had little competition in the late 1930s. But it was not for want of trying, particularly by the Boston Red Sox, who were using Tom Yawkey's millions to turn a perennial tail ender into a contender. In 1938 the Red Sox climbed to second place behind the talent Yawkey had purchased: Lefty Grove, Jimmie Foxx, Joe Cronin, Doc Cramer. They even added a young star fresh from the minors in second baseman Bobby Doerr.

In 1939 the Red Sox completed the changing of the guard—their own, and that of baseball itself. "If there was ever a man born to be a hitter it was me," their new prospect wrote years later. He was fresh, sassy and skinny. He impressed everyone with his hitting and exasperated every-

one with his offhand attitude toward fielding. His name, of course, was Ted Williams.

Williams grew up in San Diego. His father ran a photographic studio that kept him busy into the evenings, and his mother, too, was so devoted to her job with the Salvation Army that she had little time left for her children. Ted played baseball year-round, and in 1936 he signed with the San Diego Padres—a Pacific Coast League team unrelated to the expansion franchise by the same name that joined the major leagues in 1969.

Williams was 17. Like DiMaggio, he was poor, shy and unsophisticated. He stood 6′ 3″ and weighed 148 pounds. He mostly sat on the Padres bench that year—and ate, since he was anxious to gain weight and now could charge his meals to the team. Bill Lane, who owned the team, reprimanded Williams one day for regularly spending more than the daily meal allowance of $2.50. "Well, I just can't eat on $2.50 a day," Williams said. "Take it out of my check." The Padres let him eat. In 1937 he hit 23 homers, batted .291 and was hailed as an outstanding prospect. The Red Sox bought him, brought him to spring training in 1938, noted his talent and his sass and sent him to Minneapolis—another minor league city whose team played in the American Association.

Williams was 19. He hit like crazy, but was a careless fielder and an indifferent baserunner. Williams admired Minneapolis manager Donie Bush, but also made Bush's life hard. One day Bush reached the end of his rope and told the Red Sox brass that either he or Williams had to go. In that case, Bush was told, it would be him; Williams was too good a prospect to lose. He led the American Association in batting at .366, in homers with 43 and in RBI with 142.

Even at the age of 19, Ted Williams was among baseball's most confident hitters. "Wait'll you see Jimmie Foxx hit," a Red Sox player told Williams during spring training in 1938. "Wait'll Jimmie Foxx sees me hit," Williams replied.

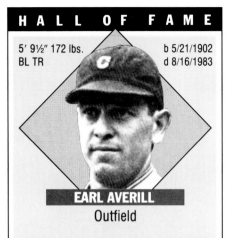

5′ 9½″ 172 lbs.
BL TR

b 5/21/1902
d 8/16/1983

EARL AVERILL
Outfield

In his very first major league plate appearance, Earl "Rock" Averill belted a home run against Detroit's Earl Whitehill. But Averill's initial success was a long time coming—his debut came at the relatively advanced age of 26.

Averill, the son of a logger from Snohomish, Washington, was a minor league star from 1926 through 1928, hitting .342 and slugging 79 home runs for the Pacific Coast League's San Francisco Seals. The Seals were reluctant to part with their star center fielder, but in 1929 they relented, selling Averill to Cleveland for a reported $50,000.

During his rookie season, Averill hit .331 and led the AL with 388 putouts. Between 1929 and 1938, Averill batted .322 and averaged 189 hits, 108 RBI and 115 runs scored each season. He played in 673 consecutive games from 1931 through 1935, and was the only outfielder selected for each of the first six All-Star games. In 1936 he hit a career-high .378 and led the AL with 232 hits. His most notorious hit, however, occurred in the 1937 All-Star Game, when he smacked a line drive that broke Dizzy Dean's big toe.

A lifetime .318 hitter, Averill hung up his spikes in 1941 and Cleveland retired his uniform number, 3; Bob Feller and Lou Boudreau are the only other Indians to have their numbers retired. His son, Earl Douglas Averill, played in the majors from 1956 to 1963.

In 1975 the Veterans' Committee elected him to the Hall of Fame.

As a rookie in 1937, Detroit's Rudy York (above, sliding) established a major league record for home runs in a single month. He hit 18 in August; 35 for the season. York never hit as many again in his 13-year career.

In 1939 Williams won another RBI championship: this time, in the AL—an unusual achievement for a rookie. Like DiMaggio, he was given a place of honor in a tough lineup, batting fourth for the Red Sox behind Doerr, Cramer and Foxx, and in front of Cronin. Williams' rookie year was even better than DiMaggio's, at least in batting. He hit .327 with 31 homers and 145 RBI. He was immensely and admirably curious about every aspect of hitting, pressing Foxx, Cronin and others with questions about various pitchers.

Feller, DiMaggio and Williams were so good as rookies that some doubted their staying power. In 1937 the Indians and the Giants barnstormed north from spring training. Dick Bartell, the Giant shortstop, saw Feller pitch for the first time and said several pitchers in the NL were "definitely faster." If so, Bartell was in for a rough season; Feller faced him ten times that spring and fanned him nine times.

Players, writers and fans argued whether Feller was as fast as Lefty Grove or Walter Johnson. In one way he was better. Neither Grove nor Johnson had much of a curveball in their early years, but Feller quickly developed one of the sharpest curves in the game. He was just wild enough to keep batters loose.

As an 18-year-old phenom in 1937, Feller was a hothouse flower. He missed two months with a sore arm, then had trouble winning despite impressive strikeout totals. On July 18 of that year, a crowd of 58,884 turned out at Cleveland Stadium to watch him face the Yankees and DiMaggio: baseball's most spectacular young players going head-to-head. The day was DiMaggio's. He doubled and tripled, then came up in the ninth with the bases loaded and the score tied, 1–1. Earle Combs, coaching first base for

Though his numbers weren't as spectacular as some of the other rising stars' in the AL, Athletics left fielder Bob Johnson was among the most consistent sluggers of the decade. From 1933 through 1941—his first nine years in the majors—Johnson hit .299 and averaged 27 homers, 102 runs scored, 107 RBI and 86 walks a season.

Cleveland third baseman Ken Keltner hit 26 homers as a rookie in 1938, then withstood the sophomore jinx in 1939 by hitting .325 with 97 RBI and leading AL third basemen in putouts, double plays and fielding percentage. On July 17, 1941, he stopped Joe DiMaggio's hitting streak at 56 games with two spectacular fielding plays.

New York, stole the catcher's sign and, as Feller pitched, yelled that a curveball was coming. DiMaggio hit it into the left center field stands for a grand-slam homer.

Feller won only nine games in 1937. In 1938 he won 17 and led the league in strikeouts for the first of seven times. Going into the final game of the season, Feller was virtually tied for the strikeout lead with Bobo Newsom, the colorful right-hander who won 20 games that season for the seventh-place St. Louis Browns. Feller and Newsom both pitched their teams' final day of the season. After the St. Louis game, Newsom phoned Feller in the Cleveland clubhouse.

Newsom: "Listen, it's been a hell of a race for strikeouts, hasn't it?"
Feller: "Sure has."
Newsom: "I think I beat you out. I struck out ten today. What kind of a game did you have?"
Feller: "Well, I lost four to one, Bobo."
Newsom: "That's too bad."
Feller: "But I struck out eighteen."

It was a new AL record for strikeouts in a nine-inning game, since surpassed by Nolan Ryan with 19 and Roger Clemens with 20. Feller was on his way. In 1939 he fully realized his promise, winning 24 and losing 9—the first of six 20-win seasons, despite four seasons in the Navy during World War II. He was baseball's best pitcher, and he was only 20 years old.

DiMaggio didn't have a bad year in 1939, either. The Yankees won going away. No one had hit .400 since Bill Terry of the Giants in 1930, but with three weeks remaining in the 1939 season, DiMaggio was at .408. He came down with a painful ailment in his left eyelid that made him blink and made it

An unusual triangle was formed in 1940, as Boston outfielder Dom DiMaggio (right) found himself linked to two great players and rivals—his brother Joe (left) and his teammate Ted Williams (center). But Dom was a fine player in his own right, topping .300 four times and being generally acknowledged as in his brother's class as a defensive center fielder.

difficult for him to keep his eye on the ball. The Yanks were coasting to their fourth straight pennant, so manager Joe McCarthy could have benched DiMaggio. "If I take you out," McCarthy told his young star, "they'll say I did it to make you a .400 hitter and they'll call you a cheese champion. So my advice, Joe, is to stay in there and do the best you can. What do you say?"

DiMaggio said he would play. His batting average skidded 27 points, winding up at .381—the league's best and his career high. He hit 30 homers and drove in 126 runs—his fourth of seven straight seasons with more than 100 RBI. As for a .400 batting average, Williams achieved that in 1941.

In Feller, DiMaggio and Williams, the AL had three bright young stars who dominated the game into the 1950s. The old order was fading. Ruth played his last game in 1935, Bill Terry in 1936, Rogers Hornsby and Frankie Frisch in 1937 and Lou Gehrig in 1939. Dizzy Dean, Lefty Grove, Jimmie Foxx, Al Simmons and the Waner brothers played into the 1940s, but only as part-timers.

As sluggers, DiMaggio and Williams were matched in stature by Detroit's Hank Greenberg, who also bridged the gap between decades, coming to the Tigers in 1933 and starring in the 1940s as well. All three played in the AL, as did most of the slugging stars who preceded them: Ruth, Gehrig, Foxx, Simmons. The AL consistently outhit the NL in the 1930s, scoring more runs every season from 1931 to 1942—which happened to be the rookie year of Stan Musial, the NL's answer to DiMaggio and Williams. ◗

Joe DiMaggio (opposite, left) and Bob Feller (right) were both rookies in 1936, but by the time Feller played in his first World Series 12 years later, DiMaggio had already played in seven. "I'd like to thank the good Lord for making me a Yankee," he once said.

Mel Ott

From the very beginning Giant manager John J. McGraw knew that Mel Ott was an original. Well, not actually from the very beginning. Upon meeting the stubby, small-town kid from Louisiana, McGraw figured he had been sold a bill of goods by the scout who had raved about this 16-year-old catcher. But then McGraw saw Ott hit.

The first thing he noticed was Ott's strange habit of hiking his lead foot high off the ground as he began his stroke. Ott held his hands down low too and choked up on the bat. But when the pitch came in, his swing became a thing of beauty, level and smooth and as consistent as a Swiss watch. No matter what the tryout pitcher threw, Ott timed it perfectly and lined hits to the right field wall. McGraw was fascinated. What struck him most was that despite all the movement in the swing, Ott's head remained still. "He's like a golfer," McGraw told a coach watching the performance. "His body moves but those eyes never leave the ball."

From that day in 1925 on, Ott was McGraw's personal project. McGraw refused to send him to the minors, fearful that some coach would ruin his exquisite swing. First, he told Ott that his catching days were over—his thick legs, McGraw realized, weren't flexible enough to stand the daily pounding. He assigned the teenager a spot on the bench—right next to McGraw himself. Game after game, the manager would critique what was happening on the field for his student, carping about bad plays and warning the youngster, "Don't ever let me catch you doing that." Ott listened, at least partly out of fear, but he

learned. "More than anything he taught me how to anticipate plays," he later explained.

Ott had plenty of study time. His first two seasons, 1926 and 1927, he did little more than pinch-hit. He struck out in his first major league at-bat, but hit .383 in 35 games the first year and .282 in 82 games the next. By 1928 McGraw thought his protégé was ready, and on May 10, Ott became the Giants' starting right fielder, celebrating his promotion with four RBI. He stayed in the lineup 19 more years.

By his 21st birthday, Ott was a shining star. He batted .322 and hit 18 homers in 1928, but he was only warming up. The next year his average climbed to .328 while his RBI total soared to 151 and his homers to 42. He was the archetypal American hero, so lovable that not even Dodger fans booed him. Not only was he quiet and unassuming, but he also was the classic overachiever. Through the 1930s, he became the most feared home run hitter in the National League—this despite the fact that he was only 5' 9" and weighed 170 pounds.

Part of his success clearly had to do with his environment. Rarely were a player and a ballpark better suited for each other than Ott and the Polo Grounds. He was a lefty and a dead-pull hitter; the right field corner was a mere 257 feet away. In fact, of his 511 career homers, 323 came at home, the most any major league player has ever hit in one park. And he pleased the home crowd with his fielding as well. The cozy lower right field stands became known as "Ottville," and fans who could afford pricey box seats bought tickets out there instead so they could

Timing, not physical strength, was the key to Mel Ott's power. The 5' 9", 170-pound slugger said, "It was a matter of connecting at exactly the right place in the swinging arc. That way I was able to get every pound behind the ball."

get closer to him. "Master Melvin," as he was called, repaid them with one fielding gem after another, regularly gunning down runners with his powerful arm. Once, legend has it, he threw a ball 400 feet in spring training.

But he was most revered for his timely bat. Pitchers routinely put him on with men on base, which helps explain why he walked more than 100 times in each of ten seasons and held the NL record for bases on balls—1,708—until Joe Morgan broke it in 1982. "Ott beats you and he does it over and over again," said Pirates Hall of Famer Pie Traynor. "You get in a tight spot, the score tied or close and then Ottie breaks up the game. He was the only one who had that kind of stuff." A case in point was the 1933 World Series—Ott's first—against the Washington Senators. He had four hits in the Giants' first-game victory, then won the fifth game and the world championship with a tenth-inning homer.

For many years, he was the league's dominant player, winning the NL home run title three times and tying for the lead three other times. He hit two or more homers in one game 49 times. Twice he scored

six runs in one game, and for eight consecutive years he had more than 100 RBI. He led the Giants to pennants in 1933, 1936 and 1937, and when the team began to slide in the early 1940s, he was, at the age of 32, named player-manager with the hope that he could inspire the New York club back to the top.

But Ott proved a far better player than manager. The Giants finished third in 1942, his first year at the helm, and never did any better during the next five and a half seasons under him. It was said that he couldn't handle pitchers and that he was too soft with his veteran players. It was Ott about whom Leo Durocher uttered his famous aspersion, "Nice guys finish last." Ironically, Durocher replaced him as the Giants' manager halfway through the 1948 season.

But Ott had already made his mark. Without hesitation, the Giants retired his number, 4, and in 1951 he was voted into the Hall of Fame. He worked briefly as a minor league manager in Oakland, then became a broadcaster for the Detroit Tigers. On a foggy November night in 1958 he and his wife were involved in a head-on car collision. A week later the Little Giant was dead.

In hopes of pleasing manager John McGraw, Ott (opposite) used to practice sliding in his hotel room, using pillows to cushion the impact. A great hitter and fielder, Ott was most of all a winner. "He did more to help the other team lose than almost anybody else," wrote Bill James.

MEL OTT

Outfield, Third Base
New York Giants 1926–1947
Hall of Fame 1951

GAMES	2,732
AT-BATS	9,456
BATTING AVERAGE	
Career	.304
Season High	.349
SLUGGING AVERAGE	
Career	.533
Season High	.635
HITS	
Career	2,876
Season High	191
DOUBLES	
Career	488
Season High	37
TRIPLES	
Career	72
Season High	10
HOME RUNS	
Career	511
Season High	42
TOTAL BASES	5,041
EXTRA-BASE HITS	1,071
RUNS BATTED IN	
Career *(8th all time)*	1,860
Season High	151
RUNS	
Career *(9th all time)*	1,859
Season High	138
WORLD SERIES **1933, 1936–1937**	

The Cubs
Come Through

Galan, Herman, Lindstrom, Hartnett, Demaree, Cavaretta, Hack, Jurges, Klein

The 1935 Chicago Cubs (above) were solid all around—hitting, pitching and defense. The combination translated into 100 wins and a pennant. Pictured from left are left fielder Augie Galan, second baseman Billy Herman, utility infielder Freddie Lindstrom, catcher Gabby Hartnett, center fielder Frank Demaree, first baseman Phil Cavarretta, third baseman Stan Hack, shortstop Billy Jurges and right fielder Chuck Klein.

Cubs catcher and hero Gabby Hartnett was given a police escort (preceding page) off the field on September 28, 1938, after his blast carried through the darkness into the Wrigley Field bleachers, beating the Pirates and vaulting the Cubs to the NL pennant.

harlie Grimm was a man of many talents. He sang, and he played the banjo left-handed. He painted portraits and designed furniture. He was a raconteur; no one told funnier baseball stories than Grimm. Given an audience—and he often had one —Grimm could entertain with magic tricks or tell jokes in a phony German accent. He was a master of pantomime. As a player, he led his infield teammates in a pantomimed infield drill —without a ball—that entertained a generation of Chicago fans. Al Capone and John Dillinger, among others, came out to Wrigley Field early to see the show. In later years, as a third-base coach, Grimm still mimicked plays and players.

Cub fans loved him, and they had good reason, because Grimm was at the heart of the Cubs organization in the midst of its last period of success. The Cubs were never a dynasty, but for a decade they won pennants every three years: 1929, 1932, 1935, 1938. Grimm contributed to that record, first as a player—he was a strong left-handed hitter and led National League first basemen in fielding for seven seasons—and then as a manager.

He took his banjo and his ukelele on road trips, and his teammates crowded around him on the trains and in the hotels. The Cubs of the early 1930s needed relaxing entertainment because they were managed by Rogers Hornsby. Although he was a great player, the "Rajah" was a stern, unfriendly manager. Riggs Stephenson, the Cubs' star left fielder, typified his teammates' attitude about Hornsby when he said, "I never done anything to that man. I wonder why he don't talk to me."

When he did talk, Hornsby was blunt to the point of cruelty. One day a father came to Wrigley Field to watch his son try out. The boy didn't hit very well, but the proud father nevertheless asked Hornsby what he

On August 2, 1932, Charlie Grimm (left, with his daughter May Gene) replaced the irascible Rogers Hornsby as Cubs manager. The team responded by winning 37 of their last 57 games to win the pennant by four games over Pittsburgh.

Rogers Hornsby's face might have helped sell ice cream to fans in Wrigley Field in 1932, but his relationship with his players and the Cubs' front office was so sour that even though he managed the team for most of the season, the team denied him a World Series share.

thought of the young man's chances. "I can spit farther than he can hit a ball," Hornsby replied.

Hornsby was the Pete Rose of his day. Although he didn't bet on baseball games, he was an avid gambler whose racetrack wagers cost him dearly, both in the pocketbook and in public esteem. In 1927 he was sued by a partner who contended that Hornsby owed him $92,000—money Hornsby had borrowed and bet at the racetracks. Testimony disclosed that in a four-month period from December 1925 to March 1926, Hornsby's racetrack wagers totaled $327,995—roughly the equivalent of $2.5 million today. Hornsby's bets were legal, earning him nothing worse than disapproval from Commissioner Kenesaw Mountain Landis, a man who tolerated no wrongdoing among baseball players. But Hornsby was in debt, having also lost heavily in the 1929 stock market crash. In 1932 newspapers disclosed that the Cub manager had borrowed about $11,000 from several of his players.

Landis suspected that Hornsby was inspiring certain of his players to play the ponies. He called a hearing, and the Hornsby scandal was big news for days. Guy Bush, a Cub pitcher, was accused of placing bets in partnership with Hornsby, and Landis asked both of them whether it was true that "you contracted with a couple of ladies known as blondes" to carry bets from the Cubs' clubhouse to neighborhood bookies. "This is a lot of bunk," Hornsby replied. Bush expressed outrage: "That is a helluva story to be telling about a man that is married," he said. Once again, the commissioner could find no grounds for action. But William Veeck, the Cubs' general manager, was fed up with Hornsby's behavior and his managing style. On August 2, 1932, he fired Hornsby and replaced him with first baseman "Jolly Cholly" Grimm.

5' 11" 180 lbs.   b 7/7/1909
BR TR

BILLY HERMAN
Second Base

In the 1930s cleanup hitters like Lou Gehrig, Al Simmons and Mel Ott got all the attention; batting fourth and driving in runs allowed them to shine. But somebody had to be on base for them to drive in. Throughout the decade, second baseman Billy Herman did the job for the Chicago Cubs. Batting second, Herman knew what his role was: "In those days, teams had maybe one or two power hitters and the rest of us had to move it around." And Herman moved it around as well as anyone. An accomplished bat handler, he hit to all fields, sacrificing power for control and consistency, compiling an impressive .304 lifetime average and a .433 average in ten All-Star games. "I didn't swing and miss much," he said. It was true; in 1935 he struck out only once in every 23 at-bats.

Herman was a great defensive player, too. He led the league in putouts at his position seven times—an NL record. His skills helped the Cubs to win pennants in 1932, 1935 and 1938. But his reputation as one of the game's most intelligent players got him traded to the Brooklyn Dodgers in 1941; Jimmie Wilson, the Cubs' manager, saw Herman as a threat to his job. Had Wilson known that Herman's managing record would be 189–274 in four seasons, he wouldn't have worried.

But Herman's lack of success as a manager does not diminish his success as a player. After all, hitters like Billy Herman helped make guys like Gehrig, Simmons and Ott look good.

The Cubs won only two games in the 1935 World Series against Detroit, and Lon Warneke got the win in both of them. Warneke tossed a four-hit shutout in Game 1, then pitched six shutout innings in a 3–1 Game 5 win.

At the time, the Cubs were in second place, five games behind the Pirates. Under Grimm's light touch, they shot to the top, winning 14 straight games and 20 out of 25. Not that everything went smoothly. This was, after all, Chicago in the speakeasy era, and the Cub players had a diverse circle of acquaintances. Shortstop Billy Jurges was shot one evening by a showgirl he had befriended. Her name was Violet Popovitch Heindel-Valli. She shot herself, too. Jurges refused to press charges, and he and Miss Heindel-Valli both recovered and resumed their careers, Jurges learning to endure cries of "Bang! Bang!" from rival bench jockeys.

In the meantime, the Cubs needed a replacement shortstop. They found a good one in Mark Koenig, a former Yankee star who had faded back to the minor leagues. Koenig came up for the final 33 games of a hot 1932 pennant race and batted .353, although some of the Cubs considered him to be an interloper. The Cubs clinched the pennant September 20 when Hazen "Kiki" Cuyler tripled with the bases loaded to beat the Pirates and give Bush his 19th win of the season.

The Cubs were good and getting better. Billy Herman, a future Hall of Famer, was a rookie at second base; Stan Hack, who was to star for years to come, was a rookie at third. Lon Warneke won 22 games, led the National League in earned runs with an average of 2.37 and sported one of the more melodious nicknames to grace the 1930s. Warneke hailed from Mt. Ida, Arkansas; they called him "the Arkansas Humming Bird."

The Cubs drew well during the Depression, partly because so many Chicago women took advantage of free "Ladies' Day" tickets, a ploy admittedly designed to attract accompanying gentlemen at the full tariff.

The record for attendance was set June 27, 1930, when Wrigley Field was packed with 51,556 fans—30,476 of them women admitted without charge. Newspapers ran stories on the phenomenon, and one reporter talked to an elderly lady who had been swept into Wrigley Field by the crowd. "I was just minding my business, walking down Addison Street," she said, "when all of a sudden I was inside the ballpark. I had no intention of watching a ball-game. But I couldn't get out. So I just stayed."

The Cubs were no match for the Yankees in the 1932 World Series, made memorable by Babe Ruth's "called shot" home run. The Cub players voted Rogers Hornsby not a penny of World Series money, even though he had managed the team for two-thirds of the season. They voted only a half share to Koenig, giving his former teammates on the Yankees ample fodder for Series bench-jockeying, and enraging Commissioner Landis. As punishment, Landis didn't send the Cub players their Series money until the following January.

The Cubs fell short in 1933 and 1934, but Grimm was highly regarded by the Cubs' management and not only stayed on, but was given the additional title of club vice president. Asked his managerial philosophy, Grimm replied, "Keep 'em happy." But not at all costs. When the Cubs installed a new public address system in late 1934, Grimm had to be reassured that no music would be played over it during pregame warm-ups. The people in the booth, he felt, could not be depended upon to play the right music to match the rhythm of certain drills, and it would end up throwing the players off. At about that time, Grimm put aside his banjo and his uke, inspiring Edward Burns of the *Chicago Tribune* to write, "has

Continued on page 154

Cubs center fielder Freddie Lindstrom got cut down trying to steal by two future Hall of Famers—Tiger catcher Mickey Cochrane and second baseman Charlie Gehringer (above)—in Game 1 of the 1935 World Series. The Cubs won the opener, 3–0, but lost to the Tigers in six games.

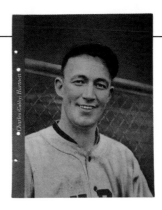

Charles Gabby Hartnett

Gabby Hartnett

History seemed to follow Gabby Hartnett around in the 1930s. Hartnett was behind the plate when Babe Ruth hit his famous "called shot" in Game 3 of the 1932 World Series. He was behind the plate when the Giants' Carl Hubbell struck out five future Hall of Famers in a row—Ruth, Gehrig, Foxx, Simmons and Cronin—in the 1934 All-Star Game. And he was at the plate on September 28, 1938, as darkness fell over Wrigley Field in the bottom of the ninth, with the game tied, 5–5, and the Cubs trailing the Pirates in the pennant race by half a game. Hartnett hit a long drive that came to be known as the "homer in the gloamin'," a belt that boosted the Cubs to the National League flag.

Hartnett played 19 seasons with Wrigley Field as his home. He was one of the most popular players in Chicago, so popular that when Hartnett signed an autograph for mobster Al Capone's son, a newspaper photographer snapped the three of them together. When Commissioner Landis saw the photo in the newspaper he reprimanded Hartnett, who reportedly told Landis, "If you don't want anybody to talk to the Big Guy, Judge, you tell him."

For most of his career, Hartnett was acknowledged as the finest all-around catcher in the league, and he had the numbers to prove it. He caught at least 100 games in 12 seasons, and with 233 home runs ranks fourth all time among National League catchers. An outstanding defensive catcher, Hartnett led the league six times each in fielding percentage and assists. But if it hadn't been for an errant bit of judgment by a Giants scout, he might have spent his career in New York.

The eldest of 14 children, Hartnett signed with Worcester, Massachusetts, of the Eastern League in 1921. Giants manager John McGraw was looking for a hard-throwing catcher and sent scout Jesse Burkett to take a look at the 20-year-old Hartnett. Burkett wired back that although Hartnett was a solid 6' 1" and 195 pounds, his hands were too small for him ever to be a big-league catcher. Later that season—on the advice of scout Jack Doyle—the Cubs bought Hartnett's contract for $2,500. Doyle liked Hartnett's play—and also liked his face. "Hartnett had a strong puss," Doyle said.

Before Hartnett left for spring training in 1922, his mother told him to keep his mouth shut during the trip. That advice earned him his most popular nickname; Hartnett sat silently next to Dean Sullivan, sports editor of the *Chicago Herald Examiner.* "You're certainly a gabby guy," Sullivan finally said, and a nickname was born.

By 1924 Hartnett was the Cubs' starting catcher, and in 1925 he set a major league record for home runs by a catcher with 24. In 1929 the Cubs won the pennant, but Hartnett had injured his arm in spring training, and caught just one game all season. He came back strong in 1930 and had his finest year, boosting his home run record to 37, adding 122 RBI and posting a .339 average. Hartnett went on to anchor Cub pennant-winners in 1932 and 1935, then took over as player-manager midway through the 1938 season, when he led the Cubs to another pennant, climaxing their late-season surge with his memorable twilight homer.

Hartnett called a great game, handled pitchers as well as anyone and is said to have missed just three foul pops in 1,790 games behind the plate. Pitchers loved him, but Dizzy Dean, the Cardinal great who went 7–1 for the Cubs in 1938, paid him the ultimate compliment. "If I had that guy to pitch to all the time," Dean said, "I'd never lose me a game."

Gabby Hartnett was the epitome of the all-around catcher. Not only could he hit, catch and throw, but he fired up pitchers and annoyed batters better than any catcher of his era. "He gets it out of you," said teammate Charlie Root.

GABBY HARTNETT

Catcher
Chicago Cubs 1922–1940
New York Giants 1941
Hall of Fame 1955

GAMES	**1,990**
AT-BATS	**6,432**
BATTING AVERAGE	
Career	**.297**
Season High	**.354**
SLUGGING AVERAGE	
Career	**.489**
Season High	**.630**
HITS	
Career	**1,912**
Season High	**172**
DOUBLES	
Career	**396**
Season High	**32**
TRIPLES	
Career	**64**
Season High	**9**
HOME RUNS	
Career	**236**
Season High	**37**
TOTAL BASES	**3,144**
EXTRA-BASE HITS	**696**
RUNS BATTED IN	
Career	**1,179**
Season High	**122**
RUNS	
Career	**867**
Season High	**84**
WORLD SERIES	**1929, 1932, 1935, 1938**
MOST VALUABLE PLAYER	**1935**

21 STRAIGHT

On September 3, 1935, the Chicago Cubs were in third place, 2½ games behind the league-leading Cardinals. But with 18 straight games before the home fans, the Cubs became unstoppable. They won all 18 and continued the streak when they went to St. Louis on September 25. The Cubs clinched the NL pennant with their 20th victory in the first game of a doubleheader on September 27, and took the second game to set the modern record for consecutive games won without a tie.

Date	Opponent	Score
September 4	Phillies	8–2
September 5	Phillies	3–2 (11)
September 6	Phillies	3–2 (10)
September 7	Phillies	4–0
September 9	Braves	5–1
	Braves	2–1
September 10	Braves	4–0
September 11	Braves	15–3
September 12	Dodgers	13–3
September 13	Dodgers	4–1
September 14	Dodgers	18–14
September 15	Dodgers	6–3
September 16	Giants	8–3
September 17	Giants	5–3
September 18	Giants	15–3
September 19	Giants	6–1
September 21	Pirates	4–3
September 22	Pirates	2–0
September 25	Cardinals	1–0
September 27	Cardinals	6–2
	Cardinals	5–3

Leo Durocher said Cubs second baseman Billy Herman (above) "had become universally accepted as the classic #2 hitter in baseball, an absolute master at hitting behind the runner."

the frowning dignity of the vice presidency cloyed the minstrel poesy that once mused within that wholesome bosom?"

The Cubs pulled a risky move before the 1935 season, trading veteran slugger Babe Herman and two good pitchers—Hornsby's erstwhile crony Guy Bush and Jim Weaver—to the Pirates. In return, they got Larry French, an able left-handed pitcher, and Fred Lindstrom, a battered veteran who could play either third base or the outfield.

The trade did not look good, and neither did the Cubs. But Jolly Cholly figured he had the right players in place. As the season started, he was 38 and suffering from lumbago, so he benched himself in favor of an 18-year-old rookie, Phil Cavarretta, at first. At second was Herman, 25, having his best year: he came away hitting .341 with a league-leading 227 hits. Gabby Hartnett, a great catcher for most of two decades, batted .344. Warneke, French, and Bill Lee pitched superbly.

The Cubs, however, seemed to be spectators at a pennant race between the Cardinals and the Giants. Nearing the end of a losing home stand in June 1935, the Cubs lost a doubleheader to St. Louis. The next day, the Cubs led by four runs going into the top of the ninth inning. With one out and the bases loaded with Cardinals, Grimm pulled pitcher Tex Carleton and brought in Larry French. Cardinal first baseman Ripper Collins greeted him with a grand-slam homer. The Cubs had lost another game. Chicago newspapers surmised that Grimm might be fired. On Labor Day, a Cub play-by-play announcer in Des Moines, Iowa—one Dutch Reagan— announced the obvious: the Cubs would have to win the rest of their games to win the pennant.

The Cubs swept four games each from the Phillies, Braves and Dodgers. Then the Giants came to Wrigley Field, fresh from winning three

After hitting over .300 in five of his first seven years with the Cubs, Hall of Fame outfielder Kiki Cuyler was given his unconditional release midway through the 1935 season. Cuyler, 37, made the Cubs look stupid by hitting .326 for the Reds in 1936.

times in St. Louis. The Cubs knocked off the visitors four in a row, and for an encore beat the Pirates twice. That made 18 straight wins. Even back then managers had to suffer questions from an occasional ignoramus. A radio reporter, uninterested in baseball and subbing for the station's regular baseball man, asked Grimm, "How's the club been doing?"

The winning streak had moved the Cubs into first place, but to finish the season they had to face the Cardinals—and the Dean brothers—in St. Louis. Warneke promptly beat Paul Dean, 1–0, for his 20th win. Dizzy Dean started the opener of a doubleheader the next day, and the Cubs rocked him for 15 hits; Lee got his 20th win, and his team clinched the pennant with a 6–2 victory. The Cubs ran their winning streak to 21 by taking the nightcap, too, for an even 100 wins on the season. Lindstrom, the veteran pickup, scored or drove in the winning run in seven of the last 21 games.

Chicago couldn't stand up to Detroit in the Series, losing four games to two, but the following year, Grimm's team was *almost* good enough to make a repeat appearance. The Cubs finished five games out in 1936 and three games out in 1937. Jolly Cholly kept clowning and kept his players loose.

Yet even Grimm's good humor was tried in 1938. The Giants, defending league champions, won 18 of their first 21 games. Grimm decided a change was needed: "One day, after we were beaten, I sat in the clubhouse, my head in my hands. I thought a while, then decided I wasn't doing the club any good. So I quit." He advised Cubs owner Philip K. Wrigley to elevate Gabby Hartnett, the scrappy catcher, to the managership. Wrigley obliged, and so did Hartnett. Grimm went home to his Missouri

A member of all three Cub pennant-winners in the 1930s, center fielder Frank Demaree had his best seasons in 1936 and 1937, years the Cubs finished second. Demaree hit .350 in 1936, and in 1937 he hit .324, with 115 RBI.

farm, where he spent one night before being summoned back to broadcast the Cubs' games.

The Pittsburgh Pirates, led by the Waner brothers—Lloyd and Paul—and Arky Vaughan, had pulled seven games ahead of their NL rivals by Labor Day, 1938. The Cubs gained on them, but during a trip East, two straight doubleheaders had left Chicago's pitching staff exhausted. They needed an act of God and they got it: a hurricane hit the East Coast September 18, and for three days no games were played in New York, Philadelphia or Boston.

Rested, the Cubs started another binge; they won seven straight and returned home. The Pirates came to Chicago September 27, leading the league by only a game and a half. Hartnett surprised everyone by starting a sore-armed right-hander who hadn't pitched for two weeks and hadn't started a game for more than a month. His name was Dizzy Dean. The Cubs had acquired him before the 1938 season, giving the Cardinals three players and $185,000. Dean's bad arm was no secret. The Cubs figured he would draw enough fans to pay for himself and perhaps help occasionally on the mound. Using guile, control, slow curves and an occasional fastball, Dean checked the Pirates through 8⅔ innings, yielding just one run. Reliever Lee came on and got the final out, and the Cubs won, 2–1, pulling within a half game of first.

The next day belonged to Gabby Hartnett. The Pirates took the lead twice, but the Cubs tied it at 5–5 after eight innings. Wrigley Field was getting dark, but the umpires decided to let the game go one inning more. Charlie Root stopped the Pirates in the top half, and the Cubs faced Mace

Brown, the National League's best reliever. With two out, nobody on base and the count 0–2, Hartnett took one final swing. "I got the kind of feeling you get when the blood rushes out of your head and you get dizzy," Hartnett later told writer Hal Totten. "A lot of people have told me they didn't know the ball was in the bleachers. Well, I did—maybe I was the only one in the park who did. I knew it the minute I hit it." Hartnett's "homer in the gloamin' " sent the Cubs into first place and is still regarded as one of the most dramatic hits in history. Fans and teammates carried him around the bases in a rite of justified jubilation.

The Cubs lost the World Series to the Yankees in 1932, to the Tigers in 1935 and to the Yankees again in 1938. Charlie Grimm returned as manager in 1944 and guided a makeshift team to the pennant in the wartime year of 1945. A long drought followed, and a National League pennant has never graced Wrigley Field since. But Cub fans with long memories—*very* long memories—can look back fondly on Jolly Cholly Grimm, Gabby Hartnett and the good old days of the 1930s. ◉

Cub catcher-manager Gabby Hartnett (left) made a winner out of pitcher Charlie Root (right) with his "homer in the gloamin' " to put the Cubs in first place on September 28, 1938. Three days later, Root returned the favor with a pennant-clinching 10–3 win over the Cardinals.

Trying Times

As the Great Depression tightened its grip on America in the 1930s, the nation turned inward and sought sanctuary in its most cherished institutions: the family, the church and the ballpark. While most fans couldn't afford to actually see a game, they could perhaps spare two cents for a newspaper, or even better, listen to a game through the magic of radio. With their own lives made small by hunger and deprivation, they escaped into the exploits of larger-than-life heroes like Ruth and Ruffing, Gehrig and Grove. Baseball was rarely better, and the daily hum of the regular season lent a reassuring constancy to American life. Although there may have been little else, there was still a World Series each fall and a new season each spring.

For baseball, the 1930s brought radical change both in the way the game was played and in the way it was perceived. In 1939 the age of televised baseball was ushered in, as NBC's Bill Stern (top) broadcast an intercollegiate game between Columbia and Princeton. In New York, John McGraw's 31-year reign as manager of the Giants ended in 1932, when Bill Terry (right, with young Cecil Haley) took over.

Prosperity was just around the corner throughout the 1930s, but the lines were awfully long. Entrepreneurs sold all-American sandwiches in the street (top), while those who couldn't scrape together three cents could get some Salvation Army soup (above). Desperate times called for desperate measures, as some took the concept of "selling oneself" to an extreme (right).

A lot of attention—serious and otherwise—was focused on the ball itself in the 1930s. Experts from the National Bureau of Standards (top right) used an air cannon to test the liveliness of baseballs prior to the 1938 season, while Indians third baseman Ken Keltner (above) dropped a ball off the top of the 708-foot Terminal Tower in Cleveland into the waiting mitt of catcher Henry Helf. The catch broke the previous record of 550 feet set by Gabby Street in 1908 when he caught a ball thrown from the top of the Washington Monument. Red Sox fans would have liked members of the 1930 New York Yankees arrested, but it was just fun and games as the Yankee lineup (right) stood tall at a Boston police station.

And you thought they just played baseball. Cincinnati's Frank McCormick (above) could leap large newsreel cameras in a single bound, while Athletics slugger Jimmie Foxx (top right) was a leather-draped gunslinger and Detroit's Mickey Cochrane (right) played a mean alto sax.

The Luckiest Man

Even without Babe Ruth batting in front of him, even without the pennants and the pinstripes and the illness that tinged his legend with tragedy, Lou Gehrig would be remembered today as one of baseball's greatest players. Gehrig led the American League in home runs three times and in RBI five times. He played every Yankee game for almost 14 years, and he was a model of consistency, hitting .340 lifetime. For 11 seasons—1927 through 1937—he *averaged* 153 RBI. With Gehrig playing first base, the Yankees won seven pennants and six World Series. In 34 World Series games, he hit ten homers, drove in 35 runs and batted .361.

Yet Gehrig's fame might be greater had he not been a Yankee. He played ten seasons in Babe Ruth's shadow and three in Joe DiMaggio's. He lacked Ruth's color and DiMaggio's grace. "Some ballplayers have natural-born ability," Gehrig told sportswriter Jack Sher. "But I wasn't one of them. You take a player like Joe DiMaggio. Now there's a natural. Sometimes I wonder how in the world I was ever able to make it."

Gehrig was humble in his work and bashful among his peers. The ebullient, wisecracking Ruth always seemed to *play* baseball, while Gehrig stolidly *worked* at the game. Ruth was a better player than Gehrig, but then Ruth was better than anyone else who ever played the game. And Gehrig wasn't far behind him. As Ruth himself said, "There's only one man who ever had a chance of breaking my record, and that's Lou Gehrig."

Ruth's personality enhanced his fame and his popularity among other players. Gehrig's shyness detracted from his celebrity status. Gehrig had more education than Ruth—he attended Columbia University for two years. Nevertheless, while Ruth joked and chattered and charmed sportswriters

and everyone else, Gehrig lacked self-confidence and was a poor communicator. He once told sportswriter Fred Lieb, "You know, when some of the writers come up to me and ask me questions, they think that I'm rude because I don't answer right. But I'm so scared I'm almost shitting in my pants."

The two men were close friends off the field until a dispute between Christina Gehrig, Lou's mother, and Claire Ruth, Babe's wife, split them apart. But two men were never more different. As Claire herself said, "Surely Babe was ridiculous when he left a ten-dollar tip where fifty cents would have been generous. But Lou's dimes were just as silly."

Gehrig's notorious frugality probably had something to do with his humble beginnings. His parents were poor immigrants from Germany. They worked in a fraternity house at Columbia University, Christina cooking and cleaning, Heinrich stoking the furnace and doing maintenance work. Lou—"little Heinie," as the fraternity boys called him—played ball and otherwise hung around.

Lou worked hard in high school and, on the side, waited tables at the fraternity house. A football scholarship got him into Columbia—and into a fraternity himself, though not the one where he and his parents had worked. Far from contributing to his self-esteem, fraternity membership humbled him all the more. He couldn't dress or talk like his fraternity brothers, most of whom came from upper-class backgrounds, and he was treated as an outsider.

While he was in college, Gehrig's parents became ill. Over the protests of his mother, he left Columbia in 1923 after his sophomore year; the Yankees had offered him a $1,500 signing bonus and a $3,000 contract, and

In September 1933, at the age of 30, Gehrig moved out—over his mother's objections—and married Eleanor Twitchell, a sometimes songwriter (above). In 1934 Gehrig won the Triple Crown with 49 home runs, 165 RBI and a .363 average.

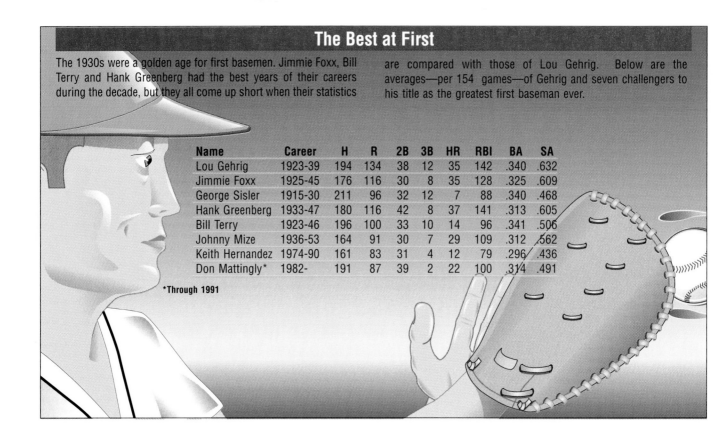

The Best at First

The 1930s were a golden age for first basemen. Jimmie Foxx, Bill Terry and Hank Greenberg had the best years of their careers during the decade, but they all come up short when their statistics are compared with those of Lou Gehrig. Below are the averages—per 154 games—of Gehrig and seven challengers to his title as the greatest first baseman ever.

Name	Career	H	R	2B	3B	HR	RBI	BA	SA
Lou Gehrig	1923-39	194	134	38	12	35	142	.340	.632
Jimmie Foxx	1925-45	176	116	30	8	35	128	.325	.609
George Sisler	1915-30	211	96	32	12	7	88	.340	.468
Hank Greenberg	1933-47	180	116	42	8	37	141	.313	.605
Bill Terry	1923-46	196	100	33	10	14	96	.341	.506
Johnny Mize	1936-53	164	91	30	7	29	109	.312	.562
Keith Hernandez	1974-90	161	83	31	4	12	79	.296	.436
Don Mattingly*	1982-	191	87	39	2	22	100	.314	.491

*Through 1991

he accepted, knowing that the salary would allow him to pay his parents' medical bills and to contribute to their support.

He started out as a clumsy fielder and became acceptable at first base only through hard work. Late in his career, Gehrig described his fielding progress: "In the beginning, I used to make one terrible play a game. Then I got so I'd make one a week, and finally I'd pull a bad one about once a month. Now, I'm trying to keep it down to one a season."

Gehrig was always a talented hitter, but his most spectacular feats always seemed to be preempted by other memorable events. At Philadelphia's Shibe Park on June 3, 1932, Gehrig hit four consecutive home runs, two of them to center field and two to right. He hit the first three against George Earnshaw, the Athletics' ace right-hander. Roy Mahaffey relieved, and as the dejected Earnshaw headed for the showers, his manager, Connie Mack, called him back. "Wait, George, I want you to see how Mahaffey pitches to Gehrig," Mack said. Gehrig hit Mahaffey's next pitch into the center field seats. "I see, Connie. May I go now?" said Earnshaw.

In the ninth inning, a leaping catch by Al Simmons robbed Gehrig of a fifth homer. Four straight home runs! "Well, Lou, nobody can take today away from you," said Joe McCarthy, the Yankee manager. But McCarthy was wrong. Coincidentally, John McGraw announced his retirement that day, after 31 years as manager of the New York Giants. McGraw's resignation—and not Gehrig's four homers—led the sports pages.

Ruth's "called shot" home run was far and away the highlight of the 1932 World Series, which the Yankees won in four games from the Chicago Cubs. In fact, Ruth hit two homers in that game. So did Gehrig, who batted .529 for the Series, with nine runs and eight RBI. "When I get to bat," Gehrig once

Ruth and Gehrig clowned around a bit before Opening Day at Philadelphia's Shibe Park in 1932. But once the season started they got serious. The pair combined for 75 home runs and 288 RBI during the season, then pounded the Cubs into submission in a four-game World Series sweep.

After Ruth left the Yankees, Gehrig flirted with a Hollywood career, even donning a leopard skin in order to pose as Tarzan. But Gehrig's media blitz was short-lived. The one film he starred in, Rawhide, was a disaster.

said, "people are still talking about what Ruth has done. If I stood on my head and held the bat in my teeth, none of the fans would pay the slightest attention. But I'm not kicking."

In 1931 Ruth and Gehrig both hit 46 home runs, but again fate deprived Gehrig of his chance to outshine Ruth. One day during the season, with two out and Lyn Lary on first base, Gehrig homered to right. Lary thought the ball had been caught, and trotted into the dugout. Gehrig trotted around the bases, passing the spot where Lary had left the baselines. Lary was declared out, the inning was over, and Gehrig's homer didn't count. Not until 1934, when Ruth was 39 and on his last legs, did Gehrig hit more homers in a season than the Babe.

Ruth's salary eventually reached $80,000. Gehrig peaked at $39,000 in 1938, and when his hitting fell off to a mere .295, 29 homers and 114 RBI, the Yankees cut his salary by $5,000.

Gehrig was always willing to work for his pay. His first few years, he sent almost all his earnings to his parents; when he reported to the Yanks' spring-training camp in 1924 he had only $12. He confided his plight to sportswriter Dan Daniel: "Things are pretty tough, Dan. I can't seem to find a job, not even washing dishes." Daniel told Gehrig that he shouldn't look for outside work but should ask Miller Huggins, the Yankee manager, for money. "Oh, I couldn't do that," Gehrig replied. Daniel made the request for Gehrig, and the Yanks were spared the ridicule that would have resulted had their prize prospect been found washing dishes for his meal money. Before the 1930 season, Ruth proposed to Gehrig that they should bargain for more money together; with the team's two power hitters holding out, Babe argued, the Yankees would have to pay them

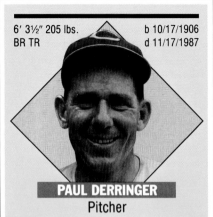

PAUL DERRINGER
Pitcher

6' 3½" 205 lbs.
BR TR
b 10/17/1906
d 11/17/1987

Paul Derringer had all the basics— a fastball, a change-up and a mean curve—when the world champion St. Louis Cardinals brought him up to bolster their pitching staff in 1931. Though envisioned as a spot reliever, Derringer nailed down a starting slot by Memorial Day. At season's end, his record stood at 18–8, and his .692 winning percentage led the majors, a feat never before accomplished by a rookie.

Early in 1933 the faltering Cards traded Derringer to an even worse team—the Cincinnati Reds. Derringer pitched 19 games in which he allowed three runs or less, and his 3.30 ERA was the best of his career up to that point. But incredibly, he also lost 27 games that season—the most in the majors.

The Reds' fortunes, and Derringer's record, drastically improved in the following years. He won 22 games in 1935 and hit his stride between 1938 and 1940, posting three consecutive seasons with 20 or more wins. His best year was 1939, when he went 25–7 and topped the majors with a .781 winning percentage.

Cincinnati won the NL pennant in 1939 and 1940. In the 1940 World Series against Detroit, Derringer's record was 2–1, including a complete-game victory in Game 7 to give the Reds the world championship.

In the early 1940s Derringer began to fade, and he was sold to the Chicago Cubs in January 1943. He had one winning season left in his arm: in 1945 he went 16–11 with the Cubs, then retired with a lifetime 223–212 record.

Appropriately, Yankee pitcher Lefty Gomez (11) registered the final out of the 1937 World Series. Gomez took the throw from Gehrig and beat Joe Moore (5) to the bag, completing a 4–2 win in Game 5. Gomez had tossed a six-hitter to win Game 1.

whatever they wanted. But it just wasn't in Gehrig's character. "I don't think so," he told Ruth.

Gehrig was a manager's delight. Joe McCarthy, the Yankee manager for Gehrig's last eight seasons, recalled, "What a wonderful fellow that Gehrig was! Always hustled. Never gave a moment's trouble. Just went out every day and played his game and hit the ball. I'll say he hit the ball, and in all directions—right, left, center. No, I never asked him to bunt, not once in eight years. I don't think that would have been very good strategy."

If he had not considered himself such a plodder, Gehrig might not have forced himself to play 2,130 consecutive games—the astounding record for which he is best remembered. He was 21 when he started his streak on June 1, 1925, appearing as a pinch hitter, though most remember the following day, when he filled in at first base for the Yankee regular, Wally Pipp. He was 35 when he played his final game on April 30, 1939. He could no longer play well, and the reason—though he didn't know it—was that he was suffering from an incurable disease that was wasting his body and, before long, would kill him.

But Gehrig had never let physical ailments stop him—one reason why he was able to set the record for most consecutive games played. He fractured a toe in 1934, yet kept playing. He was beaned, knocked unconscious and sent to the hospital with a concussion. The next day, he hit three triples. Late in Gehrig's career, doctors x-rayed his hands. They found 17 fractures, all of which had healed by themselves. Gehrig had broken every finger of both hands at least once and had never sought medical treatment.

Top Row: Colonel Jacob Ruppert (Owner), Bump Hadley, Pat Malone. Middle: Monte Pearson, Lou Gehrig. Bottom: Jake Powell, Red Rolfe, George Selkirk.

NEW YORK YANKEES
1936 WORLD CHAMPIONS

Top Row: John Murphy, Charlie Ruffing, Joe McCarthy (Manager). Middle: Lefty Gomez, Tony Lazzeri. Bottom: Bill Dickey, Frank Crosetti, Joe DiMaggio.

Gehrig batted cleanup for two of the Yankees' three dynasties. The first won pennants in 1926, 1927, 1928 and 1932 with the most devastating one-two punch in baseball history: Ruth followed by Gehrig. Ruth left the Yankees after the 1934 season, and Joe DiMaggio came up in 1936, took Ruth's number-three spot in the lineup and helped Gehrig launch the second dynasty.

When Ruth left, Gehrig made a stab at the limelight. He hired a public relations man and starred in a dreadful Western movie called *Rawhide*. He threw parties for the press and signed on to do a live radio commercial for a breakfast cereal. He botched the commercial, felt uncomfortable in the role of hail-fellow-well-met and resumed his quiet ways.

But his hitting was anything but quiet. Joe McCarthy's Yankees of the late 1930s are sometimes eclipsed in memory by the Yankee dynasties featuring Ruth and Mickey Mantle. But McCarthy's champions rank among the best, and not just because of Gehrig and DiMaggio.

The Detroit Tigers won the AL pennant in 1934 and 1935, but the Yankees were second both years, and in 1936 they were again contenders. Only two starters remained from the Yankee Murderers' Row of a decade before—Gehrig at first base and Tony Lazzeri at second—but a new generation of stars was taking over. Frank Crosetti played shortstop. Red Rolfe was establishing himself as the league's best third baseman, and Bill Dickey as its best catcher. DiMaggio, Jake Powell and George "Twinkletoes" Selkirk played the outfield, and veterans Red Ruffing and Lefty Gomez led a solid pitching staff. For four years, starting in 1936, McCarthy's Yankees laid waste to the rest of the American League; they won the pennant by 19½ games in 1936, 13 in 1937, 9½ in 1938 and 17 in 1939. Eddie Brannick,

Continued on page 172

Led by future Hall of Famers Lou Gehrig, Joe DiMaggio and Bill Dickey, the 1936 Yankees scored an average of seven runs a game during the regular season. They kept it up in the World Series, averaging seven runs a game in a six-game win over the Giants.

Bill Dickey

Bill Dickey was the first Yankee to know about Lou Gehrig's illness. It was only fitting. For six years they were roommates. They went to movies together, ate meals together, played bridge together. But theirs was more than a friendship of convenience. They were kindred spirits, modest men of few words who played baseball with a consistency and dedication that provided ballast for the Yankee dynasty and who ultimately set standards of excellence that endured for decades.

Dickey couldn't match Gehrig's record of consecutive games played, but he was as constant as any catcher could be. For 13 straight seasons, beginning in 1929, he caught more than 100 games. In time, every finger and the thumb on his throwing hand had been broken at least once by foul tips. Usually, no one knew about it.

Unlike Detroit's Mickey Cochrane, Dickey was not a fiery field general; he led by quiet example, with poise and savvy. During the 1930s and 1940s, Dickey knew the strengths and weaknesses of AL batters inside and out, which made him a masterful handler of pitchers. They showed their respect by doing what he asked. There's the story of Marius Russo, who before one World Series game in 1941 was told to spend a half hour with Dickey going over the Dodgers' hitters. The meeting, which lasted ten seconds, consisted of Russo telling Dickey that he would throw whatever pitches the catcher called. He did just that and won with a four-hitter. Pitchers on other teams were just as appreciative of Dickey's value. Cleveland's Bob Feller once said that if he had Dickey catching him, he would win 35 games a year.

Dickey had little more than raw talent when he broke in with the Yankees in 1928. His arm was strong but erratic, so he worked on his wild tosses by going to the outfield and throwing to a spot on the wall for 20 minutes every day. He moved into the starting lineup the next year and soon he was a defensive standout, feared by baserunners throughout the league. In 1931 he went 125 straight games without a passed ball; it was one of four years that he committed only three errors while playing in more than 100 games.

But Dickey would have been quickly forgotten, particularly in the Yankees' intimidating lineup, had he been only a slick catcher. Once manager Miller Huggins broke him of his habit of swinging from his heels and got him to choke up, Dickey became a slashing hitter. He hit over .300 eleven times, and his lifetime average was an impressive .313. He wasn't considered a home run hitter, although he belted at least 22 homers a season from 1936 through 1939. He was best known as a clutch hitter; some say he was the best one in the powerhouse New York batting order. Gehrig once estimated that Dickey's bat was worth 300 runs a season.

Dickey remained with the Yankees through 1943. And just when people were beginning to dismiss him as an aging veteran, he hit the winning homer in the 1943 World Series.

After a stint in the Navy, Dickey returned to the Yankees as player-manager in 1946. He wasn't cut out for managing and resigned 14 games before the end of the season. Two years later, he returned to New York as a coach, and Casey Stengel gave him the job of molding a rough-edged, awkward-looking kid named Yogi Berra. Dickey continued to help young Yankee catchers, such as Elston Howard, through the 1950s. His coaching skills were highly praised; Howard called Dickey "a genius. Nobody teaches baseball better than he does."

Bill Dickey never led the league in any offensive category, but he was a key to the Yankee machine in the 1930s and 1940s. Dickey, said Tiger great Charlie Gehringer, "made catching look easy."

BILL DICKEY

Catcher
New York Yankees 1928–1943, 1946
Hall of Fame 1954

GAMES	**1,789**
AT-BATS	**6,300**
BATTING AVERAGE	
Career	**.313**
Season High	**.362**
SLUGGING AVERAGE	
Career	**.486**
Season High	**.617**
HITS	
Career	**1,969**
Season High	**176**
DOUBLES	
Career	**343**
Season High	**35**
TRIPLES	
Career	**72**
Season High	**10**
HOME RUNS	
Career	**202**
Season High	**29**
TOTAL BASES	**3,062**
EXTRA-BASE HITS	**617**
RUNS BATTED IN	
Career	**1,209**
Season High	**133**
RUNS	
Career	**930**
Season High	**99**
WORLD SERIES	**1932,**
	1936–1939, 1941–1943

Gehrig took advantage of Giants right fielder Jimmy Ripple in Game 3 of the 1937 World Series (below, top to bottom, and at right). Gehrig singled to right and made a wide turn around first. When Ripple threw behind him, Gehrig kept on going and beat first baseman Johnny McCarthy's throw to second baseman Burgess Whitehead.

secretary of the New York Giants, saw the Yanks play one day and was asked what he thought of them. His reply gave the team a nickname: "window breakers," he said.

McCarthy was a good psychologist and a strict disciplinarian. He and Gehrig imbued the players with a winning attitude, a strict work ethic and pride that extended beyond the field. "You're Yankees," McCarthy told his players. "Act like it." On the road, Yankee players wore coats and ties to dinner. On the field, they devoted themselves to batting practice, fielding practice and every detail of play. No card playing or other idle activities sullied McCarthy's clubhouse.

The 1930s became known as the era of American League superiority, but it was mostly Yankee superiority. After winning the 1927 and 1928 World Series in four games each, the Yanks swept the Cubs in four in 1932, beat the New York Giants in six in 1936 and in five in 1937. They swept the Cubs again in 1938 and the Cincinnati Reds in 1939. Seven pennants, seven world championships, 28 World Series wins and only three losses.

Although renowned for their slugging, the Yankees prided themselves on pitching and defense. Red Ruffing won 20 or more games every season from 1936 through 1939, and Lefty Gomez wasn't far behind. The Yankees had by then copied Branch Rickey's farm system, using their vast treasury to make it one of the best. The 1937 Newark Bears, a storied Yankee farm team, yielded outfielder Charlie Keller and second baseman Joe Gordon—stars of Yankee teams to come—not to mention a dozen other solid major leaguers.

In April 1937 the Yankees got a head start on a practice they later made famous—outbidding other teams for a promising free agent. Back then, the reserve clause in every player's contract tied him to his team until he was sold, traded or released. But Commissioner Landis, a foe of farm-system operations, tried to make sure major league teams strictly followed the rules concerning the control of minor league players. He ruled that the Cleveland Indians had tried to protect a young outfielder by keeping him in the minors and out of the spotlight. Landis granted the player—Tommy Henrich—his free agency. The Yankees promptly signed him for $25,000—a star's salary. In 1937, his rookie year, Henrich hit .320 and went on to earn the nickname of "Old Reliable." With DiMaggio, Keller and Henrich, the Yankees had an All-Star outfield that helped keep them on top for years.

By 1936, the Yanks were baseball's best team, and they only got better. The cry went up, "Break up the Yankees!" But no one could. Tom Yawkey's money had bought him a strong Red Sox team: in 1938 Jimmie Foxx batted .349, hit 50 homers and drove in 175 runs; Ben Chapman hit .340; shortstop-manager Joe Cronin batted .325; and Lefty Grove won one of his nine ERA championships. But the Red Sox were never in the pennant race. The following year, Boston brought up Ted Williams, and still, the Red Sox finished second, never threatening the regal Yankees.

G ehrig started strong in 1938. He was 34, but his skills seemed as sharp as ever, and his streak of consecutive games passed 2,000—although his wife, Eleanor, unsuccessfully urged him to cut it off at 1,999 games, just to relieve the pressure. Around midseason, Gehrig fell into a slump. His coordination slipped, and he felt tired. His solution

For most players, a .295 average, 29 home runs and 114 RBI would be a great season. But for Lou Gehrig (above), his 1938 numbers hinted at the debilitating disease that ended his career less than a year later.

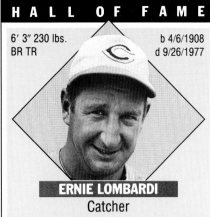

6' 3" 230 lbs.
BR TR

b 4/6/1908
d 9/26/1977

ERNIE LOMBARDI
Catcher

He was perfectly cast as a catcher: Ernie "Schnozz" Lombardi, a big, lumbering man with a rifle arm and a nose so big it extended precariously beyond his mask. Lombardi anchored the Cincinnati Reds from 1932 through 1941 and the New York Giants from 1943 through 1947. He batted over .330 in four consecutive seasons with the Reds, and twice led the NL in batting average, something no other catcher has ever done. When he retired after 17 years in the majors, he had a lifetime .306 average.

That he hit so well was miraculous because he was so slow that infielders could play him 10 to 15 feet behind their normal positions. But Lombardi compensated by hitting the ball so hard that pitcher Carl Hubbell, no faint heart, said,"I thought he might hurt me, even kill me, with one of those liners."

Lombardi was solid behind the plate as well. He caught at least 100 games a season for 8 years, and he caught both of Johnny Vander Meer's consecutive no-hitters. In 1938 he was named league MVP. But Lombardi is often remembered for his famous "snooze" in the fourth and final game of the 1939 World Series, when Yankee Charlie Keller charged the plate and knocked him over, and Joe DiMaggio scored from first as Lombardi lay there, unable to recover his senses or the ball. Lombardi was roasted in the press, even though the Series-winning run had scored before Keller crashed into Lombardi.

Lombardi was elected to the Hall of Fame in 1986.

Bill Dickey hit over .300 eleven times in his career, but got his biggest thrills with his shin guards on. "I loved to make a great defensive play," he said. "I'd rather do that than hit a home run."

was typical Gehrig: extra batting and fielding practice. It didn't work. His timing and power were off. In the World Series he got four hits, all singles. When manager McCarthy was asked what he thought was wrong with Gehrig, he answered, "I wish I had more players on this club that would be so off in their play that they could give me 200 runs."

After the Series, a doctor diagnosed Gehrig's problem as a gall bladder ailment and put him on a bland diet. Gehrig charged into spring training in 1939 determined to regain his skills—and instead watched them slip further. Ground balls went through his legs. He had trouble getting to first base in time to take throws from other infielders. He batted poorly, and even when he hit the ball squarely, it would droop over the infield for a single or loop into an outfielder's glove.

He was 35, and most observers attributed his problems to age, but his teammates knew better. Gehrig's roommate, Bill Dickey, later said, "I knew there was something seriously wrong with him. I didn't know what it was, but I knew it was serious. We were in the room one day, and Lou stumbled as he walked across the floor. I was reading a paper and looked up to see what he had stumbled over, but there was nothing there. I was going to ask him what had happened, but he had a strange look on his face and I didn't say anything.

"A few days later he was standing looking out the window and I was sitting behind him, talking to him, and I saw one leg give way, just as though somebody had tapped him sharply at the back of the knee joint. He looked around quick, to see if I had noticed it, I guess, but I didn't say anything."

The season opened with Gehrig playing first base, but his plight was apparent. In the clubhouse one day he leaned down to tie a shoe and fell

on the floor; his teammates pretended they didn't notice. Eleanor said he sometimes came home after games and cried.

The sports pages were full of stories about Gehrig's decline. A few fans started to jeer him. At Griffith Stadium in Washington on Sunday, April 30, 1939, Gehrig played his 2,130th consecutive game. He came up four times with runners on base and failed to get anything resembling a hit. The season was eight days old, and Gehrig was hitting .143. He had four hits, all singles.

Bad as that was, Gehrig got the final message from his teammates. A ground ball was hit to Yankee pitcher Johnny Murphy. Gehrig got to first barely in time to take the throw. It was a routine play; Gehrig knew that. Yet Murphy and the other infielders congratulated him. "Nice play, Lou," Murphy said.

The Yankees flew to Detroit. After a day off, Gehrig sought out Joe McCarthy in the hotel. Accounts of their conversation differ slightly, but whatever the words, Gehrig told his manager to take him out of the lineup. McCarthy urged him to stick with the team and rest, in hopes that his skills would return.

That afternoon, as Yankee captain, Gehrig took the lineup card to the home plate umpire, who glanced at it and was startled to see Babe Dahlgren listed as the first baseman. "Hey, what's this, Lou?" he said. He looked up at Gehrig; tears were streaming down Gehrig's face. The public address announcer told the fans that Gehrig's streak had come to an end, and the Detroit partisans gave him a big ovation. In the Yankee dugout, Lefty Gomez, the wisecracking pitching ace, put his arm around Gehrig's shoulder and comforted him with a joke. "Hell, Lou," Gomez said, "it took 15 years to get you out of the game. Sometimes I'm out in 15 minutes."

With Gehrig gone in 1939, the Yankee tradition was carried on by young sluggers like Charlie "King Kong" Keller. Keller drove in 83 runs in just 111 games as a rookie, then scored an insurance run (above) in a three-run, tenth-inning rally to complete a four-game Yankee sweep over Cincinnati in the World Series.

Continued on page 178

Red Ruffing

There are turning points in every player's career, but few can be pinpointed as precisely as Red Ruffing's. On May 5, 1930, Ruffing, a burly right-hander, was on his way to another dismal season with the equally dismal Boston Red Sox. Ruffing had lost 25 games in 1928 and 22 more in 1929 for the cellar-dwelling Sox. He led the majors in losses both seasons, and his 0–3 mark in the first few weeks of 1930 carried his lifetime record to an appalling 39–96 with a .289 winning percentage.

Then it happened. On May 6, 1930, Ruffing was traded to the Yankees and began a career that yielded 231 wins, six world championship rings and a plaque in Cooperstown. "I was so tickled to death I couldn't wait 'til I got there," he recalled.

Ruffing deserved a break. The son of an Illinois coal miner, Ruffing had been a hard-hitting first baseman and outfielder as a teenager, playing for a mining company team. But when he was 15, a mining-car accident cost him four toes on his left foot, forcing him out of baseball for a year. Unable to run well, Ruffing turned to pitching and rode a blazing fastball into the majors in 1924.

Not only did Ruffing's fortunes improve when he was traded to the Yankees six years later, so did his pitching. In five full seasons with Boston, his ERA fell below 4.00 only once. It stayed above 4.00 his first two seasons in New York, then dropped under 4.00 for his next 13 seasons, and four times dipped under 3.00. And when Ruffing had his best years, so did the Yankees. In 1932 he went 18–7 with a 3.09 ERA—second in the AL to Lefty Grove—and a league-leading 190 strikeouts, and the Yankees won their first pennant in four years. Ruffing's four 20-win seasons came in a row, coinciding with the Yankees' four straight world championships from 1936 to 1939. And his consistency was remarkable; his records those years were 20–12, 20–7, 21–7 and 21–7. He pitched World Series openers in 1938 and 1939, turning in two complete-game wins and allowing just a single run each time. His Series totals include seven wins —second only to Whitey Ford—and just two losses, a 2.63 ERA and seven complete games.

When Ruffing wasn't winning games with his arm, he was doing it with his bat. At 6′ 1½″ and 205 pounds, Ruffing was a powerful hitter. His 36 home runs rank third among pitchers behind Wes Ferrell and Bob Lemon, but Ruffing is the all-time leader in doubles with 98 and RBI with 273. He was used as a pinch hitter 228 times in his 22-year career, and his .269 lifetime average includes eight seasons in which he hit over .300. In 1932 he pitched a shutout against Washington and won the game with a homer in the tenth, calling it "one of my greatest feats in baseball."

Ruffing pitched on two more Yankee pennant-winners in 1941 and 1942, then lost two years to military service. He returned in July 1945, and, at 41, went 7–3 in 11 starts, then went 5–1 in 1946. Pitching for the Yankees undoubtedly helped his won-lost record, but being on a team renowned for its hitters also kept his pitching efforts from being fully appreciated. Ruffing's 273 wins include 48 shutouts, more than Bob Feller, Lefty Grove or Carl Hubbell. And his 335 complete games have since been surpassed by only one man—Warren Spahn. The glory of the Yankees in the 1930s may have belonged to sluggers like Joe DiMaggio and Lou Gehrig, but the label "staff ace" belonged to Ruffing.

RED
RUFFING

Right-Handed Pitcher
Boston Red Sox 1924–1930
New York Yankees 1930–1942, 1945
Chicago White Sox 1947
Hall of Fame 1967

GAMES	**624**
INNINGS	
Career	**4,344**
Season High	**289⅓**
WINS	
Career	**273**
Season High	**21**
LOSSES	
Career	**225**
Season High	**25**
WINNING PERCENTAGE	
Career	**.548**
Season High	**.750**
ERA	
Career	**3.80**
Season Low	**2.89**
GAMES STARTED	
Career	**536**
Season High	**34**
COMPLETE GAMES	
Career	**335**
Season High	**25**
SHUTOUTS	
Career	**48**
Season High	**5**
STRIKEOUTS	
Career	**1,987**
Season High	**190**
WALKS	
Career *(9th all time)*	**1,541**
Season High	**118**
WORLD SERIES	**1932,**
	1936–1939, 1941–1942

Overlooked among Yankee sluggers of the 1930s was pitcher Red Ruffing, who hit over .300 five times in the decade. And he could pitch too, posting a .648 winning percentage with the Yankees from 1930 through 1939.

The Yankee infield in 1938 included three players with at least 80 RBI. (From left) Gehrig was going gray but still knocked in 114 runs at first; second baseman Joe Gordon had 97 RBI; third baseman Red Rolfe had 80; adding defensive balance was shortstop Frankie Crosetti, who led AL shortstops in putouts, assists and double plays.

In June, at his wife's urging, Gehrig checked into the Mayo Clinic in Rochester, Minnesota. Dr. Harold C. Habein, the clinic's chief diagnostician, greeted him in the lobby and was shocked to see Gehrig's shuffling walk. He shook Gehrig's hand, excused himself and walked into Dr. Mayo's office. Habein had watched his mother's decline before her death, and she had walked and looked like Gehrig. "My God," he said to Mayo, "the boy's got amyotrophic lateral sclerosis!" Tests proved him right. On June 19, Gehrig's 36th birthday, the Mayo Clinic issued this statement:

> This is to certify that Mr. Lou Gehrig has been under examination at the Mayo Clinic from June 13 to June 19, 1939, inclusive.
>
> After a careful and complete examination, it was found that he is suffering from amyotrophic lateral sclerosis. This type of illness involves the motor pathways and cells of the central nervous system and in lay terms is known as a form of chronic poliomyelitis (infantile paralysis).
>
> The nature of this trouble makes it such that Mr. Gehrig will be unable to continue his active participation as a baseball player inasmuch as it is advisable that he conserve his muscular energy. He could, however, continue in some executive capacity.
>
> —H.C. Habein, M.D.

Gehrig wrote to Eleanor back home: "There is a 50-50 chance of keeping me as I am. I may need a cane in 10 or 15 years. Playing is out of the question. . . . They seem to think I'll get along all right if I can reconcile myself to this condition, which I have done but only after they assured me there is

No one ever had bigger shoes to fill—or got a bigger pat on the back—than Babe Dahlgren (12), the 26-year-old whose job it was to fill in when Lou Gehrig (above) took himself out of the lineup on May 2, 1939, after playing in 2,130 consecutive games.

no danger of transmission and that I will not become mentally unbalanced and thereby become a burden on your hands for life. I adore you, sweetheart."

While Gehrig went fishing with his doctors, Eleanor looked up her husband's disease at a medical library and learned that he would inevitably get worse and die within a couple of years. She never told Lou, but he almost surely knew that she knew. He returned to the team, suited up every day, carried the lineup card to the umpire and watched the action from the dugout. As the Yankees embarked from a train one day, a group of Boy Scouts recognized Gehrig, who was walking with Rud Rennie of the *New York Herald-Tribune.*

"Good luck, Lou!" the scouts yelled.

Gehrig smiled and waved to them, and said to Rennie, "They're wishing me luck, and I'm dying."

It was Bill Corum, a leading New York sportswriter, who suggested that the Yankees honor Gehrig with an appreciation day. The ceremony was scheduled between games of a doubleheader at Yankee Stadium on July 4, 1939. As Paul Gallico later wrote, Gehrig was invited to star at his own funeral.

Both Yankee teams that Gehrig anchored were there—the Yankees of 1939 and most members of the great 1927 team. Babe Ruth and Wally Pipp led a march to the flagpole as an Army band played. The weather was perfect, and 61,808 fans came out. Gehrig was in uniform, but he wore no cap, and people close enough to him could see the tears on his face.

The Mayor of New York City, Fiorello LaGuardia, gave a speech. So did James A. Farley, postmaster general. Gehrig and Ruth had not spoken

For the first time in more than 14 seasons, Lou Gehrig sat in the dugout and watched as his teammates played on May 2, 1939—and he was impressed. "I never appreciated some of the fellows I've been playing with for years," he said. "What I always thought were routine plays when I was in the lineup are really thrilling when you see 'em from off the field."

for years, but now the Babe walked up to Gehrig and threw his arms around him.

Gifts were presented from everyone imaginable, from the stadium groundskeepers to the New York Giants. Gehrig's teammates had decided to give him a trophy, and had asked John Kieran, gifted sports columnist of *The New York Times,* to write a suitable inscription. Bill Dickey brought the trophy forward and handed it to Joe McCarthy, who gave it to Gehrig. Dickey almost broke down giving a brief presentation speech.

Then it was Gehrig's turn to speak, but he could not. Sportswriter Sid Mercer, the master of ceremonies, started to make an apology for Gehrig. But McCarthy gently pushed Gehrig forward. The crowd cheered him, then fell silent. Lou had written a short speech the night before, but he spoke without reading.

"They say I have had a bad break. But when the office force and the groundkeepers and even the Giants from across the river, whom we'd give our right arm to beat in the World Series—when they remember you, that's something. And when you have a wonderful father and mother who worked hard to give you an education . . . and a wonderful wife . . ."

This was one occasion that Hollywood could not have embellished. Gehrig's voice was failing. Fans, some of them crying, leaned forward to catch his words. He spoke next of Jacob Ruppert, the Yankee owner who had died seven months earlier. "And there is one man who, I wish, could be with us here today but he . . . and Miller Huggins . . . and Joe McCarthy . . . and Ed Barrow. When you have the privilege of rooming with and knowing one of the finest fellows that ever lived, Bill Dickey . . ." Gehrig's final words were mixed with sobs—his, and those of his teammates

and the fans. "I may have been given a bad break, but I have an awful lot to live for. With all this, I consider myself the luckiest man on the face of this earth."

A silence that began when Ruth mildly criticized Gehrig's mother in 1933 ended on Lou Gehrig Day in 1939, as the Babe embraced his old friend and teammate on Gehrig's last appearance at Yankee Stadium. Two years later, Gehrig was dead.

Waiving the usual five-year waiting period, the Baseball Writers Association voted Gehrig into the Hall of Fame that summer. The Yankees retired his uniform and his number, 4; it was the first time an athlete's number had been so honored. After the 1939 season, Mayor LaGuardia offered Gehrig a job with the New York City Parole Board. Gehrig took it. He enjoyed counseling young offenders. But his illness got worse, and he had to quit the job late in 1940.

Friends continued to visit Gehrig until the spring of 1941. He fell into a coma the night of June 2. His parents rushed to his bedside, and so did Ed Barrow, the Yankee general manager. Gehrig died quietly in his wife's arms. He was 17 days short of his 38th birthday. ◑

1930s Statistics

1930

American League

	W	L	PCT	GB
Philadelphia	102	52	.662	—
Washington	94	60	.610	8
New York	86	68	.558	16
Cleveland	81	73	.526	21
Detroit	75	79	.487	27
St. Louis	64	90	.416	38
Chicago	62	92	.403	40
Boston	52	102	.338	50

League Leaders

Batting	A. Simmons, PHI	.381
Runs	A. Simmons, PHI	152
Home Runs	B. Ruth, NY	49
RBI	L. Gehrig, NY	174
Steals	M. McManus, DET	23
Wins	L. Grove, PHI	28
Saves	L. Grove, PHI	9
ERA	L. Grove, PHI	2.54
Strikeouts	L. Grove, PHI	209

World Series

Philadelphia (AL) def. St. Louis (NL) 4–2

Record Setters

Most RBI, season—190, H. Wilson, CHI (NL), 155 games

Most home runs in a season, NL—56, H. Wilson, CHI, 155 games

Most runs scored in a season, NL (since 1900)—158, C. Klein, PHI, 156 games

Highest team batting average, season, NL (since 1900)—.319, NY

Most team hits, season—1,783, PHI (NL), 156 games

Most runs scored by a team, season, NL (since 1900)—1,004, StL, 154 games

Highest team ERA, season—6.70, PHI (NL), 156 games

National League

	W	L	PCT	GB
St. Louis	92	62	.597	—
Chicago	90	64	.584	2
New York	87	67	.565	5
Brooklyn	86	68	.558	6
Pittsburgh	80	74	.519	12
Boston	70	84	.455	22
Cincinnati	59	95	.383	33
Philadelphia	52	102	.338	40

League Leaders

Batting	B. Terry, NY	.401
Runs	C. Klein, PHI	158
Home Runs	H. Wilson, CHI	56
RBI	H. Wilson, CHI	190
Steals	K. Cuyler, CHI	37
Wins	R. Kremer, PIT	20
	P. Malone, CHI	20
Saves	H. Bell, StL	8
ERA	D. Vance, BKN	2.61
Strikeouts	B. Hallahan, StL	177

1931

American League

	W	L	PCT	GB
Philadelphia	107	45	.704	—
New York	94	59	.614	13½
Washington	92	62	.597	16
Cleveland	78	76	.506	30
St. Louis	63	91	.409	45
Boston	62	90	.408	45
Detroit	61	93	.396	47
Chicago	56	97	.366	51½
Most Valuable Player		L. Grove, PHI

League Leaders

Batting	A. Simmons, PHI	.390
Runs	L. Gehrig, NY	163
Home Runs	L. Gehrig, NY	46
	B. Ruth, NY	46
RBI	L. Gehrig, NY	184
Steals	B. Chapman, NY	61
Wins	L. Grove, PHI	31
Saves	W. Moore, BOS	10
ERA	L. Grove, PHI	2.06
Strikeouts	L. Grove, PHI	175

World Series

St. Louis (NL) def. Philadelphia (AL) 4–3

Record Setters

Most career home run titles—12, B. Ruth, BOS (AL), NY (AL)

Most career slugging percentage titles—13, B. Ruth, BOS (AL), NY (AL)

Most RBI, season, AL—184, L. Gehrig, NY, 155 games

Most home runs by a pitcher, season—9, W. Ferrell, CLE (AL), 48 games

Most doubles, season—67, E. Webb, BOS (NL)

Most assists for a rookie first baseman—125, J. Burns, StL (AL) (tied by E. Bouchee, PHI [NL], 1957)

Most runs scored by a team, season, AL—1,067, NY, 155 games

National League

	W	L	PCT	GB
St. Louis	101	53	.656	—
New York	87	65	.572	13
Chicago	84	70	.545	17
Brooklyn	79	73	.520	21
Pittsburgh	75	79	.487	26
Philadelphia	66	88	.429	35
Boston	64	90	.416	37
Cincinnati	58	96	.377	43
Most Valuable Player		F. Frisch, StL

League Leaders

Batting	C. Hafey, StL	.349
Runs	C. Klein, PHI	121
	B. Terry, NY	121
Home Runs	C. Klein, PHI	31
RBI	C. Klein, PHI	121
Steals	F. Frisch, StL	28
Wins	B. Hallahan, StL	19
	H. Meine, PIT	19
	J. Elliott, PHI	19
Saves	J. Quinn, BKN	15
ERA	B. Walker, NY	2.26
Strikeouts	B. Hallahan, StL	159

Records listed in **Record Setters** still stand as of publication date.

1930s Statistics

1932

American League

	W	L	PCT	GB
New York	107	47	.695	—
Philadelphia	94	60	.610	13
Washington	93	61	.604	14
Cleveland	87	65	.572	19
Detroit	76	75	.503	29½
St. Louis	63	91	.409	44
Chicago	49	102	.325	56½
Boston	43	111	.279	64
Most Valuable Player			J. Foxx, PHI	

League Leaders

Batting	D. Alexander, BOS, DET	.367
Runs	J. Foxx, PHI	151
Home Runs	J. Foxx, PHI	58
RBI	J. Foxx, PHI	169
Steals	B. Chapman, NY	38
Wins	G. Crowder, WAS	26
Saves	F. Marberry, WAS	13
ERA	L. Grove, PHI	2.84
Strikeouts	R. Ruffing, NY	190

World Series

New York (AL) def. Chicago (NL) 4–0

Record Setters

Most World Series batting .300 or over—6, B. Ruth, NY (AL), 1921, 1923, 1926, 1927, 1928, 1932

Most pennants won, manager—10, J. McGraw, NY (NL), 1904, 1905, 1911, 1912, 1913, 1917, 1921, 1922, 1923, 1924 (tied by Casey Stengel, NY [AL] 1949, 1950, 1951, 1952, 1953, 1955, 1956, 1957, 1958, 1960)

Most World Series games lost, manager, career—28, J. McGraw, NY (NL)

Most times struck out in a World Series game—5, G. Pipgras, NY (AL), October 1, 1932

Most assists by a rookie second baseman—527, Billy Herman, CHI (NL)

Most putouts by a right fielder, season, NL—392, Babe Herman, CIN

National League

	W	L	PCT	GB
Chicago	90	64	.584	—
Pittsburgh	86	68	.558	4
Brooklyn	81	73	.526	9
Philadelphia	78	76	.506	12
Boston	77	77	.500	13
New York	72	82	.468	18
St. Louis	72	82	.468	18
Cincinnati	60	94	.390	30
Most Valuable Player			C. Klein, PHI	

League Leaders

Batting	L. O'Doul, BKN	.368
Runs	C. Klein, PHI	152
Home Runs	C. Klein, PHI	38
	M. Ott, NY	38
RBI	D. Hurst, PHI	143
Steals	C. Klein, PHI	20
Wins	L. Warneke, CHI	22
Saves	J. Quinn, BKN	8
ERA	L. Warneke, CHI	2.37
Strikeouts	D. Dean, StL	191

1933

American League

	W	L	PCT	GB
Washington	99	53	.651	—
New York	91	59	.607	7
Philadelphia	79	72	.523	19½
Cleveland	75	76	.497	23½
Detroit	75	79	.487	25
Chicago	67	83	.447	31
Boston	63	86	.423	34½
St. Louis	55	96	.364	43½
Most Valuable Player			J. Foxx, PHI	

League Leaders

Batting	J. Foxx, PHI	.356
Runs	L. Gehrig, NY	138
Home Runs	J. Foxx, PHI	48
RBI	J. Foxx, PHI	163
Steals	B. Chapman, NY	27
Wins	L. Grove, PHI	24
	G. Crowder, WAS	24
Saves	J. Russell, WAS	13
ERA	M. Pearson, CLE	2.33
Strikeouts	L. Gomez, NY	163

World Series

New York (NL) def. Washington (AL) 4–1

Record Setters

Most years leading in walks—11, B. Ruth, NY (AL)

Highest slugging percentage, career (13 or more seasons), NL—.578, R. Hornsby, StL, NY, BOS, CHI, 1915–1933

Highest pinch-batting average, career, AL—.300, B. Fothergill, DET, 1922–1933

Most putouts by a second baseman, season, NL—466, Billy Herman, CHI

Most consecutive games without being shut out—308, NY (AL), August 3, 1931–August 2, 1933

National League

	W	L	PCT	GB
New York	91	61	.599	—
Pittsburgh	87	67	.565	5
Chicago	86	68	.558	6
Boston	83	71	.539	9
St. Louis	82	71	.536	9½
Brooklyn	65	88	.425	26½
Philadelphia	60	92	.395	31
Cincinnati	58	94	.382	33
Most Valuable Player			C. Hubbell, NY	

League Leaders

Batting	C. Klein, PHI	.368
Runs	P. Martin, StL	122
Home Runs	C. Klein, PHI	28
RBI	C. Klein, PHI	120
Steals	P. Martin, StL	26
Wins	C. Hubbell, NY	23
Saves	P. Collins, PHI	6
ERA	C. Hubbell, NY	1.66
Strikeouts	D. Dean, StL	199

1930s Statistics

1934

American League

	W	L	PCT	GB
Detroit	101	53	.656	—
New York	94	60	.610	7
Cleveland	85	69	.552	16
Boston	76	76	.500	24
Philadelphia	68	82	.453	31
St. Louis	67	85	.441	33
Washington	66	86	.434	34
Chicago	53	99	.349	47

Most Valuable Player — M. Cochrane, DET

League Leaders

Batting	L. Gehrig, NY	.363
Runs	C. Gehringer, DET	134
Home Runs	L. Gehrig, NY	49
RBI	L. Gehrig, NY	165
Steals	B. Werber, BOS	40
Wins	L. Gomez, NY	26
Saves	J. Russell, WAS	7
ERA	L. Gomez, NY	2.33
Strikeouts	L. Gomez, NY	158

World Series
St. Louis (NL) def. Detroit (AL) 4–3

Record Setters
Most career home runs, AL—708, B. Ruth, BOS, NY, 1914–1934

Most RBI, career, AL—2,192, B. Ruth, BOS, NY, 1914–1934

Most extra-base hits, career, AL—1,350, B. Ruth, BOS, NY, 1914–1934, 506 doubles, 136 triples, 708 home runs

Most total bases, rookie season—374, H. Trosky, CLE (AL) (tied by T. Oliva, MIN [AL], 1964)

Most extra-base hits, rookie season—89, H. Trosky, CLE (AL), 45 doubles, 9 triples, 35 home runs

National League

	W	L	PCT	GB
St. Louis	95	58	.621	—
New York	93	60	.608	2
Chicago	86	65	.570	8
Boston	78	73	.517	16
Pittsburgh	74	76	.493	19½
Brooklyn	71	81	.467	23½
Philadelphia	56	93	.376	37
Cincinnati	52	99	.344	42

Most Valuable Player — D. Dean, StL

League Leaders

Batting	P. Waner, PIT	.362
Runs	P. Waner, PIT	122
Home Runs	M. Ott, NY	35
	R. Collins, StL	35
RBI	M. Ott, NY	135
Steals	P. Martin, StL	23
Wins	D. Dean, StL	30
Saves	C. Hubbell, NY	8
ERA	C. Hubbell, NY	2.30
Strikeouts	D. Dean, StL	195

1935

American League

	W	L	PCT	GB
Detroit	93	58	.616	—
New York	89	60	.597	3
Cleveland	82	71	.536	12
Boston	78	75	.510	16
Chicago	74	78	.487	19½
Washington	67	86	.438	27
St. Louis	65	87	.428	28½
Philadelphia	58	91	.389	34

Most Valuable Player — H. Greenberg, DET

League Leaders

Batting	B. Myer, WAS	.349
Runs	L. Gehrig, NY	125
Home Runs	H. Greenberg, DET	36
	J. Foxx, PHI	36
RBI	H. Greenberg, DET	170
Steals	B. Werber, BOS	29
Wins	W. Ferrell, BOS	25
Saves	J. Knott, StL	7
ERA	L. Grove, BOS	2.70
Strikeouts	T. Bridges, DET	163

World Series
Detroit (AL) def. Chicago (NL) 4–2

Record Setters
Most walks, career—2,056, B. Ruth, BOS (AL), NY (AL), BOS (NL), 1914–1935, 2,036 in AL, 20 in NL

Highest slugging percentage, career—.690, B. Ruth, BOS (AL), NY (AL), BOS (NL), 1914–1935

Most putouts by a shortstop, career—5,139, R. Maranville, BOS (NL), PIT (NL), CHI (NL), BKN (NL), StL (NL), 1912–1935

Most putouts by a rookie right fielder—322, I. Goodman, CIN (NL)

First night game—Philadelphia (NL) at Cincinnati (NL), Crosley Field, May 24, 1935

National League

	W	L	PCT	GB
Chicago	100	54	.649	—
St. Louis	96	58	.623	4
New York	91	62	.595	8½
Pittsburgh	86	67	.562	13½
Brooklyn	70	83	.458	29½
Cincinnati	68	85	.444	31½
Philadelphia	64	89	.418	35½
Boston	38	115	.248	61½

Most Valuable Player — G. Hartnett, CHI

League Leaders

Batting	A. Vaughan, PIT	.385
Runs	A. Galan, CHI	133
Home Runs	W. Berger, BOS	34
RBI	W. Berger, BOS	130
Steals	A. Galan, CHI	22
Wins	D. Dean, StL	28
Saves	D. Leonard, BKN	8
ERA	C. Blanton, PIT	2.58

Records listed in **Record Setters** still stand as of publication date.

1930s Statistics

1936

American League

	W	L	PCT	GB
New York	102	51	.667	—
Detroit	83	71	.539	19½
Chicago	81	70	.536	20
Washington	82	71	.536	20
Cleveland	80	74	.519	22½
Boston	74	80	.481	28½
St. Louis	57	95	.375	44½
Philadelphia	53	100	.346	49

Most Valuable Player — L. Gehrig, NY

League Leaders

Batting	L. Appling, CHI	.388
Runs	L. Gehrig, NY	167
Home Runs	L. Gehrig, NY	49
RBI	H. Trosky, CLE	162
Steals	L. Lary, StL	37
Wins	T. Bridges, DET	23
Saves	P. Malone, NY	9
ERA	L. Grove, BOS	2.81
Strikeouts	T. Bridges, DET	175

World Series
New York (AL) def. New York (NL) 4–2

Record Setters
Most runs scored, rookie season, AL—132, J. DiMaggio, NY, 138 games

Most RBI, game, AL—11, T. Lazzeri, NY, May 24, 1936

Most double plays by a first baseman, career, NL—1,708, C. Grimm, CHI, 1918–1936

Most total bases, team, season—2,703, NY (AL), 155 games

Most RBI by a team, season—995, NY (AL), 155 games

Most RBI by a team, World Series game—18, NY (AL) vs. NY (NL), October 2, 1936

National League

	W	L	PCT	GB
New York	92	62	.597	—
Chicago	87	67	.565	5
St. Louis	87	67	.565	5
Pittsburgh	84	70	.545	8
Cincinnati	74	80	.481	18
Boston	71	83	.461	21
Brooklyn	67	87	.435	25
Philadelphia	54	100	.351	38

Most Valuable Player — C. Hubbell, NY

League Leaders

Batting	P. Waner, PIT	.373
Runs	A. Vaughan, PIT	122
Home Runs	M. Ott, NY	33
RBI	J. Medwick, StL	138
Steals	P. Martin, StL	23
Wins	C. Hubbell, NY	26
Saves	D. Dean, StL	11
ERA	C. Hubbell, NY	2.31
Strikeouts	V. Mungo, BKN	238

1937

American League

	W	L	PCT	GB
New York	102	52	.662	—
Detroit	89	65	.578	13
Chicago	86	68	.558	16
Cleveland	83	71	.539	19
Boston	80	72	.526	21
Washington	73	80	.477	28½
Philadelphia	54	97	.358	46½
St. Louis	46	108	.299	56

Most Valuable Player — C. Gehringer, DET

League Leaders

Batting	C. Gehringer, DET	.371
Runs	J. DiMaggio, NY	151
Home Runs	J. DiMaggio, NY	46
RBI	H. Greenberg, DET	183
Steals	B. Chapman, BOS, WAS	35
	B. Werber, PHI	35
Wins	L. Gomez, NY	21
Saves	C. Brown, CHI	18
ERA	L. Gomez, NY	2.33
Strikeouts	L. Gomez, NY	194

World Series
New York (AL) def. New York (NL) 4–1

Record Setters
Most consecutive games won, pitcher—24, C. Hubbell, NY (NL), July 17, 1936–May 27, 1937

Highest winning percentage, pitcher, season, AL (minimum 16 decisions)—.938, J. Allen, CLE

Most putouts by a third baseman, career, NL—2,291, P. Traynor, PIT, 1920–1937

Most errors committed by a third baseman, career, NL (since 1900)—323, P. Traynor, PIT, 1920–1937

Highest home run percentage, rookie season—9.3, R. York, DET (AL)

Highest slugging average, rookie season, AL—.651, R. York, DET

Highest fielding average, rookie third baseman—.978, D. Gutteridge, StL (NL)

National League

	W	L	PCT	GB
New York	95	57	.625	—
Chicago	93	61	.604	3
Pittsburgh	86	68	.558	10
St. Louis	81	73	.526	15
Boston	79	73	.520	16
Brooklyn	62	91	.405	33½
Philadelphia	61	92	.399	34½
Cincinnati	56	98	.364	40

Most Valuable Player — J. Medwick, StL

League Leaders

Batting	J. Medwick, StL	.374
Runs	J. Medwick, StL	111
Home Runs	J. Medwick, StL	31
	M. Ott, NY	31
RBI	J. Medwick, StL	154
Steals	A. Galan, CHI	23
Wins	C. Hubbell, NY	22
Saves	M. Brown, PIT	7
	C. Melton, NY	7
ERA	J. Turner, BOS	2.38
Strikeouts	C. Hubbell, NY	159

1930s Statistics

1938

American League

	W	L	PCT	GB
New York	99	53	.651	—
Boston	88	61	.591	9½
Cleveland	86	66	.566	13
Detroit	84	70	.545	16
Washington	75	76	.497	23½
Chicago	65	83	.439	32
St. Louis	55	97	.362	44
Philadelphia	53	99	.349	46
Most Valuable Player				J. Foxx, BOS

League Leaders

Batting	J. Foxx, BOS	.349
Runs	H. Greenberg, DET	144
Home Runs	H. Greenberg, DET	58
RBI	J. Foxx, BOS	175
Steals	F. Crosetti, NY	27
Wins	R. Ruffing, NY	21
Saves	J. Murphy, NY	11
ERA	L. Grove, BOS	3.08
Strikeouts	B. Feller, CLE	240

World Series

New York (AL) def. Chicago (NL) 4–0

Record Setters

Most consecutive no-hit games—2,
J. Vander Meer, CIN (NL), June 11 and 15, 1938

Most World Series games won, no defeats—6,
L. Gomez, NY (AL), 1932, 1936, 1937, 1938

Most earned runs allowed, season (since 1900)—
186, B. Newsom, StL (AL), 330 innings

Most walks allowed, season, AL—208,
B. Feller, CLE

Most putouts by a left fielder, career, AL—4,395,
G. Goslin, WAS, StL, DET, 1922–1938

Most errors by a left fielder, career (after 1900)—
195, G. Goslin, WAS (AL), StL (AL), DET (AL),
1922–1938

National League

	W	L	PCT	GB
Chicago	89	63	.586	—
Pittsburgh	86	64	.573	2
New York	83	67	.553	5
Cincinnati	82	68	.547	6
Boston	77	75	.507	12
St. Louis	71	80	.470	17½
Brooklyn	69	80	.463	18½
Philadelphia	45	105	.300	43
Most Valuable Player				E. Lombardi, CIN

League Leaders

Batting	E. Lombardi, CIN	.342
Runs	M. Ott, NY	116
Home Runs	M. Ott, NY	36
RBI	J. Medwick, StL	122
Steals	S. Hack, CHI	16
Wins	B. Lee, CHI	22
Saves	D. Coffman, NY	12
ERA	B. Lee, CHI	2.66
Strikeouts	C. Bryant, CHI	135

1939

American League

	W	L	PCT	GB
New York	106	45	.702	—
Boston	89	62	.589	17
Cleveland	87	67	.565	20½
Chicago	85	69	.552	22½
Detroit	81	73	.526	26½
Washington	65	87	.428	41½
Philadelphia	55	97	.362	51½
St. Louis	43	111	.279	64½
Most Valuable Player				J. DiMaggio, NY

League Leaders

Batting	J. DiMaggio, NY	.381
Runs	R. Rolfe, NY	139
Home Runs	J. Foxx, BOS	35
RBI	T. Williams, BOS	145
Steals	G. Case, WAS	51
Wins	B. Feller, CLE	24
Saves	J. Murphy, NY	19
ERA	L. Grove, BOS	2.54
Strikeouts	B. Feller, CLE	246

World Series

New York (AL) def. Cincinnati (NL) 4–0

Record Setters

Most consecutive games played—2,130,
L. Gehrig, NY (NL), June 1, 1925–April 30, 1939

Most career grand slams—23, L. Gehrig, NY (AL),
1923–1939

Most consecutive games scoring one or more runs,
season, AL—18, R. Rolfe, NY, August 9–
25, 30 runs

Most winning percentage titles, pitcher—5,
L. Grove, PHI (AL)

Most ERA titles—9, L. Grove, PHI (AL)

Most runs batted in, rookie season—145,
T. Williams, BOS (AL), 149 games

Most bases on balls, rookie season (after 1900)—
107, T. Williams, BOS (AL), 149 games

Most home runs in a World Series by a rookie—
3, C. Keller, NY (AL)

National League

	W	L	PCT	GB
Cincinnati	97	57	.630	—
St. Louis	92	61	.601	4½
Brooklyn	84	69	.549	12½
Chicago	84	70	.545	13
New York	77	74	.510	18½
Pittsburgh	68	85	.444	28½
Boston	63	88	.417	32½
Philadelphia	45	106	.298	50½
Most Valuable Player				B. Walters, CIN

League Leaders

Batting	J. Mize, StL	.349
Runs	B. Werber, CIN	115
Home Runs	J. Mize, StL	28
RBI	F. McCormick, CIN	128
Steals	L. Handley, PIT	17
	S. Hack, CHI	17
Wins	B. Walters, CIN	27
Saves	B. Bowman, StL	9
	C. Shoun, StL	9
ERA	B. Walters, CIN	2.29
Strikeouts	C. Passeau, CHI, PHI	137
	B. Walters, CIN	137

Records listed in **Record Setters** still stand as of publication date.

INDEX

FOR FURTHER READING

Dick Bartell, with Norman L. Macht, *Rowdy Richard: A Firsthand Account of the National League Baseball Wars of the 1930s and the Men Who Fought Them,* North Atlantic Books, 1987.

Robert S. Boone and Gerald Grunska, *HACK: The Meteoric Life of One of Baseball's First Superstars,* Highland Press, 1978.

Robert W. Creamer, *Babe: The Legend Comes to Life,* Simon and Schuster, 1974.

G. H. Fleming, *The Dizziest Season: The Gashouse Gang Chases the Pennant,* William Morrow and Company, Inc., 1984.

Hank Greenberg, edited by Ira Berkow, *Hank Greenberg: The Story of My Life,* Times Books, 1989.

John B. Holway, *Blackball Stars,* Meckler Books, 1988.

Murray Polner, *Branch Rickey: A Biography,* Atheneum, 1982.

Curt Smith, *Voices of the Game: The First Full-Scale Overview of Baseball Broadcasting, 1921 to the Present,* Diamond Communications, Inc., 1987.

PICTURE CREDITS

Front Cover: Joe DiMaggio by *Sports Illustrated*/Acme Photos

Back Cover: Jimmie Foxx and Lou Gehrig by UPI/Bettmann Newsphotos

Opening Spread: New York Daily News Photo

Hack and the Rabbit Ball
UPI/Bettmann Newsphotos; 7 Thomas Carwile Collection/Renée Comet Photography; 8 National Baseball Library, Cooperstown, New York; 10 (left) National Baseball Library, Cooperstown, New York; 10 (right) National Baseball Library, Cooperstown, New York; 11 (left) AP/Wide World Photos; 11 (right) UPI/Bettmann Newsphotos; 12 Thomas Carwile Collection/Renée Comet Photography; 13 Thomas Carwile Collection/Renée Comet Photography; 14 (left) National Baseball Library, Cooperstown, New York; 14 (right) National Baseball Library, Cooperstown, New York; 15 (left) Ron Menchine Collection/Renée Comet Photography; 15 (right) National Baseball Library, Cooperstown, New York; 16 (left) National Baseball Library, Cooperstown, New York; 16 (right) Ron Menchine Collection/Renée Comet Photography; 17 (left) AP/Wide World Photos; 17 (right) *The Sporting News;* 18 Thomas Carwile Collection/Renée Comet Photography; 19 AP/Wide World Photos; 20 National Baseball Library, Cooperstown, New York; 21 (left) AP/Wide World Photos; 21 (right) Thomas Carwile Collection/Renée Comet Photography.

The Last of the Breed
22 National Baseball Library, Cooperstown, New York; 23 Ron Menchine Collection/Renée Comet Photography; 24 AP/Wide World Photos; 25 (left) National Baseball Library, Cooperstown, New York; 25 (right) Ron Menchine Collection/Renée Comet Photography; 26 (left) Ron Menchine Collection/Renée Comet Photography; 26 (right) Dennis Goldstein Collection; 27 Missouri Historical Society; 28 Ron Menchine Collection/Renée Comet Photography; 29 (left) UPI/Bettmann Newsphotos; 29 (right) Temple University Libraries Photojournalism Collection; 30 Ken Felden; 31 (left) Mark Rucker Collection; 31 (right) The

Historical Society of Pennsylvania; 32 (left) UPI/Bettmann Newsphotos; 32 (right) National Baseball Library, Cooperstown, New York; 33 Burton Historical Collection, Detroit Public Library; 34 Ron Menchine Collection/Renée Comet Photography; 35 (top) Mark Rucker Collection; 35 (bottom) National Baseball Library, Cooperstown, New York; 36 (all) Ron Menchine Collection/Renée Comet Photography; 37 UPI/Bettmann Newsphotos; 38 UPI/Bettmann Newsphotos; 39 The Bettmann Archive; 40 Thomas Carwile Collection/Renée Comet Photography; 41 National Baseball Library, Cooperstown, New York; 42 AP/Wide World Photos; 43 Thomas Carwile Collection/Renée Comet Photography.

Hard Times
44 The Bettmann Archive; 45 Ron Menchine Collection/Renée Comet Photography; 46 (left) Ron Menchine Collection/Renée Comet Photography; 46 (right) The Bettmann Archive; 47 AP/Wide World Photos; 48 (left) AP/Wide World Photos; 48 (right) Thomas Carwile Collection/Renée Comet Photography, © 1932 Time Inc., reprinted by permission; 49 (left) AP/Wide World Photos; 49 (right) Ron Menchine Collection/Renée Comet Photography; 50 Ron Menchine Collection/Renée Comet Photography; 51 National Baseball Library, Cooperstown, New York; 52 National Baseball Library, Cooperstown, New York; 53 AP/Wide World Photos; 54 (left) AP/Wide World Photos; 54 (right) UPI/Bettmann Newsphotos; 55 (left) AP/Wide World Photos; 55 (right) UPI/Bettmann Newsphotos; 56 Ron Menchine Collection/Renée Comet Photography; 57 Thomas Carwile Collection/Renée Comet Photography; 59 AP/Wide World Photos; 60 National Baseball Library, Cooperstown, New York; 61 John Holway Collection; 62 Ron Menchine Collection/Renée Comet Photography; 63 UPI/Bettmann Newsphotos; 64 (left) Ron Menchine Collection/Renée Comet Photography; 64 (right) Ron Menchine Collection/Renée Comet Photography; 65 Cleveland Public Library.

The Gashouse Gang
66-67 The Bettmann Archive; 68 (left) Culver Pictures; 68 (right) AP/Wide World Photos; 69 (left) AP/Wide World Photos; 69 (right) Dennis Goldstein Collection; 70 AP/Wide World Photos; 71 (left) National Baseball Library, Cooperstown, New York; 71 (right)

AP/Wide World Photos; 73 (left) National Baseball Library, Cooperstown, New York; 73 (right) AP/Wide World Photos; 74 Ron Menchine Collection/Renée Comet Photography; 75 AP/Wide World Photos; 76 FPG International; 77 Ron Menchine Collection/Renée Comet Photography; 78 (top) Ron Menchine Collection/Renée Comet Photography; 78 (bottom) UPI/Bettmann Newsphotos, courtesy of Cleveland Public Library; 79 (left) Thomas Carwile Collection/Renée Comet Photography; 79 (right) Thomas Carwile Collection/Renée Comet Photography; 80 AP/Wide World Photos; 81 AP/Wide World Photos; 82 National Baseball Library, Cooperstown, New York; 83 UPI/Bettmann Newsphotos; 84 Ron Menchine Collection/Renée Comet Photography; 84-85 UPI/Bettmann Newsphotos; 86 (left) UPI/Bettmann Newsphotos; 86 (right) National Baseball Library, Cooperstown, New York; 87 AP/Wide World Photos; 88 Burton Historical Collection, Detroit Public Library; 89 (left) AP/Wide World Photos; 89 (right) Ron Menchine Collection/Renée Comet Photography.

Inside the Park
90 New York Daily News Photo; 90-91 New York Daily News Photo; 92-93 UPI/Bettmann Newsphotos; 94-95 UPI/Bettmann Newsphotos; 96-97 New York Daily News Photo.

By Popular Demand
98 *The Sporting News;* 99 Ron Menchine Collection/Renée Comet Photography; 100 UPI/Bettmann Newsphotos; 101 AP/Wide World Photos; 102 (left) National Baseball Library, Cooperstown, New York; 102 (right) David Scherman/ *Life Magazine* © 1939 Time Inc., reprinted by permission; 103 David Scherman/*Life Magazine* © 1939 Time Inc., reprinted by permission; 104 Ron Menchine Collection/Renée Comet Photography; 105 (left) The Western Reserve Historical Society; 105 (right) National Baseball Library, Cooperstown, New York; 106 AP/Wide World Photos; 107 (left) Thomas Carwile Collection/ Renée Comet Photography; 107 (right) Ron Menchine Collection/Renée Comet Photography; 108 Ron Menchine Collection/Renée Comet Photography; 109 UPI/Bettmann Newsphotos; 110 Ron Menchine Collection/Renée Comet Photography; 112 *The Sporting News;* 113 (left) Thomas Carwile Collection/ Renée Comet Photography; 113 (right) Ron Menchine Collection/Renée Comet Photography; 114-115 The Historical

Society of Pennsylvania; 116 *The Sporting News;* 117 AP/Wide World Photos; 118 (top) National Baseball Library, Cooperstown, New York; 118 (bottom) National Baseball Library, Cooperstown, New York; 119 AP/Wide World Photos; 120 Thomas Carwile Collection/Renée Comet Photography; 121 (left) UPI/ Bettmann Newsphotos; 121 (right) Ron Menchine Collection/Renée Comet Photography; 122 UPI/Bettmann Newsphotos; 123 National Baseball Library, Cooperstown, New York.

The Changing of the Guard
124 UPI/Bettmann Newsphotos; 125 (left) Thomas Carwile Collection/Renée Comet Photography; 125 (right) Ron Menchine Collection/Renée Comet Photography; 126 AP/Wide World Photos; 127 (left) AP/Wide World Photos; 127 (right) UPI/Bettmann Newsphotos; 128 National Baseball Library, Cooperstown, New York; 129 UPI/Bettmann Newsphotos; 130 Thomas Carwile Collection/Renée Comet Photography; 131 (left) UPI/Bettmann Newsphotos; 131 (right) AP/ Wide World Photos; 132 Ron Menchine Collection/ Renée Comet Photography; 133 Ron Menchine Collection/Renée Comet Photography; 134 UPI/Bettmann Newsphotos; 135 (top) UPI/Bettmann Newsphotos; 135 (bottom) Thomas Carwile Collection/Renée Comet Photography;136 (left) Ron Menchine Collection; 136 (right) AP/Wide World Photos; 137 AP/Wide World Photos; 138 (left) National Baseball Library, Cooperstown, New York; 138 (right) AP/Wide World Photos; 139 (left) National Baseball Library, Cooperstown, New York; 139 (right) National Baseball Library, Cooperstown, New York; 140 UPI/Bettmann Newsphotos; 141 UPI/ Bettmann Newsphotos; 142 Ron Menchine Collection/Renée Comet Photography; 143 *The Sporting News;* 144 FPG International; 145 UPI/ Bettmann Newsphotos.

The Cubs Come Through
146-147 UPI/Bettmann Newsphotos; 148 Ron Menchine Collection/Renée Comet Photography; 149 (left) National Baseball Library, Cooperstown, New York; 149 (right) Ron Menchine Collection/Renée Comet Photography; 150 (left) UPI/Bettmann Newsphotos; 150 (right) AP/Wide World Photos; 151 AP/Wide World Photos; 152 Thomas Carwile Collection/Renée Comet Photography; 153 (top) UPI/Bettmann Newsphotos courtesy Cleveland Public Library; 153 (bottom) AP/Wide World Photos; 154 (left) Ron Menchine Collection/Renée Comet Photography; 154 (right) National Baseball Library, Cooperstown, New York; 155 (left) National Baseball Library, Cooperstown, New York; 155 (right) Ron Menchine Collection/Renée Comet Photography; 156 (left) AP/Wide World Photos; 156 (right) National Baseball Library, Cooperstown, New York; 157 AP/Wide World Photos; 158 (top) Courtesy of Cleveland State University; 158 (bottom) The Burton Historical Collection, Detroit Public Library; 159 (top) AP/Wide World Photos; 159 (bottom left) AP/Wide World Photos; 159 (bottom right) AP/Wide World Photos; 160 (top left) UPI/ Bettmann Newsphotos; 160 (top right) The Bettmann Archive; 160 (bottom) Dennis Goldstein Collection; 161 (left) National Baseball Library, Cooperstown, New York; 161 (top right) National Baseball Library, Cooperstown, New York; 161 (bottom right) Dennis Goldstein Collection.

The Luckiest Man
162-163 UPI/Bettmann Newsphotos; 164 AP/Wide World Photos; 165 (left) UPI/Bettmann Newsphotos; 165 (right) National Baseball Library, Cooperstown, New York; 167 (left) UPI/Bettmann Newsphotos; 167 (right) Amateur Athletic Foundation of Los Angles; 168 (left) National Baseball Library, Cooperstown, New York; 168 (right) UPI/Bettmann Newsphotos; 169 Thomas Carwile Collection/Renée Comet Photography; 170 Ron Menchine Collection/Renée Comet Photography; 171 (top) AP/Wide World Photos; 171 (bottom) Culver Pictures Inc.; 172 (all) UPI/Bettmann Newsphotos; 173 New York Daily News Photo; 174 (left) UPI/Bettmann Newsphotos; 174 (right) AP/Wide World Photos; 175 New York Daily News Photo; 176 Ron Menchine Collection/Renée Comet Photography; 177 (left) National Baseball Library, Cooperstown, New York; 177 (right) AP/Wide World Photos; 178 AP/Wide World Photos; 179 AP/Wide World Photos; 180 UPI/Bettmann Newsphotos; 181 Brown Brothers.

Decade Statistics
182 (both) Ron Menchine Collection/ Renée Comet Photography; 183 (top) Ron Menchine Collection/Renée Comet Photography; 184 (bottom) Thomas Carwile Collection/Renée Comet Photography; 185-186 (all) Ron Menchine Collection/Renée Comet Photography.

ACKNOWLEDGMENTS

The author and editors wish to thank:

Peter P. Clark, Tom Heitz, Bill Deane, Patricia Kelly, Dan Bennett, Frank Rollins and the staffs of the National Baseball Library, Cooperstown, New York; Helen Bowie Campbell and Gregory J. Schwalenberg, Babe Ruth Museum, Baltimore, Maryland; Ellen Hughes and Robert Harding, National Museum of American History, Smithsonian Institution, Washington, D.C.; George Hobart and Mary Ison, Prints and Photographs Division, Library of Congress, Washington, D.C.; Marcey Silver, The Historical Society of Pennsylvania, Philadelphia, Pennsylvania; Dennis Goldstein, Atlanta, Georgia; Thomas Carwile, Petersburg, Virginia; John Holway, Alexandria, Virginia; Mark Rucker, Saratoga Springs, New York; Clarence "Lefty" Blasco, Van Nuys, California; Caroline Tell, Washington, D.C.; Morris Eckhouse, South Euclid, Ohio; Catherine J. Phillips, Ferndale, Michigan; Bob Davids, Washington, D.C.; Adrienne Aurichio, New York, New York; Lillian Clark, Cleveland Public Library, Cleveland, Ohio; Deborah Cohen, *LIFE* Picture Service, New York, New York; Renée Comet, Renée Comet Photography, Washington, D.C.; Sarah Antonecchia, UPI/Bettmann Newsphotos, New York, New York; Mrs. Meredith Collins, Brown Brothers, Sterling, Pennsylvania; Tom Logan, Culver Pictures, New York, New York; Stephen P. Gietschier, *The Sporting News,* St. Louis, Missouri; Karen Carpenter and Sunny Smith, *Sports Illustrated,* New York, New York; Nat Andriani, AP/Wide World Photos, New York, New York; Joe Borras, Accokeek, Maryland; Dave Kelly, Library of Congress, Washington, D.C.; Julie Harris, Arlington, Virginia; Maria F. Negron, Falls Church, Virginia; Nick Cappetta, Alexandria, Virginia; Dorothy A. Gergel, Springfield, Virginia; Jayne E. Rohrich, Alexandria, Virginia.

Illustrations: 9, 52, 58, 72, 166 by Dale Glasgow.

World of Baseball is produced and
published by Redefinition, Inc.

WORLD OF BASEBALL

Editor	Glen B. Ruh
Design Director	Robert Barkin
Production Director	Irv Garfield
Senior Writer	Jonathan Kronstadt
Features Editor	Sharon Cygan
Text Editor	Carol Gardner
Picture Editing	Rebecca Hirsh
	Louis P. Plummer
Design	Edwina Smith
	Sue Pratt
	Collette Conconi
	Monique Strawderman
Copy Preparation	Anthony K. Pordes
	Ginette Gauldfeldt
	Kimberly Fornshill Holmlund
Editorial Research	Janet Pooley
	Mark Lazen
	Ed Dixon
Index	Lynne Hobbs

REDEFINITION

Administration	Margaret M. Higgins
	June M. Nolan
Fulfillment Manager	Karen DeLisser
Marketing Director	Harry Sailer
Finance Director	Vaughn A. Meglan
PRESIDENT	Edward Brash

Library of Congress Cataloging-in-Publication Data
Low and outside/William B. Mead
     (World of Baseball)
     includes index.
     1. Baseball—United States—
     2. History—20th century.
I. Title. II. Series.
GV863.A1M435   1990   90–32136
796.357'0973—dc20
ISBN 0–924588–07–1

CONTRIBUTORS

William B. Mead splits his writing time
between two diverse specialties: baseball and
personal finance. He is the author of *Baseball
Goes to War, The Official New York Yankees
Hater's Handbook, Two Spectacular Seasons*
and, for World of Baseball, *The Explosive
Sixties*. The closest Mead ever came to the
major leagues was as an eager participant in a
Baltimore Orioles fantasy camp.

Henry Staat is Series Consultant for World of
Baseball. A member of the Society for
American Baseball Research since 1982, he
helped initiate the concept for the series. He is
an editor with Wadsworth, Inc., a publisher of
college textbooks.

Ron Menchine, an advisor and sports collector,
shared baseball materials he has been collecting
for 40 years. A radio sportscaster and sports
director, he announced the last three seasons of
the Washington Senators.

The editors also wish to thank the following
writers for their contributions to this book:
Randy Rieland, Washington, D.C.; Robert
Kiener, Washington, D.C.; Regina Dennis,
Alexandria, VA; Michael Leccese, Washington,
D.C.; Andrew Keegan, Alexandria, VA

This book is one of a series that celebrates
America's national pastime.

Redefinition also offers World of Baseball Top
Ten Stat Finders.

For subscription information and prices, write:
     Customer Service, Redefinition, Inc.
     P.O. Box 25336
     Alexandria, Virginia 22313

The text of this book is set in Century Old
Style; display type is Helvetica and Gill Sans.
The paper is 70 pound Warrenflo Gloss supplied
by Stanford Paper Company. Typesetting by
Intergraphics, Inc., Alexandria, Virginia. Color
separation by Lanman Progressive, Washington,
D.C. Printed and bound by Ringier America, New
Berlin, Wisconsin.